The

and Human

Michael Changaris, Psy.D.

TOUCH

The Neurobiology of Health, Healing, and Human Connection

Michael Changaris, Psy.D.

LifeRhythm

LifeRhythm and Core Evolution Publications
PO Box 806, Mendocino, CA 95460, USA
Books@LifeRhythm.com I www.LifeRhythm.com

Editing by Deborah Freeman
Design by Dragon Design, Germany

Cataloging-in-Publication-data for this book is available from the Library of Congress.

Note: This book is intended only as an informative guide for those wishing to know more about touch and health issues. In no way is this book intended to replace, countermand or conflict with the advice given to you by your practitioner. The ultimate decision concerning care should be made by you and if you choose so with your practitioner.

Information in this book is general and is offered with no promise or guarantees for health or healing on the part of the author or of LifeRhythm Publication. The author and publisher disclaim all liability in connection with the use of this book. The names and identifying details of people associated with events described in this book have been changed. Any similarity to actual persons is coincidental.

LifeRhythm books are available at special discounts for bulk purchases by Institutes, Universities or other organizations.
Please contact us for more information: www.LifeRhythm.com I Books@LifeRhythm.com

Table of Contents

Chapter 1

Beginnings

The very possibility of human life starts with touch. The intertwining of fingers as a couple walks out of a movie, the profound wordless communication of safety and connection that forms the basic stability of love, all is rooted in touch. Swimming in the womb, an infant explores the extent of its own body through touch, motion, and the swirls of amniotic fluid against its skin. Infants who receive regular touch from their parents are cognitively more mature than infants who do not. Infants who do not have enough touching, holding, and play can die from a disease called "wasting." In effect, without touch, the child loses its will to live.

The first true connection with a parent or a care provider is the skin-on-skin contact of being held. Teenagers who are touch-deprived have an increased risk of violence. Supportive touch can be healing for a marriage, and can reduce the inevitable stresses of adult life. For older adults, touch can be a lifeline of connection and communication between family members when words no longer come easily. From birth to death, touch plays a vital role in human development and living a happy, engaged life.

Touch can be profoundly damaging to the body and psyche, or it can lead to health, safety and healing. Both torture and kindness happen through touch! Lack of human contact can be as damaging as experiencing some of the most violent, aggressive acts. The type, quality, and quantity of human touch can change the course of a life. Touch affects brain development, the expression of neurochemicals, childhood behavior, marital satisfaction, infant-parent bonding, and mental health over a lifetime.

Despite the wealth of data about its importance to human health, touch has been an understudied and at times even a taboo topic for physical and mental health providers. People in hospitals are often touch-deprived, and most touch they receive comes in the form of a medical and often painful intervention. The isolation people feel at these times can be profound. Unfortunately, psychotherapists often do not realize and address the impact touch-deprivation has on their clients. Without effectively using touch as an intervention in treatment, psychotherapists are literally leaving people out of touch with their world.

Womb Matters

A mother holding her child in her arms knows that her child feels pain. She knows that if her child is cold, or hungry, or is vaccinated in the pediatrician's office, her child feels pain. However in earlier years, medical authorities argued that very young children did not feel pain. Even those who did believe infants felt pain argued that the infant would not remember it. As late as 1985, infants had extensive surgeries without any anesthesia. The medical field believed the child was not yet aware enough—that the memory centers in the brain were not fully formed; thus the infant would never remember the pain. In fact, pain does affect infants: an infant's brain is a powerful memory device—recording events at a rate that adults could never match.

There are times when the rush to reduce our world to an experiment leads scientists to "throw out the baby with the bath water." Researchers discounted time in the womb as a key part of human development except in extreme cases of prenatal exposure to toxins. However, a wealth of data indicates a different conclusion. In one of his lectures, Stanford University's "stress expert" Robert Sapolsky described the metabolic programing occurring in-utero: "Environment does not begin at birth. Environment begins as soon as you have an environment. As soon as you are a fetus, you are subject to whatever information is coming through mom's circulations. Hormones, levels of nutrients. (...) Be a Dutch Hunger Winter fetus and half a century later, everything else being equal, you are more likely to have high blood pressure, obesity or metabolic syndrome. That is environment coming in a very unexpected place. (…)" That is the power of the time in the womb. It is in the womb that the child first hears, through the water bathing its skin, the soft lilt of their mother's voice.

Do prenates learn even in the womb? To decide this, researchers played babies the music they love the most—the sound of their mothers' voices. Mothers were recorded while talking to their infants. Another woman recorded the same script, and the newborns were exposed to both recordings. Infants don't speak, but their body language clearly indicates when they like something. Researchers closely observed the infants, recording and coding all of their behaviors. They observed the eye blinks, twists and turns—every movement. It is no surprise that infants tend to turn towards things they like, and turn away from or ignore things they don't. These researchers showed that infants, even just out of the womb, preferred their mother's voice to that of a stranger.

I sat with a friend who was pregnant. She held her stomach, not consciously aware that she was stroking her belly with the unique kind of love a mother gives to her child. This type of maternal behavior affects a child's development. The prenate's neural chemistry develops through a complex interaction between genetics, environment and behaviors. This interaction is also part of the falling in love process of a mother and her child. Studies indicate that the dialogue between infant and mother starts in the womb.

Moody Tuesday

Pregnancy can be quite stressful at its best. Despite the fact that for many women pregnancy is a joyous experience, for others pregnancy is fraught with low mood and anxiety. A body of literature indicates that pregnancy is the time when women display the highest prevalence of mental health challenges. Some of this has to do with the natural anti-depressant effect of estrogen and the fluctuations in hormones during pregnancy. Even considering the tendency in medicine (due to its culture of male domination) to over-pathologize normal expression of emotion by women, the research is relatively clear.

Some research indicates that nearly one-fifth of women present with depressive symptoms during pregnancy. Many precipitating factors for depression during pregnancy are rooted in social stressors, including lack of partner support, poverty, poor support for family needs in the work place, or domestic violence.

Regardless of the cause, depression is a very difficult experience. It robs a person of the most basic joys, offering instead a feeling of hopelessness. In a carefully constructed study, levels of key neurotransmitters associated with depression [serotonin (a neurotransmitter related to happiness in the moment), dopamine (related to pleasure and appetite) and cortisol (the stress hormone)], were measured in pregnant women. Women who were depressed had fundamental differences in their levels of these neurotransmitters compared to women who were not depressed. After their birth, researchers measured the infants' neurotransmitter levels. The infants whose mothers were depressed had a similar neurochemical profile to that of their mothers', while the infants whose mothers were not depressed had a neurochemical profile similar to their happier mothers' profile. These findings indicate that the dialogue between a mother's body and her prenate may tune the expression of neurochemicals in the infant's brain.

Fear and stress are common during pregnancy. I have sat with many patients and friends as they explored fears around giving birth and taking care of their child, and fears around the health of their child. It is a profound and important time. One woman I worked with was able to get a monthly massage throughout the course of her pregnancy. The regular touch soothed her stress and the discomfort of the physiological changes in her body, and even at times her normal anxiety about the future. It may be possible to help couples learn to do this (massage) for each other. In all probability, teaching couples to provide massage for each other would be beneficial for both them, and their developing fetus.

Anxiety is normal; however it is possible to develop skills that shift us from anxiety to rest. Supporting mothers and families in this way may be vital for child health; thus supporting families to manage stress during pregnancy could, and should, be a real public health goal. Anxiety during pregnancy also influences child development. Children of mothers with high levels of anxiety during pregnancy demonstrate more behavioral problems in their first years of life.

Anxiety is our body attempting to help us protect ourselves. All people feel anxiety at times. It helps us mobilize a defense against a threat. However, our bodies are designed to feel anxious, and then return to rest. It is possible for the anxiety system to become stuck. For people who experience excessive anxiety, a simple daily task can feel like being required to give an impromptu speech to one-thousand people!

Anxiety and anger are part of the same system—often referred to as the fight-flight system. Anxiety is flight (a.k.a. fear). Anger is fight. Preeminent touch researcher Dr. Tiffany Field assessed one-hundred-sixty-six pregnant women during their second trimester, classifying them into two groups: high-anger and low-anger. Fetuses within the wombs of mothers with high amounts of anger were more active, and exhibited developmental delays. Dr. Field also found that neonates whose mothers were in the high-anger group had higher levels of cortisol (stress hormone), and lower levels of serotonin (a neurotransmitter involved in feeling happy in the moment, and in depression), and dopamine (a neurotransmitter involved in happiness, pleasure, motivation, ADHD, and addiction).

You can see happiness in the brain. Happy people have more activation in the left hemisphere of the front-brain—the prefrontal cortex (PFC)—while depressed people have greater activation in the right hemisphere of the prefrontal cortex. Dr. Field measured the neonates' brain activity using a device called the electroencephalogram (EEG). She found that the neonates of high-anger mothers also had greater activation in the right frontal lobe (PFC) of the brain.

Some of Dr. Field's most interesting findings in this research were the impacts of anger on sleep. One of the most difficult parts of early parenting is the sleep schedule. You can see the rings under the eyes of new parents, and the war weary comments like "She's not quite sleeping through the night yet." Dr. Field noted disorganized sleep patterns in neonates of the high-anger group, and lower scores on an assessment using the Neonatal Behavioral Assessment Scale, also known as the Brazelton Scale This neonatal measure determines the strengths and weaknesses of newborns by assessing twenty-eight behavioral items and eighteen reflex assessments, as noted by the Brazelton Institute. Unlike other neonatal assessments (the Apgar score), the Brazelton Scale's result is not reflected in one number; instead it provides parents with a spectrum of data about their infant's strengths and weaknesses.

Dr. Field has conducted many studies on touch and health. Some of her research indicates that we can reduce some of the impacts of stress factors by implementing healthy touch as a part of family health during pregnancy.

Stress does not just affect one part of our lives. It affects every part of our lives. Stress during pregnancy impacts the entire mother-child dyad—from neurochemistry to genetic expression. For the infant, maternal stress plays a large role in their developing brain and hormonal functioning. This is a powerful statement. It points out that maternal stress— which can be managed in myriad ways—will affect the way the brain develops. The brain is built over time, one layer on the other. Deficiencies early in development can have profound impact on the life of a child. Since time in the womb has profound effects on the development of a child's brain, managing stress during pregnancy might be one of the most effective things we could do to help "level the playing field" for newborns. There is a large amount of research focused on the impact of economic deprivation and stress, and the results are clear: lower birth weight, premature birth, and some behavioral problems *are* related to prenatal stress.

She said that she was lonely and feeling hopeless. I sat with her as she explored the feelings. She talked about how often her body hurt since she had become pregnant. She decided to go to a massage therapist, and as she worked with this therapist, she cried for the first time since learning she was pregnant. The tension in her body—the fear she was holding—softened. The next time we met, her face looked more relaxed and she smiled for the first time in a long while. Depression is a major stressor on both mother and child, and touch is a powerful tool to help depressed mothers feel better.

In 2004, Dr. Field conducted a study of pregnant women experiencing depression. The women divided into two groups, with each group receiving a different intervention. Researchers measured brain chemistry levels—particularly those neurotransmitters involved in depression—dopamine, serotonin and cortisol. One group's intervention consisted of a classic and effective relaxation technique called progressive muscle relaxation. The other group received a massage. By the end of the sixteen-week study, women receiving massage showed increased serotonin and dopamine levels and reduced cortisol levels, compared to women practicing the relaxation skill. While this study did not measure levels in the babies after their birth, it is probable there would be differences in their neurotransmitter levels as well.

Prenatal Development

Imagine for a moment that you don't even know how to move your hand. Imagine that you have never seen anything and sound itself has never reached your brain. This is the experience of life before the senses develop. As your hand moves, the warm, supportive world around you moves too. It might take considerable time to realize your hand is different from the movement itself. In the womb, touch is the first sensation a prenate develops, while vision is the last. Touch is the base of our sensory world; it is the first way we learn to relate with others and ourselves. This sense develops as the neonate begins to explore its limbs in the whooshing warmth of amniotic fluid. Touch has several key developmental moments in the womb. The first occurs at about eight weeks. If you brush the cheek of an eight-week old prenate with a cotton swab, she will turn away from it. By the second trimester this pattern changes, and the prenate starts to turn towards touch. At fourteen weeks, the entire body of a prenate, except for the top of the head and back, responds to touch. At about the same developmental period of fourteen weeks, the prenate begins touching its own face. Self-touch is a way of exploring the world and of soothing oneself. Explorations the prenate makes about its own body may underlie the development of brain systems. By sixteen weeks, the prenate displays rooting response (part of what an infant needs for successful nursing). Many of the movements that the prenate makes are practice for future abilities outside the womb.

Our senses are the way that we explore our contact with the world and ourselves. At the earliest stages of development, a prenate appears to make random movements. While from our view these movements look random, it may be a much deeper and intentional process from the perspective of the prenate. As these movements occur, the prenate's brain develops a map of the inside of the body.

When I was in training as a psychologist, I took a course about neuroscience from a professor who appeared to get a kind of glee out of showing us our startle response. He would tell a story—the room would quiet as we became wrapped up in the tale—and "BOOM!" He would slam his hands together. The entire room full of people would jump a foot into the air. That is our startle response and it is vital to our health on many levels—but startle is not present in a fetus from conception.

At eight weeks, the fetus displays a "startle" response. Startle is a key part of stress physiology. It is what allows us to notice danger and produce a defensive strategy. Jolts of many kinds can produce startle in a prenate. Sounds, bright lights, and sudden movements their mother makes all can induce a startle response. If we are in a state of stress, we startle more easily. Since the infant and the mother are in body-mind-brain dialogue, maternal stress may influence an infant's startle response. A pregnant woman who is supported and is relaxed exhibits lower stress response, which may affect the startle response in the infant they carry. In all likelihood, a study examining the relationship between maternal stress and infant startle response would provide powerful information.

The Chicken or the Gene

What drives development? Is development a predetermined script read from the letters of our DNA—like a group of actors reading Shakespeare—each performance the same script reinterpreted by a different actor? Or is the development of a human being a dialogue between the genetic code, the mother, and the experience of the fetus?

Studies have begun answering this question. In developmental psychology's early years, the accepted view was that human development follows a script. Now, advances in tools and techniques and the resulting data may completely transform our understanding of human development.

What could a chicken teach us about how we develop? In evolutionary biology there is a concept known as conservation, which points to a basic biological principle: When nature designs a solution to a problem, it keeps using it. If DNA were the script for life repeated without the impact of experience, one would expect that experience would have little or no effect on the course of human development. However, there are interesting findings that challenge the assumption that we are just our genes.

If the environment does not matter, the small movements a developing chick makes in its egg would not matter either, at least regarding how bones develop. However, a study uncovered something quite remarkable: both human bodies and chicken bodies have cartilage and bone. If you want to feel cartilage, touch the tip of your nose. Move it back and forth. It is both solid and moveable. That is the function of cartilage. Cartilage in our ribcage allows us to breathe. If all our cartilage were turned to bone, we would be prisoners in our own body, unable to move at all! This study on the movement of prenatal chicks in their eggs produced results with shocking implications: Researchers kept one group of chicks from moving within their eggs. The chicks that could not move did not develop any cartilage at all, they developed only bones! The movements an unhindered chick makes within its egg appear to interact with its genetic code; telling it to make cartilage in one area and bone in another.

Under normal conditions, a chicken developing within its egg is exposed to its mother's voice; it recognizes those sounds when it breaks free of its egg. If a chicken fetus is overly stimulated by too much shaking, it emerges unable to recognize the sounds of the chicken species. The shaking interrupts the chick's audio learning. Similarly, if the shaking occurs during the development of vision, the chick has difficulty recognizing visual cues.

The sequencing of an animal's exposure to sensory experience is vital. Hearing develops just before vision. Fetal ducklings and rats exposed to light prior to the visual developmental period actually lose their ability to hear. The light's impact catalyzes the development of vision and overrides the development of hearing. This may have some profound implications for human development and neurological conditions. Sensory development requires the right type of stimulus at the right time. Just as in "The Story of the Three Bears," optimal sensory development requires a Goldilocks Zone—where conditions are just right!

Developmental Principles

For the prenate within the womb, there are several principles of development: First, development moves from head to toe. Second, development of organs moves from basic functions to functions that are more specialized. Unlike Athena, the Goddess of Wisdom in Greek mythology, a liver does not spring forth fully formed as a liver, but smaller. In fact, a human liver develops only the functions necessary for supporting the fetus at its current stage of development. Initially the developing human heart has only two chambers, because two are enough to manage the demands of circulation at that stage of development. Over the course of prenatal development as the body's demands increase, the heart expands to four chambers. This implies that the demands of the physical systems of the body on a specific organ may be a trigger for further development of that organ. Finally, the third major principle of development is that it occurs in the order of importance, starting with organs vital for surviving and then moving on to less vital organs or functions. While these are general principles and not sacrosanct laws, they do accurately describe the pattern of human development. Touch, as the first sense to develop, may play a powerful role in fetal development within the womb.

Learning in the Womb

All these findings beg a very deep question: "Does the fetus learn?" There are several indications that indeed the prenate does learn.

Three basics are required for learning: The first is the ability to sense the environment. Without sensing mechanisms to receive feedback about the world, no learning is possible. The second is being able to recognize organized relationships in the environment, either within the self (moving an arm), or in the environment. For the most part, our world is a series of predictable relationships, which brings us to the third vital part of learning: an observation of relationships between things needs to be remembered. Truly, learning is the recognition and storage of relationships!

A prenate has a startle response. We all do. If you are sitting quietly, absorbed in the task at hand, and suddenly there is a loud sound, you will probably jump. A prenate is no different. It will throw its arms and legs wide and brace when it hears a loud sound or experiences some other intense occurrence. The prenate's startle response also brings about an increase in its heart rate.

Habituation is a term psychologists and developmental biologists use to describe a simple process—an ability to ignore things if they are irrelevant. If your desk were located near a door that creaks loudly when people use it, you would begin to recognize that sound and stop jumping. The prenate is the same. It can notice the sound, but if it happens over and over, then like the adults in Aesop's Fable, "The Boy Who Cried Wolf," the mind stops creating a startle response. In effect the mind is saying, "I have seen this before and it was not that interesting the last time." This ability may be a vital precursor to cognitive development. In other words, to be able to habituate you need to receive sensory information, recognize a relationship (the door creaks and it is not a threat), and store the relationship you noticed in memory. In fact, if a prenate cannot habituate to startle (learn to ignore things that are not a threat), they exhibit profound decreases in their intelligence and cognitive abilities throughout life.

Movement in the Womb

Prenates move around, kick the walls of their mother's uterus, and change positions. The prenate has the ability to act within its environment. A prenate floating in the warm, safe womb does not simply lie down on the job. It is active and exhibits a wide range of behaviors and movements. One reason a prenate moves is so it can practice. The prenate practices breathing motions throughout gestation. Although there is no air in the womb, the prenate practices in order to be ready for when it must switch from taking in oxygen via its mother, to taking air into its own lungs.

Bonding with care providers is another important reason for some of the behaviors a prenate practices. For example, drinking amniotic fluid may help a prenate learn to recognize its mother by smell, which may also affect the latching-on process during initial breastfeeding. The sound of its mother's voice filtering through the fluid surrounding a prenate develops the infant's recognition of and appreciation for her and her voice. Another prenatal behavior—the sleep-wake cycle while in the womb—is crucial to optimal fetal development. Disruptions in the development of sleep-wake patterns negatively affect the development of a prenate—possibly impacting its entire lifespan. It is very possible that with good research, protocols to retrain sleep-wake cycles will be developed—even for those with disruptive in-utero programming.

Touch in Infant Development

Once a child is born, the role of interactive touch becomes much greater. Touch is vital for human development. If deprived of touch during infancy, a child has adverse changes in their development that can last a lifetime.

In the early 20th century, children who did not have access to parental care were placed in orphanages. These orphanages were crowded and under-staffed, but in most, the children were well fed. Despite getting enough nutrition, infants were dying. Concerned people began a campaign to find out why this was happening. Austrian psychoanalyst and physician Rene Spitz believed that lack of love, or lack of important parental relationships, was what was hurting and even killing these infants, not contagious disease or some other physical insult. Dr. Spitz observed that some infants, those more appreciated by staff, received more interaction and cuddling—and these infants survived.

Despite his many critics, Dr. Spitz set out to test and prove his theory by comparing a group of infants being raised by their incarcerated mothers (from the very nature of prisons, these infants were exposed to many germs and diseases), to a group of orphanage infants being raised in sterile isolation. (In a fruitless effort to reduce the alarming infant mortality rate of more than one in three infants, many orphanages hung sterile sheets between cribs to reduce germs and disease.) Dr. Spitz's findings were nothing less than stunning: Thirty-seven percent of the institutionalized infants perished. Not one of the babies raised by their incarcerated mothers died.

In 2007, results of another controlled trial of orphanage versus foster care (in Romania—notorious for its deplorable orphanages) proved irrefutably that foster children receiving more "parental" love and touch than institutionalized children, developed much more optimally. They grew faster, they were happier—some were even significantly smarter! In short, unlike the unfortunate orphanage infants, the fostered babies were not suffering from the deepest starvation of all: a profound lack of loving touch.

Continual lack of touch and care causes an infant to simply give up. In the beginning, an infant cries, asking for care; when none is forthcoming, the crying escalates. Its tiny body writhes in tension, rigid with desperation as it wails for the care that it must have to survive. Over time, if no one comes, sheer exhaustion quiets the baby, leading to even less care. If this dreadful cycle continues, the infant will just give up—stop eating, stop drinking, stop crying, and quietly die.

There is a simple solution. It does not require a billion-dollar research program or passing a drug to market after rigorous clinical trials. The solution is there in the environment that an infant's physiology is designed for. The solution is touch. If an infant is held, it survives.

An infant has a genetic code that tells it how to survive, but the code requires a family to activate it. A family provides many things, but three of the basics are security, love, and nourishment. The institutionalized infants were getting two of the three, but that was not enough. To an infant, love communicated by touch, by contact with their caregiver, is as vital as food. Without touch, babies perish.

There is a growing body of research examining the impact on brain development of growing up in an orphanage without adequate love and support. Much of this research is conducted on children who come to the United States from countries that do not provide good regulation of their orphanages. In some of these orphanages, children are tied to their beds and ignored for hours on end. Studies show that children who survive such profound touch deprivation experience dramatically adverse changes in the way their brains function. Touch starvation in these communities is rampant and its consequences can be deadly. The real tragedy is that this is preventable.

We all can see that tying children down would change their functioning. It makes sense. However, even small disruptions in maternal care at key periods of development can impact a child for life. One would expect that large-scale maternal deprivation would lead to changes, but minor deprivation? When a baby chimpanzee is separated from its mother for as little as two weeks, there are adverse changes in how that chimpanzee responds to stress for the remainder of its life. The same result holds true for humans.

Brain-derived neurotrophic factor (BDNF) is a neurochemical responsible for learning, neuroplasticity (how the brain changes), and healing for body systems. In one study, rats who suffered maternal deprivation were put into a water maze, a technique that is often used to measure how well an animal can learn. The rat is placed into a milky fluid so it cannot see, let alone touch the ground. It must swim until it finds a platform hidden below the surface of the water. Although rats can swim, they don't enjoy it; they want to get to dry land as soon as possible, thus being in a water maze is stressful. Rats that did not receive enough maternal touching had less BDNF production after stress. Their entire brain was deprived of this neurochemical. The researcher made a striking conclusion: Rats that were touch-deprived early in life lacked the protection of BDNF under stress, and this lack led to significant health impacts across their life span.

Another study in rats may offer profound implications for the development of future therapies. This group of researchers was looking at the intergenerational impact of stress on female rats. Researchers used two groups of rats. One group encountered a stressful situation just after their birth. The other group was allowed to develop in a more natural and thus less stressful environment. As with the water maze study referenced above, this study found that small amounts of stress at an early age adversely influenced functioning throughout the stressed group's lifetime. This result clearly points to things we can do to help our society develop in a more beneficial manner. It shows that providing support for mothers and their infants in their early development will have long-term positive impacts on a generation.

However, this study went two very important steps further: The researchers observed the rats developing and eventually helped them connect with a mate. After the female rats mated and conceived, the researchers watched the developing fetuses and the rat pups that were eventually born. They observed that rat mothers subjected to stress early in their own development did not lick their pups, and displayed less maternal care than unstressed rat mothers display. Stress during pregnancy not only affected the stress response of a single generation of rats later in life, it also had an impact on the succeeding generation!

The impact of our choices today on the generations to come has long been a popular subject for discussion. Here demonstrated is the biology of one generation's childhood stress directly influencing the stress levels of their offspring. Observable change at a physiological level between two generations is a shocking and very exciting finding.

However, the researchers went on to measure one more critical variable. They wanted to determine whether it is possible to change the course of a rat's life by making changes in its environment. Researchers added what is known as an "enriched environment" to the lives of all the rats born, whether their mothers had been subjected to stress early in their lives, or not. What they found is riveting! *All* of the rats in the enriched environment demonstrated improved physical and cognitive development. This implies that despite the profoundly negative impact of stress on a developing fetus and the infant it becomes, implementing simple steps can positively influence the trajectory of a life! For both humans and rats, touch is an important part of an enriched environment, and a vital part of ideal human development—

about which the field of psychology is deeply concerned. Yet the field has almost completely ignored the impact of touch on the developing human. A greater understanding of touch and its role could lead to implementing more and better medical and clinical interventions to help heal a wide range of health conditions, in addition to helping people learn to live a more fulfilling life.

Kangaroo Care

He was born far too soon and the first hours of his life were diffi-cult. His doctor told the parents that their infant son would not long survive. The new mother asked for her son to be brought to her, and placed with his belly to her chest, skin-to-skin. She began weeping silently as he breathed. She had carried him in her womb for months and now she was losing him. She could not bear to miss a single moment.

Her husband, very excited about becoming a father at last, sat in shock, thinking that this was the end for his infant son. In his over-whelming pain, all he wanted was to hold his baby boy, so the new father took off his shirt, climbed onto the hospital bed and together with his wife, held their baby during what they believed would be the last few moments of his life. As the infant lay on his mother's chest, cocooned between his parents, the heat of her body began to warm his tiny body. Contact with his mother's body began to reduce the infant's stress levels. After an interminable amount of time, rather than grow-ing shallower, his breathing deepened and the rate increased. The infant began making small movements and his breathing and heart rates continued stabilizing.

For what seemed like another infinite length of time, his parents held and loved their boy, preparing to let him go, if that was what had to happen. Happily, it did not. They sent for their doctor, who replied through a nurse that their baby was dying and sent his deep condo-lences. More time passed and the parents finally resorted to trickery to convince the doctor to return. When the doctor returned to re-exam-ine their baby, he confirmed that the infant's vital signs had stabilized and he was growing stronger by the minute. The baby boy lay on his mother's stomach—alive. Several years later, he is a rambunctious child who enjoys playing with his younger brother.

There is a remarkable dialogue going on between a mother's body and that of her infant. Is it possible that in the above instance, skin-to-skin contact between mother and child helped keep this baby alive? For years, the assumption was that newborn care provided by medical professionals was best—allowing the mother to rest. However, as we have seen, short-term deprivation of maternal care has dramatic impacts on an infant that can last a lifetime. Because of the overwhelming data, there has been a push to change the old practice of separating an infant from its mother during their time in hospital care.

Kangaroo care has been around for more than thirty years now. At its heart, kangaroo care means providing ongoing skin-to-skin contact between an infant and its mother. Based on the simple, but far-reaching idea that a newborn child is most likely to thrive in its parents' arms, kangaroo care proposes that human children, like kangaroos, are born completely dependent on their parents; hence, the human infant is uniquely evolved to live specifically within the environment of the mother-infant relationship, and more broadly in a family system.

Human infants, especially those who are born prematurely, will die if they are not kept warm. Over time, modern medicine developed incubators designed to keep a child's temperature high enough to survive by creating a tightly controlled environment. Medical professionals believed the incubator provided the best means of regulating temperature, thus helping infants survive and thrive. However, warmth is not all that a mother's body provides. Over the past thirty years, kangaroo care has amassed an impressive body of data supporting its use. One initial finding was that yes, just like an incubator, kangaroo care is very effective at keeping an infant warm. However, there are additional surprising and very important findings:

When placed in an incubator, a baby's temperature stays within a healthy range, but fluctuates widely within that range. However, when placed against its mother's chest in skin-to-skin contact, the infant's temperature is more stable. This is a well-documented phenomenon called thermal regulation. What happens in thermal regulation is that the mother's body adjusts its temperature to regulate the infant's temperature. If the infant's body temperature drops one degree, the mother's body raises her temperature one degree to compensate. Thus, the infant and mother body-to-body connection creates the environment needed for optimal infant health.

The mother-child skin-to-skin bond is profound, as demonstrated by a study of a small sample of mothers who bore twins and used kangaroo care. Researchers found that as one twin's body-temperature dropped, the mother's temperature on that side increased. The mother's other side synchronized with her other twin!

This co-regulation or interactive regulation does not stop at temperature. The skin-to-skin contact brings about changes in an infant's stress response that can be demonstrated by measuring cortisol. Skin-to-skin contact between a mother and her infant reduces its cortisol levels, or rather, its stress response; whereas infants placed in an incubator demonstrate "protest distress" response. They fuss and cry to get the attention of their caregivers. When mere crying fails to attract attention, the crying escalates to screaming until the infant's body is racked with sobs. If attention is still not forthcoming, the infant—exhausted—becomes rigid, before finally collapsing and giving up. This wrenching process leads to changes in the infant's stress response, and to poor respiration. A child in kangaroo care exhibits a more even pattern of breathing, while a child in an incubator shows quick bursts of breath, followed by long pauses between breaths.

Skin-to-skin contact also affects oxytocin, which is a neurochemical involved in many aspects of human functioning that plays two key roles in social interactions: The first role is the creation of a very strong sense of bonding (connection and love). The second role is the creation of a buffer against stress. When an infant is nestled with its mother skin-to-skin, there is an increase in secretion of oxytocin in both mother and child. Oxytocin secretion also increases in fathers who participate in kangaroo care, bringing about a stronger bond of love and connection between father and child. There are data indicating that fathers who participate in kangaroo care also feel closer to their partner, and their partner feels closer to them. In families, it is often this sense of bonding and closeness that enables members to be willing to work through problems and keep offering support, despite too little sleep and other emotional stresses of parenting.

Another important effect of oxytocin is reducing pain. Deep in the brain is a structure called the periaqueductal grey (PAG), a part of the reptilian brain. The PAG is evolutionarily the oldest part of the brain and is present in all animals, even reptiles. When we experience pain, a set of fibers fire and send an imperative signal to our brain that something is injuring our body. However, this first pain system does not tell us where the pain is located. It could be our back, our foot or our finger; all we know is that it hurts!

Then a second system fires, which enables us to "orient" to the location of the pain. Finally, a third pain system fires, telling our body to calm the pain signal down. From deep within our brain, the periaqueductal gray tells our body that it is safe to turn off the pain signal, and one of the neurochemicals involved in this process is oxytocin.

There are many studies showing that simply holding the hand of a person in pain helps reduce their pain-level. One classic study had individuals in a Functional Magnetic Resonance Imaging machine (fMRI machine, which has revolutionized study of the mind by letting researchers look at the brain as it works) plunge their hands into a bucket of icy water. One of the groups was allowed to hold the hand of a loved one. The other group had no external support. Not surprisingly, the group holding the hand of a loved one had less activation in the pain regions of their brain than the group without support. Sometimes it takes a research study and an expensive piece of equipment to confirm what any parent could tell you: Hugs help pain.

In the hospital, one of the more painful events for an infant is a heel-stick (done when an infant needs blood drawn). Infants undergoing a heel-stick cry intensely. They scrunch up their faces and wail! In Australia, a group of researchers found that infants receiving kangaroo care cried less from the heel-stick procedure and calmed more quickly afterwards.

Does touch have any connection with learning? One of the first indicators of infant learning is habituation. As demonstrated earlier, habituation is present even in the womb and is foundational to learning. When first donning a shirt, one is aware of the fabric on the skin, but after a few moments the sensation fades and one is no longer conscious of it. (Although some people within the autistic spectrum may continuously feel a scratchy tag or the thin seam at the toe-end of a sock.) With what we've learned thus far, it comes as no surprise that infants who receive kangaroo care have a more mature pattern of habituation than those who do not.

Orienting—the basic ability to locate the source of a sound, a sight, or a smell, is another primary response in all mammals and most lizards. Making a connection between an event and a cause is what forms the basis of all later learning. Orienting supports an individual to begin the process of discovering connections between cause and effect. Incidental learning is the learning that occurs simply because one exists. Driving to work each day, one learns about the street signs, the way traffic flows at different times of day—even who comes out with their morning coffee and at what time. An infant's brain is highly primed for this type of learning, awash in a sea of neurochemicals that change the rate of neuroplasticity (how the brain rewires itself in response to experience). The ability to orient to important events in the environment begins in the womb with the development of the startle response, and further develops through interaction with the environment outside the womb. Once again, it won't be surprising to learn that infants receiving kangaroo care have a more mature orienting response than infants who do not.

Along with the ability to connect cause with effect, one of our most seminal abilities is to act to create change. We learn about the world through figuring out what we can accomplish. This takes the coordinated ability to move body and mind to achieve a purposeful goal. In the womb, the prenate's brain sends out bursts of signals to the body and the limbs move. As the limbs begin to move, feedback from sensations in the limbs tells the brain *how* the limbs move. This map becomes part of a motor system in the brain. (The hand maps to the hand region of the brain.) In the period immediately after birth, the motor system has to contend with many new experiences. This requires the infant to explore again the wild and uncharted regions of its own body in its new world. At first, movements are a bit jerky and do not seem to be directed at anything. As it explores the inner space of its body, the infant starts directing movements towards a goal and accomplishing it. This is always bittersweet for parents; while it is wonderful to see their child progress, it typically results in much more hair-pulling and high-speed grabs for breakable objects. Infants receiving kangaroo care experience an increase in the maturity of their motor systems over infants who do not.

Another interesting finding is that infants who receive skin-to-skin contact also have increased eye gaze. My close friend, after the birth of his child, would say jokingly that his favorite show these days was "Baby TV." He and his wife talked about getting lost gazing at their child. The depth of heart and meaning passing between them as they gazed at one another seemed to defy explanation. It is no surprise that touch plays a role in this process. Eye gazing happens most when an infant is snuggled right in the arms of their parents. The social connection that is established with touch may prime the social connection through the eyes. Infant-mother eye gaze is how the social brain begins to develop. Reciprocal eye gaze is how an infant first sees another person who sees them. This is the foundation of how we begin to understand our own emotional life and the emotional life of others. Premature infants often lag behind full-term infants in this ability. Eye gaze has an important function for parents too. It helps parents feel more connected and may stimulate oxytocin production, increasing bonding between parent and child. Not surprisingly, eye contact is markedly different in children with autistic spectrum disorders.

All parents, but especially those of premature infants, worry whether their child will develop normally or not. This can lead to unnecessary parental stress and difficulty bonding. If a child has a difficulty, it needs to be recognized and addressed; however, consistently viewing a child as a problem can set up other difficulties. Often, infants who receive kangaroo care are perceived by their parents as more normal, leading to increased maternal and paternal sensitivity, and healthier parent-infant interactions. Multiple studies of kangaroo care have found that infants who receive skin-to-skin contact are more likely to have a higher body mass index, a good indicator of infant health and of the developing maturity of the infant.

One of the difficulties for premature infants is developing self-regulation. Self-regulation is a conglomeration of abilities that continues developing over a lifetime. Some of these abilities include self-soothing after an emotional event, sleep-regulation, waking and eating, and more advanced skills such as managing complex time demands. The foundation of self-regulation hits maturity by the age of twenty-three, but continues to develop throughout life.

The first patterns of sleep, activity, rest, and enjoyment of different tastes, develop in the womb. Once a child is born, it faces new challenges that push the child to develop the capacity to regulate its own needs. Premature infants who receive kangaroo care have a more mature, regular sleep-wake cycle. As any new parent knows, the ongoing strain of regular nocturnal arousals, midnight screaming, and inconsolable emotional responses, can strain a family and the relationship between parents.

Premature infants have a greater tendency to be unable to reduce or "modulate" their emotional reactions. All infants have limited ability to self-soothe; however, premature infants have far less self-soothing ability than do full-term infants. Studies show that premature infants who receive kangaroo care have a higher threshold for tolerating negative emotional experiences. Premature infants who receive regular skin-to-skin contact are better able to "regulate" or calm their own emotions: an example would be returning from a crying fit to a more baseline level of positive or neutral emotions. Being able to regulate emotions is associated with an ability to tolerate novelty, or new situations, pay attention to complex environmental events, and other factors in infant learning. A six-month follow-up showed that children who received kangaroo care experienced a higher quality of maternal interactions (increased shared attention between mother and infant), were more likely to explore their environment, and were better able to tolerate independence.

Brain Development and Touch—Zero to Two Years

The world inside the womb is vastly different from the world outside the womb. The brain of a prenate and infant is wide open and *driven* to develop. During the first few years of life, the infant brain bathes in neural chemicals that help it learn and develop a map of the world, its own body, and the inner world of others. For years, debate raged in the field of psychology over whether a child was simply born to its fate, driven by the force of biology, or if it developed (as John Locke, the famous Enlightenment philosopher believed) from a "blank slate" by learning, and interaction with the world. Like answers to most polarized arguments, both views are quite correct for the most part and incorrect in one respect: they were both wrong to discount the opposing view. While much of brain development occurs relatively independently of experience, much of brain development *depends* on experience.

In the last ten years, an organizational paradigm for principles of brain development has emerged. The brain develops according to three main principles: experience-independent, experience-expectant, and experience-dependent processes.

Experience-Independent Processes: biologically driven development that occurs as long as there are no major disruptions to the DNA from mutation, or factors that regulate how the genes are expressed (epigenetic factors).

Experience-Expectant Processes: parts of brain functions and structures primed for development. They require the right type of external events and interactions with care providers to develop; nonetheless, the brain is ready to learn this type of information.

Experience-Dependent Processes: require direct learning. Most of what psychology calls "crystallized knowledge" falls into this category. These are things like the name of a friend's dog or the lead singer of the Beatles, or where you can get a good pizza in your hometown.

Early Brain Changes

The child seems to be getting ready for the world in the last few months before its birth. The last trimester in the womb is one of major brain development. The brain is changing, sculpting, wiring and rewiring.

This process continues over the first year of life, during which many infants show a dramatic increase in the volume of gray-matter (the cell bodies of the neurons in the brain). The brain nearly doubles in size over the course of this first year (106 % increase in year one, 18 % in year two). While this growth is a biological process, it is also driven by the child's interactions and experiences. To put this in perspective, the brains of children who suffer profound neglect can be up to thirty-eight percent smaller as they enter their teen years, than the brain of a child with a normal upbringing.

The brain continues developing in the second year of life. Some of this development involves choosing the "best" circuits to keep, and is less related to change in size. While the sensory motor areas develop more quickly in utero, in the first and second years of life the sensory and motor regions of the brain grow more slowly than does the frontal lobe. The infant or toddler, learning to explore the world and its body's ability to affect the world, is also learning about the way things work. In the womb, there are far fewer things with which to engage. Outside the womb, there is more need for physical motion to be purposeful, and related to cause and effect. The frontal lobe structures of the brain are deeply involved in this process. During the first eighteen months of life outside the womb, the right half of the brain develops more quickly than the left. In the first year of life, the largest areas of development in the mid-brain limbic, or subcortical region, are the amygdalae and the thalamus. The amygdalae have gained notoriety over the last few years for their role in decision-making, anger, aggression, fear, stress, and post-traumatic stress disorder.

Many functions of the amygdalae are related to how we deal with frustration and aggression. An infant who has a dirty diaper and is uncomfortable will scrunch up its face and howl. When a child howls or a parent is frustrated, there is a good chance that the amygdalae are involved. When a father changes the diaper and soothingly sings to his infant, the infant calms down and the amygdalae begin to fire less. During infancy, the amygdalae are undergoing profound development, laying down tracks of neurons and patterns of behavior that can last a lifetime.

Touch changes how the amygdalae function. Soothing touch is known to reduce amygdalae activation and reduce cortisol production (a neurochemical in the catecholamine family that plays a large role in the stress response). Holding an infant reduces its stress response. Infant massage has a powerful impact on stress hormone production, not only in infants, but also in their mothers. Additionally, parents that regularly touch their infant report higher relationship satisfaction with their partner.

The thalamus, known as the relay station for the brain, is a key region of development in the infant. It is the first stop for all the sensory information we get from the world and our bodies—with the exception of smell. Some evolutionary biologists believe that smell is one of the first senses to arise; hence the brain develops around it. What is certainly true is that the sense of smell bypasses the thalamus, going straight to the amygdalae. This may be why certain aromas bring such strong memories and emotions to the surface for some people.

The thalamus is a *vital* area of the brain, one of those slightly enigmatic regions that appears to have some specific functions but is more involved in *all* brain functions than in any particular one. The thalamus also plays an important role in sleep; some have argued that it sends a pulse wave throughout the entire brain, helping the brain synchronize and enter into a sleep state. This pulsing wave may be a reason we say we "fall" asleep—the feeling of dropping down may be a part of the brain entering into a deeper state of rest.

Another vital region of the brain, the hippocampus, is less developmentally active than the thalamus during the first two years of life. A surgery brought awareness of the hippocampus into mainstream culture and first gave researchers a glimpse into this region of the brain and the role it plays in human life. A man known to researchers as HM had a profound case of epilepsy, a condition that causes seizures. In a grand-mal seizure, one part of the brain begins to fire in a synchronized pulsing pattern, and other regions begin to join the pattern until the entire brain is firing. This sends the motor regions of the brain into contractions, causing the body to tighten all at once and the person to fall to the ground in spasms. After years of treatment, HM was not getting better. One of the treatments of last resort for seizures is to sever the main brain fibers (corpus callosum) that allow communication between the left and right halves of the brain, thus stopping the seizure from propagating. HM underwent surgery to sever the corpus callosum, but his hippocampus was damaged.

When HM awakened after the surgery, he was fine in many respects (in fact the surgery did stop his seizures), but he lacked the ability to form long-term memories. He could not remember new names or places, and although he did have some ability to learn new procedures or physical tasks, he could not remember learning them! The hippocampus is vital in the storage and retrieval of information, known as declarative memory. It appears not to play as large a role in learning actions or behaviors, such as walking, or expressing emotions. It is interesting, albeit not surprising, to note that during the first two years of life the hippocampus is not developing as quickly as other regions of the infant brain. In the past, this led some theorists to make a critical error in their attempts to understand human development. They assumed that if the hippocampus was not growing, the child was not learning; therefore early experience did not matter. The infant *is* learning. The hippocampus *is* developing, just more slowly than the other more procedural memory systems.

It is also interesting that while declarative memory (memory of events, people,) is not developing very rapidly in the first two years— the executive system *is* developing quickly. This executive system, or front-brain, relates to thinking, planning, organizing, and understanding. These first two years of life tune the senses and the brain. During its first months of life, an infant will hear and attend to all the sounds of all human languages. As the child ages, the mind begins to tune towards the sounds of the child's native language. However, it may be that a good part of our higher-order planning and organizing is not fueled by verbal understanding, but by a wordless knowing. Perhaps this is why intuition plays such a large role in learning and creativity. The foundation of our knowing may have a non-verbal component that is under-recognized due to the current cultural bias in this "information age."

Connection between infant and caregiver is a sensory relationship. It is a relationship of anticipated experiences. Touch and holding are primary in this early relationship. As the child explores the world, the parents' touches and physical connection become signals of safety. When a child falls, touch soothes both the physical and the emotional pain. Touch is integral to the developmental stages of early life. Disruption of the process of tuning the mind and senses can cause long-term disruptions in brain development. Happily however, if brain development veers off course, there are many chances throughout childhood to use touch to help nudge the brain back toward its optimal developmental path.

Chapter 2

The Role of Touch in Child Development

A small boy with jet-black hair bursts into tears after a fall. He looks back at his mother two feet away; she smiles, unworried, and picks him up as his chest heaves. His breath calms as his body sinks into his mother's arms. In another minute, he is scrambling hurriedly down her body to resume playing. As his mother watches him run off, her husband puts his hand on her shoulder and smiles. They look at each other in silent communion for a moment before they go back to parenting and help resolve a dispute between children. Touch plays a vital role in the family—supporting development of social bonds and feelings of love and helping the family survive the inevitable stresses of life. Touch supports us as we maneuver through small challenges like skinned knees, and even bigger life-events like buying or losing a home, or changing jobs.

Research into the importance of touch has proven that it is vital for childhood development. In studies of both humans and animals, the quality and quantity of touch impacts the rates of physical growth and brain development. The family is the ecosystem within which a child develops; touch and human contact create and nurture the health of the family ecosystem. Understanding the types of touch, the relationship between developmental-stages and family touch, and the biological mechanisms of touch can help a suffering family reach a new level of health and joy.

Touch in the Family—Childhood

The family is a tapestry of interactions. Smiles, gestures, laughter, confrontations, high-fives, wrestling, and cuddles—they all knit a small group of people into a family. Touch is the glue of the family unit; it plays a role in soothing feelings of disappointment, or simply feeling better after a fall. Touch is fundamental to a child's developmental ability to learn that they can feel better after experiencing a difficult situation. The child's world is written in touch. Before there are words, there is the wordless communication of the body. The exploration of the child's ability to interact with and change the world happens first through the sense of touch. It is not surprising that early experiences of touch affect our stress levels later in life, and impact how we are in relationship to others, and how we explore the world.

In a recent study exploring the impact of touch in human development, researchers interviewed three-hundred-ninety adults about their early experiences of touch, hoping to determine whether there was a connection between family touch experienced in early childhood, and adult depression. They found that three factors played a role in adult depression: poor self-image, poor image of others, and fewer interpersonal touches throughout childhood. The touch histories of the participants in this study had strong influences on their perception of romantic partners and friends in both adolescence and adulthood. Another group of researchers videotaped one-hundred-fourteen mothers with their three-month-old infants during breast feedings. The babies who received the most nurturing touch during feedings were the least likely to show problems with depression or excessive acting-out behavior (breaking objects, yelling, throwing things when angry or upset to express the emotion) at the age of two years.

Children actually make their parents want to interact more with them when they demonstrate that they are enjoying what the parent is doing! Parents not reinforced by their child's enjoyment of the interaction are likely to reduce the rate of interactive touch rather than increase it. Children who act-out tend to be more rejecting of parental touch as well. Children more rejecting of their parents' touch were at higher risk of depression as two-year olds. Research also indicates that some mothers of these less responsive children used a diverse range of touch interactions despite their child's reluctance to accept parental touch. These children were more likely to have superior adaptation at two years of age compared with both the non-touch-rejecting children and the children who rejected touch but didn't have a persistent parent! Implementing the right touch-based tools can change problems into strengths; this has powerful implications for parenting, education, and therapy.

The importance of touch does not end when we become adults. It continues throughout our lives. The small touches of appreciation between a couple—the gestures of affection and love—are a crucial part of the foundation of a relationship. As an infant transitions to childhood, the demands on parents increase. Parents are busier at work and in the home, and sometimes the warm connection between parents and their children can give way to trying to accomplish an endless list of tasks. Allowing the duties of the day to overtake parental interactions of support and play can lead to a tipping-point in relationship, leading to intense stress on the family system, the parents' relationship, and the children in the family. As the parents cease expressing support and enjoyment of each other with small gestures, they may also stop using touch with their children as well, making the family vulnerable to stressful situations.

All couples fight. Constructive conflict is an important part of human interaction. The difference between constructive and destructive conflict has been a focus of research for some time. On a biological level, as conflict increases between two people, there is typically an increase in cortisol levels. When our face gets red and we want to say something nasty to our loved one, we can thank cortisol for the feeling! Distinguished professor of psychology, and principal investigator of the Positive Emotions and Psychophysiology Lab at The University of North Carolina at Chapel Hill, Dr. Barbara Fredrickson, found in her work on emotional resilience to stress that even a small number of positive emotions after a stressor reduces the time it takes cortisol to return to rest. A hand on the shoulder, a kind smile, or a statement of forgiveness, can increase positive emotion—allowing cortisol levels to return to rest.

A group of researchers brought forty-seven couples into the lab for a good argument. However, they gave the couples a boost. In the experimental group, each individual received a small nasal spray of oxytocin, which brought about changes in their neurochemistry. (Salivary alpha-amylase increases in men and decreases in women.) Interestingly, during these arguments the men in the experimental group demonstrated behaviors that were more constructive. In another study, oxytocin reduced the secretion of cortisol in individuals with low emotion regulation skills, buffering against the adverse effects of cortisol. Unfortunately, at present we cannot publicly buy bottles of oxytocin to spray into our nostrils; however, there are skills we can use and ways we can choose to act, that will increase our excretion of oxytocin.

The Family and the Ancestral Human Mammalian Milieu

"The ancestral human mammalian milieu" is the ecology of social and environmental conditions present during human evolution. Over the course of human history, people have developed within a context. If we understand the features of this context, we can see some of the basic conditions needed for the health and wellbeing of children and families.

A central factor in the development of the ecology of the family system and child development is touch. Researcher Darcia Narvaez lists several ways touch plays a role in the development of the child. One of the first is consistency of touch. Looking at early records of human interactions and current groups of hunter-gatherers, we find that touch is constant from the beginning of life. For long periods of their early development, children are held almost constantly, and kept near parents or caregivers. Narvaez and Gleason also note that the caregivers provide appropriate responses to the feeling states and bodily needs of children. In the ancestral milieu, breastfeeding occurs frequently and on demand, as often as two or three times per hour in the early postnatal period. Research on long-term health, shows that drinking mother's milk plays an important role in developing strong immune function. This has led to an increased amount of breast-milk pumping; however, touch during breastfeeding may also affect long-term immune functioning; the skin-to-skin contact during breast-feeding may significantly alter stress response and its relationship to the immune system.

It Takes a Village

A study of touch among the Bofi, a group of hunter-gatherers in central Africa, found a diverse and consistent use of touch, confirming the assumptions made in the above discussion of the ancestral milieu. This study examined three types of touch: care-giving touch—taking care of the physical needs of children; active social-affectionate touch—highly engaged and supportive; and passive social-affectionate touch. This study found that although mothers touched children most frequently, all members of the group played roles in caring for and providing supportive touch for the children. All of the care providers used passive-affectionate touch. Fathers and other care providers (extended relatives) used about the same levels of caring touch. Juvenile peers provided the highest levels of active-affectionate touch. This study clearly shows the different types of touch and their different roles in the community support system.

In the ancestral milieu, many adults raise each child. Fathers, grandparents, aunts, and close family relations play important roles in their life. This allows the child to learn from multiple adults and creates a solid support system for the family. Children in this social milieu are embedded within their social group; they are not isolated. They tend to gather for free-play in groups of children of varied ages, rather than the age-specific playgroups of contemporary Western culture.

Touch Builds Attachment within the Family

In the mid-20th century, a revolution in psychology began that is still playing out today, led by an unlikely person—German animal ethologist Konrad Lorenz. Lorenz wrote about a series of studies on what we now call attachment. He discovered that there is a critical period when infant geese attach to a care provider. Lorenz found that if goslings saw him, rather than a goose, during this period, they would follow him as if he were their parent. With his history of participating in "racial hygiene" experiments in Poland during Nazi rule, Lorenz was an unlikely mother goose; nonetheless, he is remembered in history books as "the father of ethology." He determined that this early attachment was an enduring bond. In humans, this bond is more complicated and develops over time. Many experts argue that the early bond which ensues during a "critical period" is not only vital to human development, but to the development of relationships across a lifetime. A critical period is an interval of time when key aspects of development become possible. After the critical period it becomes difficult for the same developmental processes to happen. In geese the critical period of social bonding is just after hatching; in humans this same process of "attachment" or bonding is more complex, with more milestones in its development. A critical period is often contrasted with a "sensitive period." A sensitive period is a phase in development when an individual is more receptive to certain developmental processes than at other periods.

At around the same time Lorenz was conducting his studies, a now-famous researcher named Harry Harlow was doing foundational research with monkeys on what he chose to call "love." Harry Harlow discovered something simple and yet profound, that challenged basic assumptions of in the field of psychology. One assumption was that infants bonded with their mothers through feeding. In other words, psychologists thought that the food created the social bond, not the comfort and support of touch. Harlow's research turned this thinking on its head, finding that comfort mattered more than food in social bonds.

To understand the attachment process in humans, we need to understand three key aspects of bonding: First, the attachment bond is a stable and enduring bond with a specific person or group of people. Second, the attachment relationship supports the feeling of safety and comfort. It is a source of pleasure and enjoyment in being together and provides relief from difficulties in life. Third, the threat of losing the relationship is stressful and difficult. Touch plays a role in all three aspects.

Oxytocin is one of the chemicals that mediate what researchers (animal) call pair bonding or what researchers (human) call romantic love. Sue Carter, in her now famous research, studied the effects of oxytocin on pair bonds in voles. The prairie vole mates for life. Both parents participate in the raising of the young voles. In contrast, living high in the mountains is a close relative of the prairie vole, the mountain vole. These animals are highly promiscuous and do not have stable family bonds. Dr. Carter and her research team believed these voles would be excellent animals through which to explore the biology that leads to long-term committed relationships. Devising an elegant series of studies, Dr. Carter and her team found that blocking the expression of a certain chemical group (oxytocin and vasopressin) in prairie voles increased promiscuity over stable family units. Prairie voles stopped acting like June and Ward Cleaver in "Leave it to Beaver" and began behaving like roving Don Juans. In other words, blocking these two chemicals caused prairie voles to behave like mountain voles. Humans have a more complicated mating structure; nonetheless these chemicals also play an important role in human bonding. For humans, touch is a major method of stimulating our natural production of oxytocin and vasopressin. Touch also plays an important role in soothing difficult emotions, and promoting feelings of safety and comfort with the people that matter to us (attachment). Attachment is recognized as a crucial part of emotional development and touch is fundamental to human attachment—yet few psychologists or therapists understand how to use touch, and how to help families use touch to support their attachment and overall health.

Childhood and Touch in Learning

Our culture is highly complex. The amount of information a young child needs to learn is staggering. Touch plays a role in the learning process: for instance, in early childhood, touch plays a role in the development of attention and motor skills. Frequently, one of the father's roles is to stimulate the child through rough play. Fathers often toss their children into the air and catch them on the way down, or hang the child upside down as the child giggles and demands,

"Again, Daddy!" In this exploration, the child is learning about human interaction, and its own body. They learn how to trust their ability to move. Playful, safe roughhousing increases bonding between father and child.

As children develop their ability to explore the world, and gain confidence that parents or caregivers are meeting their needs, they transition to school. This is a difficult time for children. Often, schools are deserts of supportive touch and have a limited number of adult-child interactions.

The lack of touch in our educational structures is a shame, because as previously discussed, touch plays an important role in children successfully learning to self-regulate, pay attention, and engage in classroom activities. One study examined touch in an early childhood education classroom. The authors of this study (Steward and Lupfer) found that although educators did touch children, anxiety about legal repercussions from misperceived touch caused most of their touch to be control-based touch, or touch aimed at direct care—comfort was provided less often. School attachment, or how closely bonded a child feels to their school as a whole, is highly predictive of that child's overall success in school. It is entirely possible that the lack of touch and physical contact is creating another needless barrier to educational success.

Attitude toward touch is one factor influencing how educators use touch and contact in their work. Thus, changes in cultural attitudes would probably influence classroom practices. Research implies that other factors also influence how touch is utilized in educational centers, such as the attitudes of educational directors about touch and contact, the understood social norms of a center, and the level of emotional support provided to the staff by directors.

This study also found that a small percentage of children received all three types of contact, while some children received little or no affectionate touch. Children considered "difficult" received more negative and less affectionate touch, which is not surprising; equally unsurprising is that the strongest predictor of affectionate touch was children's expressed affection for an educator.

One of the more tragic findings of this study is that children with traumatic histories such as neglect, physical abuse, or sexual abuse, have a tendency to act-out and are thus more likely to receive negative touch from educators. Understandably, these children are ambivalent about contact and connection with adults, and are more rejecting of their educators' support, leading to a reduction of positive touch. Considering the positive impact of oxytocin and bonding on stress and health, the most damaged children, such as survivors of abuse, could very easily suffer a downward spiral of educational failure. This is tragedy heaped upon tragedy. However, with attention to the type and quality of care in the educational setting, such tragedies could be forestalled. The negative impact trauma has on learning is under-recognized and is not managed effectively. It may be one factor leading schools to fail the children they are intended to support.

Play and Touch in Early Childhood

In 1966, psychiatrist Stuart Brown studied a notorious mass-murderer: Charles Whitman climbed a tower at the University of Texas—Austin, and began shooting people with a sniper-rifle, one by one. As Dr. Brown explored the history of the young shooter, disturbing facts emerged. Charles Whitman experienced highly repressive parenting, and a violent father who abused Charles' mother. Model student and Eagle Scout though he was, Charles was not allowed to play. He had a profound deficit in his upbringing—not of structure, but of play. In the words of Dr. Brown, Charles had never "experienced play." This remarkable insight led Dr. Brown on a journey that has lasted throughout his career. He started out studying mass-murder and ended up founding the National Institute for Play. He went on to conduct a pilot study of murderers in Texas and found that they did indeed experience a very different play history than his matched control group. Since then Dr. Brown has conducted more than six-thousand informal play interviews. While these interviews were not rigorously scientific, they indicate a powerful trend; people with deficient play histories manifest loss in productivity, mild depression, and inhibited creativity.

As children develop, their play develops. According to Dr. Mildred Parten, a play expert who categorized the stages of children's play in 1932, children develop the complexity of play across childhood. While all "stage" theories are somewhat problematic in that people are far more complex than the theories allow, in general there is an increase in the complexity of play across childhood. Dr. Parten described the process of moving from "onlooker" play—sitting in a single spot, watching other children play without joining in, to "cooperative" play—engaged social interactions, rules, and an understanding of the mind of the other child. Play is a way children engage with their environment. Far from being frivolous, play develops many skills including attention and concentration, problem solving, and conflict-resolution.

Rats, if restricted from engaging in play in their childhood and adolescence, do not display typical social behaviors in their adulthood. Even for a less socially complex animal, play is vital to understanding social roles and navigating successfully through adulthood.

Play is known to stimulate dopamine, a neurochemical that plays an important role in pleasure, reward, and what researchers call "appetitive behaviors." Appetitive behaviors include enjoyment, play, sexuality, and of course, desire to eat. Dopamine also plays a role in learning, and helps stabilize sustained attention.

Two five-year-old boys are playing with a toy when one exclaims, "Let's wrestle!" They jump up and begin rolling around, pushing, shoving, and having a good time. Most mammals exhibit this type of play; it is part of the developmental process that peaks in middle-childhood. Children explore their abilities and mastery of their bodies through contact, while also learning to exercise their imagination, manage frustration, play fairly, and have safe conflict.

Other forms of motor play are rhythmic stereotypes, and exercise-based. Rhythmic stereotype play is repetitive movement that peaks in infancy. Exercise play peaks during pre-school years and is generally aimed at increasing strength and endurance. Most children in this stage love throwing objects as far as possible, exploring the limits of their abilities, whereas for older children, accuracy may become a greater focus of play.

Children dress up, build forts, wrestle, and run; touch plays a vital role in all of these activities. Touch also stimulates some of the same brain regions activated by play. Magnetic resonance imaging of rats shows the emotion-based areas of their brains light up when they are playing. Play and touch stimulate factors that increase the rate of brain plasticity—the rate a brain can remodel itself to learn new skills. Despite so much solid evidence of how vital play is for optimal development—most schools are reducing free-play, cutting physical education, and piling on homework—ignoring evidence that children need to play more, rather than less.

One powerful finding from play research is that play builds joint attention. Joint attention is the shared attention of two or more people on a task or experience. You cannot learn in a classroom without it! Joint attention is what it takes to learn to read, or to sit still in a classroom and pay attention to a teacher. In a class, when the teacher is talking, the child and the teacher are paying attention to the same thing. Sitting in a parent's lap, a child feels safe and supported as he explores a book or a toy. In these moments, a parent uses his or her own capacity to focus and concentrate, helping their child develop these abilities. Physical contact with a parent sets in motion a neurobiological cascade that primes a child for learning.

Touch and Brain Development in Childhood

A four year old child makes soup by combining sand and water. She smashes the sand and water into a yellow mold and then tries to feed it to her mother as her mother makes "num-num" sounds before returning to her task. The interaction between child and parent affects not only behavior, but also brain development. Another child, half a world away, lived in an understaffed orphanage in Romania. The staff had no training in proper childcare. In these settings, the neglect was profound. Children were mostly unattended and some, as they became mobile, were tied to their beds. This profound lack of nurturing changes not just the behavior of a child, but also the fundamental structure of a child's brain.

If this child were adopted into a caring home by the age of six months, her brain would develop almost normally, with only a three percent reduction in total brain size. However, if the child is adopted later, her brain development would be markedly different. If she is not adopted by six years of age, there can be up to a thirty-eight percent reduction in brain size! What does this mean for intelligence? A study of children adopted from a Lebanese orphanage assessed the children's intelligence and age of adoption. Children adopted before the age of six months achieved an average intelligence quotient (IQ) score of one-hundred. This score is similar to all average children, whether born or adopted into a family. Children adopted between six months and two years of age averaged an IQ score of eighty; this is a significant difference that puts the child at risk for poor intellectual functioning. If a child is adopted after six years of age, the mean IQ score is fifty, a significant intellectual disability, and half the IQ of an average adult. With an IQ of fifty, a child will almost certainly need some form of caretaking throughout their life. One of the greatest deficits in these orphanages has been touch and physical contact. Romanian orphans adopted later in life have *significant* risk of developing autism spectrum disorder—an important finding that sheds light on the relationship between trauma, neglect, and developmental disorders.

One recent finding about touch is the discovery of a group of small fibers called the C-fibers. C-fibers send signals of supportive, affectionate, or nurturing touch to the brain. They are similar to the fibers that relay pain, itch, and temperature to the brain; however, the C-fibers appear to be stimulated by light, pleasant touch. They play an important role in the emotional communication of touch and social interaction.

The C-fibers bypass the pain pathway in the brain and synapse in the insular cortex, a part of the limbic, or the emotional-brain, that plays a role in taking signals from the body and turning them into information about our emotional and physical well-being. The C-fibers engage a circuit that includes areas of the emotional brain far beyond the insula, including the medial prefrontal cortex (mPFC). This important region of the brain is involved in thinking, planning, and regulating emotions. When we are angry or upset, this area of the brain engages and soothes the difficult feeling. These brain areas are involved in what appears to be an emotion-touch circuit designed to support emotion regulation through physical contact.

Touch and the Neuropsychological Development of Adolescents

It had been a long time since her father had hugged her. She was four-teen, starting high school, and scared, but a little too proud to admit it. Her heart pounded in her chest as father drove to her bus stop. He had stopped giving her hugs when her body began to change. It made him feel a little nervous, and he did not want to be misperceived. As a tough and bright teen, Sylvia did not want to admit that she needed anyone, let alone her father, but she knew she did. She missed the times her father would hold her in his lap and read to her, or pick her up and hug her when she was hurt. Today, mixed with the excitement of going to high school, Sylvia was feeling like she just wanted to be scooped up and held close. As she was getting out of the car at the bus stop several miles from her home, her father took her hand and said, "I love you and I am proud of you." Sylvia's shoulders, tense and pressed up nearly to her ears, lowered as he held her hand, her breath-ing deepened, and she smiled as she left the car.

Her father communicated a deep sense of safety and security to Sylvia with this contact. Her response was not simply psychological; it also resulted from a neurobiological cascade of chemicals. Human contact reduced secretion of the stress hormone cortisol, helping Sylvia shift from stress to rest. Safe contact with her father increased oxytocin, giving her feelings of love and trust. These feelings lingered with Sylvia as she climbed into the bus, making it easier for her to connect and engage with other students.

Adolescence is a time of developing adult abilities and making the transition from a largely dependent child, to a more independent young adult who can still seek help when needed. The adolescent brain is developing the ability to tolerate and make use of intense emotions, as well as learning to navigate complex social interactions. In addition, dopamine secretion increases in adolescence, driving the teen to be more impulsive and pleasure seeking, and thus more susceptible to addictions.

Most teens navigate these years with only minor difficulties, particularly if they enjoy a loving, supportive relationship with the adults in their lives, good supervision, clear structure, and positive social relationships. Of these four factors, the strongest predictor of adolescents not making major mistakes, such as getting involved in criminal behaviors, or becoming addicted to drugs or alcohol, is a loving relationship with their parent or parents. However, in their fierce drive for independence, teens are often prickly and hard to communicate with, sometimes vehemently rejecting adults offering them love and support. Safe, connected touch, hugs, and time with family and interested adults, can be powerful communicators of love and support that provide a buffer against the pulls of negative peer behaviors and the impulse to act-out.

Parents must regularly shift their role as their teens develop, from director to coach and back to director again. As any parent of a teenager knows, there are many times when an adolescent will behave in an adult and responsible manner—this is when they are coachable. Only days later, that adolescent will act with terrible judgment—these are times when the teen needs direction. Because being loved, understood, and cared for are the strongest predictors of a successful transition to adulthood, parents, relatives, and educators also must find the delicate balance between pushing new development and regularly showing the teen love for who they already are.

Adolescents—Touch and Attachment

> "If your plan is for one year, plant rice;
> If your plan is for ten years, plant a tree.
> If your plan is for one hundred years, teach children"
> ~ CHINESE PROVERB

Attachment is the predictable interaction of people in relationship— the felt-quality of connection, love, and safety in relationship to others. Psychologists and researchers like John Bowlby and Mary Ainsworth discussed an individual's attachment style—patterns of behavior that tend to cluster and manifest across multiple human relationships. Some people display a secure attachment style—predicting comfort with following direction and taking leadership, and feeling a sense of safety when interacting with others. Some individuals tend to become highly anxious or worried about their social relationships, while others tend to reject social relationships outright—minimizing their importance. During adolescence, human touch and contact are fundamental for developing healthy attachments and attachment styles.

Jen Reconnects

Jen, age fourteen, sat in family therapy with me, worrying about whether her adoptive parents cared for her at all. She held her tears back with the force of her whole body, not willing to let go in her fear of being rejected, while her adoptive mother sat nearby, ready to listen and support Jen. As I watched this exchange, I encouraged Jen's mom to let her know it was safe. Jen's body softened slightly, but she tensed again as the tears nearly poured out. I asked Jen if it would be okay if her mother sat right next to her and put her hand on her back. Jen appeared frozen as she considered her options, and then gave a small, barely perceptible nod. I instructed the mother to move slowly and sit next to her daughter. As she placed her hand on to Jen's back, Jen tensed more, and then her body began heaving with sobs. I supported her mother's efforts to console Jen until her jagged sobs gave way to more even tears, and then to a quiet connection between the two. This kind of moment often precedes a deepening of the relationship and trust between a child and his or her parents. This story is a composite of many of my sessions that have followed the same pattern of interactions. Had I asked Jen's mother to explain in words her love for her daughter, we would have missed the profound communication of safety and connection offered by safe, loving, and supportive touch.

Attachment plays several vital roles in the developmental process for teenagers and their parents. The attachment relationship becomes a relationship the teen is willing to learn from, and hopes not to damage. Because of this, teens will be willing to work hard to control their impulses, and they will act in ways that invite validation from their attachment figures. Attachment also becomes a buffer against stress and life challenges. Touch plays a vital role in creating the attachment relationship.

While attachment begins in infancy, it continues across a lifetime and, even with a disruption, an individual can develop safer and more comfortable attachments if they are given the right circumstances and opportunities.

Acting-Out and Acting-In

Some of the most difficult behaviors a teen can express fall into two categories: externalizing behaviors and internalizing behaviors. Externalizing behaviors are the ways in which teens act-out when they feel intense emotions. Internalizing behaviors are ways that teens are aggressive toward themselves when their emotional reaction is greater than their ability to deal with the feeling. One of the major predictors of adolescents acting-out is their relationship to their parents. Toddlers reported by their parents to be more rejecting of affection tend to display more externalizing behaviors in adolescence. One possible pathway for this developmental pattern is that the child's rejection of parental interaction leads to a reduction of caring and supportive touch, and an increase in punishing and rejecting touch. This increase of negative touch and decrease of positive touch profoundly affects the way children experience the interaction with their care providers; it reduces trust and increases their negative behavior. Some research shows that when children who had experienced the most rejecting touch received more caring and supportive touch, their negative behaviors decreased.

In another powerful study of adolescent behavior and touch, Dr. Field and her research team hypothesized that since touch is soothing and increases a sense of relaxation and rest, it might also have a positive impact on teens who act-out aggressively. She recruited a group of teens who were highly aggressive. In a carefully detailed manner, Field studied their rates of anxiety, aggression, and other characteristics. One group received a twenty-minute massage; the other group practiced a relaxation skill. She found that only the group receiving massage showed a decrease in the aggression scores on the Child Behavior Checklist and the Overt Aggression Scale. In the massage group, the teens were not learning aggression-management or assertiveness skills, or talking about their problems, but even so, their behaviors changed. They were in relationship! Safe, supportive, connected touch in a family may also affect attachment and adolescent behavior.

Experiencing just *one positive emotion* helps individuals return from stress to rest quickly. Safe, affectionate, supportive touch creates positive emotions.

When the body moves too slowly from a stressed to a relaxed state, it is possible that teens experience stress as being endless. They may not understand that they are able to calm down, or realize that the stress will stop. Teens can learn to soothe themselves through interactions with their parents, thus increasing their own skills. This is like taking a swimming class, as opposed to being pushed into the deep end and told to swim. How can parents help a teen develop the ability to self-soothe difficult emotions? One pattern for developing increased ability managing difficult emotions is having small, tolerable experiences of emotions, while supported by another person. Like all humans, teenagers require safe, supportive, and affectionate touch; however, it is important that adults, even as they coach teens on how to regulate their emotions, also give them opportunities to regulate their emotions independently.

Late Adolescence—Touch and Education

Professors in a college program agreed to participate in a study of the impact of touch on learning. Students in their classes were randomly assigned to two groups. Members of one group received a brief, non-coercive, supportive touch on a safe body part, such as a hand or shoulder, during a discussion with their professor. Members of the other group experienced only the discussion. Students were asked to rate their teachers on how connected they felt to them. Students who received safe, non-coercive touch were more likely to report feeling connection to their teachers than those who had the discussion alone. In addition, students in the group that received touch performed better on the next academic test than students in the other group.

Teenage Brains are a Work-in-Progress

The teen brain is not fully developed, particularly in the prefrontal cortex area related to thinking, planning, organizing, regulating behavior, and tolerating emotions. The brain's frontal lobe is highly involved in attention, concentration, and learning. As discussed previously, studies indicate safe, supportive touch activates the frontal lobe of the brain, thus supporting thinking, planning, organizing, and making good choices.

Adolescence—Touch and Stress

A group of adolescent chimpanzees sits together, engaged in grooming one another, picking parasites off their friends' skin and combing through their fur. While some human teens could benefit from better grooming, this type of behavior does much more than make the young animals clean for their day in the jungle. It reduces their stress levels. The physical contact, safety, and emotional connection of the touch reduces the neurochemicals associated with stress and increases many neurochemicals that protect the brain and body from negative impacts of stress. If a human grooms a dog, or simply pets the animal, the levels of stress hormones their body expresses decrease. Just as skin-to-skin contact with a parent relaxes an infant, safe touch often greatly relieves stress. In the short-term, nurturing touch reduces stress levels and in the long-term, touch increases an individual's resilience in stressful situations—buffering them against the effects of stress.

As we noted earlier, a short disruption of the parent child bond in infancy can have a profound impact on stress reactivity for a lifetime. The timing of stress matters too. In rat models, social stress in early-adolescence increases the secretion of norepinephrine, which plays a role in the activation of defensive strategies (for example, hiding food or fighting), depression, attention, concentration, and level of arousal (alertness). However, social stress has little impact on the behaviors of adult rats or rats in late adolescence. There may be periods in early development when social interactions become the primary stressors, and it appears that this is similar for both rats and humans. Adolescents in the middle-school years ("tweens") are more affected by social stress than are adolescents graduating from high school. Children who would have buckled under social pressure in middle school are often not even fazed in their late teen years.

Unlike infant rats, if an adolescent rat undergoes stress, it does not result in increased cortisol stress response throughout its lifetime. If the adolescent rat's mother experienced high stress levels during her pregnancy, the young rat is likely to show a de*crease* in their stress response after a stressful event. These adolescent rats may have learned to ignore the impact of the stress due to chronic exposure throughout childhood. A drop in stress response sounds like a good thing, does it not? However, stress is what helps us learn from mistakes. Some human teenagers don't seem to learn from the consequences of making bad choices. In fact, teenagers whose cortisol levels drop after experiencing a stressful situation are more likely to act-out, not modifying their choices, regardless of the consequences.

Externalize This!

In the last section we considered the pathways to developing externalizing and internalizing behaviors. Research has shown some interesting and contradictory findings about the relationship of cortisol and these behaviors. One might expect that people who exhibit externalizing behaviors would have elevated cortisol levels, and while some people did, others had low or flattened cortisol levels. This study found that while experiencing an intensely stressful event at any time during development had an impact, the developmental stage when the event occurred was even more important. If a child acted-out and demonstrated externalizing behaviors before adolescence, then during adolescence they showed a lower cortisol, or stress response. If a teen developed these behaviors in adolescence, there was often an increase in cortisol before acting-out. It is possible that prolonged exposure to cortisol causes changes in the way it is secreted and functions within a teenager's body. Internalizing behaviors (self-blame and self-aggression) that began in childhood were associated with lower morning cortisol levels in adolescents, while internalizing behaviors that began in adolescence were related to higher morning cortisol levels.

Cortisol levels *should* be higher in the morning and lower at night. This makes intuitive sense. At night, we need to lower daily stress so we can sleep, while in the morning, we need enough energy to get up and face the day. However, some individuals, including those suffering with depression, exhibit a flat stress response. Flat cortisol response relates to the most severe behavioral and emotional problems in adolescent years. In other words, if the stress system is malfunctioning— behaviors are unstable.

Human contact and touch affect both behavior and neurochemistry. Touch between caregivers and children impacts stress levels, anxiety, aggression, and externalizing and internalizing behaviors. Increasing the quantity and quality of safe, supportive, nurturing touch may have a profound impact on adolescent development.

Adolescence—Touch and Social Development

We touch each other when we feel safe, and when we feel safe, we cooperate. Touch increases oxytocin, the neurochemical involved in three important aspects of human interaction: friendship bonding, romantic bonding, and social cooperation.

Dr. Tiffany Field, director of the Touch Research Lab in Florida, has published many studies of the impacts of touch on human development and health. In the mid-90s, she and her research team conceived a powerful and far-reaching idea. Considering that rates of touch vary according to cultures, and that rates of crime vary across cultures, Dr. Field thought that she could measure the impact (if any) of rates of touch on violent behaviors. The incidences of crime and violence in the United States were rising; was it possible that the rise in teen violence related to a deficiency of emotionally connected touch?

Realizing that McDonald's restaurants provide a controlled and relatively similar environment, Dr. Field and her team conducted a study in which researchers observed the types and frequency of touching behaviors among French and American teenagers. They found that French teens touch each other more often and with a higher level of affection and care than do American teens. Interestingly, American teens had more self-touch, rather than other-touch, and displayed more aggressive touch.

Teens in French society are less likely to be violent than teens in America. These findings are correlational, which makes it impossible to say whether a deficiency of affectionate touch was a direct cause of increased violence. In research parlance—correlation is not causation. Because things "co-relate"—occur close to each other in time and space—does not mean that one causes the other. For example, ice cream consumption goes up when criminal behavior goes up. This seems profound and interesting until one finds out that there is a third cause that creates both events—temperature. Moderately hot temperatures relate with increased violence, and when people are hot— they like ice cream. It is comforting to know that ice cream consumption does not lead to a life of crime.

Dr. J. W. Prescott, creator and director of the Developmental Biology program at the National Institute for Child Health and Development, believes that touch is one of the many factors contributing to child development. Results of studies he and others conducted drawing strong correlations between violent behaviors and children who lacked appropriate amounts of affection, influenced his thinking. He stated that he could assess with eighty percent accuracy the level of violence in a culture based on the level of crying and the quality of the relationship between parents and children. In cultures where physical affection toward children is common, Dr. Prescott noted less adult violence. Touch is crucial during the teen years. Touch is vital throughout our lifespan.

Chapter 3

Adulthood: Contact and Connection

Touch and Neuropsychological Development in Adults

Do we change? This deep question has challenged humans throughout our recorded history. Are we born predetermined to be "who we are"—doomed to remain the same throughout life? Or do we develop throughout our early years, but once the frame of our personality is built, our capacity to change stops? Alternatively, is life a constant process of development and change?

Early psychological theories argued that development is slow or non-existent after childhood. However, this idea is not supported by current data. Recently it has become clear that our brains change throughout our lifespan—even into our elder years. Increasing exercise, practicing meditation, increasing the joy in one's life—these and other positive activities affect the brain and influence how we view ourselves as people.

Touch has been under-researched, despite how strongly it affects us on so many levels. Touch is a vital and vibrant part of adult life—too often ignored in how we understand adulthood and what it means to live a good life. Since humans came into existence, people have been trying to figure out how to live. Our task as adults is to examine our life—our values, how the world works, who we are—and then lead a life that reflects our insights.

Erik Erikson was a student of Sigmund Freud, and like many of Freud's students, he struck out on his own intellectual path, often challenging Freud's key concepts. Many of Freud's theories were based on the tenet that the most important development stopped upon reaching adulthood. Erikson challenged this status quo and in doing so, he had a powerful impact on the field of psychology. Erikson never completed an undergraduate degree—let alone a doctorate—nonetheless he served as a professor at many distinguished institutions, including Harvard and Yale.

Erikson was a visionary—many of his ideas are still used by modern psychologists. However, his life was not without struggle. His relationship, if any, with his biological father is unknown. When Erik was about three-years old, his mother married his stepfather, who eventually adopted Erik. During that period of his life, he was known as Erik Homberger.

Erikson lived with contradictions. He was a tall, blond-haired, blue-eyed child being raised by a family of Jewish descent, who came of age in Germany prior to the Holocaust. He was teased in his temple school for looking Nordic, and by other children for being Jewish. Like many of us, his struggles and challenges pushed him toward discovering and developing his own identity. These challenges seem to have pushed him to look deeply at the meaning of identity. In fact, some of his key contributions to the field of psychology relate to understanding the development of identity. From an early age, Erikson had to consider who he was outside of the images and reflections other people gave him. He took the name Erik Erikson (Erik, son of Erik) when he took on a role as a professor at Yale, circa 1938. (It may have been helpful for his career progress at that time not to bear a classically Jewish surname.) Erikson certainly developed and grew throughout his life, experiencing significant changes in his identity even in adulthood. This may be one reason he examined and labeled stages of human development across the life span, determining the key crisis or challenge in each stage.

Each of Erikson's stages involves a crisis that challenges our identity to grow. How we meet this crisis and transform the challenge sets the stage for the development of our identity in the next stage. The stages of development in childhood build up to the challenges of young adulthood. Thus, at the age of one year, the crisis or conflict is "trust versus mistrust" and when this resolves, the child develops a basic since of hope. This development can even manifest in late adulthood. It culminates as appreciation of the interdependence of the individual and the world, as well as a sense of relatedness to the world and others. One of Erikson's powerful insights was that if we avoid the challenges of development, we do not manifest the strengths. It is through the fire of challenge and crisis that the crux of who we are is developed.

Erikson divided adulthood into two major stages. The first stage ranges over the ages of eighteen to twenty-five years (some models expand this stage to thirty-nine years), and the developmental challenge is intimacy versus isolation. The task for this stage is developing the ability to love. Erikson pointed out that intimacy requires an acceptance of the good, the bad, the wonderful, and the ugly of oneself, and of other people. Touch plays a powerful role in developing the ability to love, and to be loved. Simple gestures of affection between friends, as well as the shaky openheartedness of the first touches between lovers, lay the foundation for trust of oneself and of others. Skin-to-skin contact increases oxytocin secretion and one of the major functions of oxytocin is social bonding, or the feeling of safety with others. As individuals resolve this stage, they are driven by alternating periods of isolation (due to fear of rejection), and real contact with others, challenging themselves to accept, trust, and love themselves and others.

The second stage ranges over the ages of twenty-five to sixty-four years (some models use thirty-five or forty to sixty-four years) and the challenge is generativity versus stagnation. "Generativity" is a term coined by Erik Erikson in 1950 to denote "a concern for establishing and guiding the next generation." The profound question of this period is "Can I lead a life that matters?" During adulthood, people strive to find meaning and purpose in how they engage with the world.

Touch plays a powerful role in this period, although its effects are often unnoticed. Touch is a vital part of adult life, affecting physical and mental health, work-related stress and success, family development, and relationship satisfaction. While in general, touch is not in the foreground of adult life in the same manner as during infancy and childhood, it is a vital and often neglected aspect of adult health. Deficits in positive and nourishing touch can adversely affect the overall quality of life.

Touch in Adult Health—Emotions and Stress

A female chimpanzee sits motionless in a field, gazing meditatively at the sky while another female chimpanzee plucks parasites off her skin and grooms her hair. Two males sit in a nearby bush. Recently, these two males had a physical altercation over a favorite food. One male has just made a gesture of peace and is trying to "make-up" with the other male by grooming his back. In highly social animals like chimpanzees, grooming behaviors are often used to reconcile differences, maintain good relationships, and sustain health.

The higher a chimpanzee ranks in her social group, the easier it is for her to find someone to groom her. This is not superficial. Chimpanzees demonstrate high levels of social aggression. (An example of human social aggression is an office coworker pulling rank over you; another classic example is a playground bully.) Chimpanzees of lower social rank often have hardened arteries and cardiovascular disease. Their hearts can look like the heart of a middle-aged individual living on burgers and fries, and like that individual, they are more likely to suffer a heart attack.

Social aggression affects animal health, but equally important is lack of social support and contact. If an animal receives regular grooming (touch) from another animal, its stress hormone levels are lower and its heart is healthier; this concept is equally true in humans.

Many of the major health problems of adulthood are not a result of a single illness or insult to the body, but the build-up of thousands of small, stressful incidents. Heart disease, diabetes, and dementia are conditions that may be caused in part by the small stresses and challenges of daily life, and such conditions are certainly exacerbated by stress. Increasing supportive touch can reduce the negative impact of these small insults over time, and may be an important part of achieving optimal health and increasing the quality of life into the elder years.

One randomized controlled study found that massage led to reduced anxiety, pain, and tension after heart surgery. The heart keeps time, beating in a rhythm. If that rhythm is off, the heart starts to fluctuate wildly, preventing it from effectively pumping blood through the body. Stress increases the chance that the heart will beat out of synchrony. Touch can reduce stress. Just as with the chimpanzees, small touches on the shoulder from friends or life-partners can add up over time to a profound reduction in human-health risk.

Massage therapy reduces symptoms of insomnia (difficulty falling or staying asleep). Sleep deprivation has extremely adverse impacts on health and mental well-being; it is in fact a very effective form of torture!

In a pilot study of diabetic women, massage led to more stable glucose levels and for some, to a reduction in prescribed medication. Touch therapies can be effective for reducing symptoms of depression, anxiety, anorexia, and post-traumatic stress disorder. Touch treatments can reduce discomfort for individuals with chronic pain, fibromyalgia, and post-injury or post-surgical pain.

Touch to Soothe the Savage Beast

When a difficult emotion seizes us, it can feel overwhelming and make it very hard to think rationally. This is more than just a feeling: the brain areas associated with planning shut down when overwhelmed by intense emotion. Touch helps soothe difficult emotions. When we feel intense emotion there are usually at least two major aspects—the physical sensations and the cognitive thought that labels the emotion. Touch impacts both aspects by increasing activation in brain areas that help the body return to rest after difficult emotions. This lessens the time one spends in the grip of negative emotions, and helps one develop confidence that a difficult emotion can be tolerated without acting-out or becoming overwhelmed. Touch also increases activation in some key brain areas related to thinking and planning. Intense emotion often shuts down functioning in these areas, making it more likely that people will do and say things that may damage their relationship or reputation. Human contact can increase activation in these areas and support an individual's ability to recognize intense emotions and choose effective responses.

Touch in Adult Life

A group of researchers fanned out across several cafeterias. They sat with clipboards and pens observing people—watching interactions between couples as they moved through the lines. Every time a man touched his significant other, they marked it down. Each time a woman touched her partner, researchers made a check mark. They estimated ages for individuals and couples. In American culture, younger adults touched each other more than older adults did; and in general, unmarried men initiated touch and touched women more often than women touched men. Other studies have explored cross-gender touch in and out of relationship; studies have even explored how often couples touch each other when their children are present, versus when they are not. Studies like this conducted around the world show that in general, people in America touch each other less frequently than do people in many other cultures.

Results from S. M. Jourard's research—frequently quoted—have inspired numerous other studies. He found that in French cafés, people touched each other about one-hundred-eighty times per hour; in London cafés there were often zero touches; one-hundred-ten touches in Puerto Rico; and in the U.S. mainland—just two touches per hour! Touch plays a role in adult life. It affects family formation, friendship, and the development of a couple and a family.

Touch Works

When he made the deal to secure his job, he shook his new boss's hand and looked him in the eye. The firm connection between them made both feel safe, and consequently, they trusted each other. Touch creates trust in relationships. Touch can even affect the bottom-line in some jobs. In a study of food-servers (wait-staff) and their tips, one group of servers gave their customers a light touch on the shoulder, and the other group did not. After the data analysis, a powerful picture emerged. Those servers who touched their customers received significantly more money in tips than servers who did not touch their customers. In another study, a small intranasal spray of oxytocin increased the likelihood that someone would report trusting another person, and hence be willing to spend their money based on that person's influence. Touch impacts trust, and trust matters in how people choose to spend their money.

Touched by Love

When they met, the hug made her feel good and connected. As she leaned into him, she felt safe. She could not describe it any better than that. He just felt safe to her; she could trust him. Touch is vital to the formation of a relationship.

Signals of romantic interest are recognizable across cultures. While most individuals cannot articulate the signs, one knows them when one sees them. People display behaviors at a non-verbal level to let another person know they are interested. Small furtive glances, a slight flick of the hair over the shoulder, a hand on the arm, can indicate romantic interest. Men will often widen their body stance, puff up, and create excuses for physical contact. In this dance of courtship and connection, there are steps and missteps. One powerful signal of interest is the blush: cheeks flush and eyes often look down and then glance back up, as if to check the impact of the blush.

This dance of flirtation and courtship develops into the first blush of romance. The first stage of a romance is steeped in touch. People hold hands, stroke each other's hair, and spend lots of time in physical contact. People report that being away from their partner is painful, much like a withdrawal from some addictive substance—a feeling that is expressed in thousands of love poems. The pain of withdrawal may well be, at least in part, physical. When a relationship begins, there is a powerful upsurge in neurochemicals affecting mood and behavior. In fact, early romantic love shares many biological similarities with addiction. The intense increase in touching and physical contact bathes the brain in dopamine (one of the main neurochemicals relating to addiction), oxytocin, and even serotonin. One could hypothesize that when an infatuated couple must separate, there are fewer quick brushes of skin, fewer kisses and less time spent in loving embrace, which leads to a drop in levels of neurotransmitters, resulting in profound feelings of longing and desire. Over the centuries, so many people have reported the addictive draw of early love—perhaps these chemicals are the body's underlying mechanism of love and bonding. Researchers find that early love is also characterized by profound feelings of anxiety, reflected by elevated cortisol levels. People in the early stage of romance are on their best behavior, wanting to impress their lover—taking care not to bring about an untimely end to their relationship.

As this early stage of romantic connection, or infatuation, fades, something more enduring often takes its place. People feel safer and more stable with their partner. The touch and connection has created a social bond—an attachment. Rates and types of physical contact may play an important role in the long-term stability of a relationship. Couples who give each other affectionate touch regularly, and offer supportive touch to each other, report higher satisfaction in their relationship.

What's in a Kiss?

As the old "Shoop Shoop" song goes, "If you want to know if he loves you so, it's in his kiss." I have listened to many people describe the power of the kiss in early romantic relationship. Some research indicates that as a relationship progresses, kisses are a vital part of it. Touching and human contact are nourishment for the relationship itself. A group of researchers at the Arizona State University measured the impact of kissing on the reported quality of a relationship. They randomly assigned couples to two groups. One group was instructed to increase their rate of kissing significantly for six weeks. The other group had no such enjoyable instructions. Not surprisingly, the couples who kissed more often reported a higher level of relationship satisfaction than the group who kissed at their normal rate. A similar outcome occurs when couples who are expecting a child are asked to increase their rates of kissing. Maybe kissing is a good medication for both members of a couple expecting children! Regular massage and touch also increase relationship satisfaction, and other studies show that expectant mothers receiving regular massage enjoy a decrease in symptoms of depression and post-partum depression.

Intimate Touch

Intimate touch and developing sexually with one's partner are also important factors in the happiness and health of a couple. While most adults have experience with sexual and intimate touch, few have taken time to learn effective ways to communicate through nourishing touch. These skills can be learned. Touch has a powerful impact on the health and well-being of adults and their families. Unsatisfying communication, touch, and sexuality are primary reasons that many marriages end, however psychologists and therapists often lack basic tools to teach the couples they treat how to enjoy these qualities with each other.

Blindness and Touch

Taking her arm, I tried to help her across the room, assuming that she must need assistance. She kindly but firmly pushed my hand away, and with some frustration said, "I will ask you for help if I need it." She proceeded to guide herself across the room, missing the stool that I had bumped my shin on during my walk to the couch.

When I was growing up, I loved books. I loved the feel and the smell and I loved sitting with a book late into the night, reading by flashlight. One of my blind friends could read in the dark! There was no way my parents could catch me if I didn't use a flashlight. I would watch my friend's hand run over the page of little raised dots of Braille—a system of writing created by Louise Braille in the 1800s, that enables people who are blind or vision-impaired, to read and write. So many raised dots for "A," so many raised dots for "B," and so on for each letter of the alphabet. I ran my finger across the Braille, unable to tell the difference between each group of dots, let alone which letter was which.

There is a tendency in our culture to want humans to have just one kind of body and one kind of mind. The truth is that we humans have many different body shapes, abilities and functions, and many different types of minds. The human mind is an amazingly robust and dynamic thing. If we lose one sense, our brain adapts by using the areas formerly dedicated to the lost sense for other purposes. Some blind individuals become excellent at maneuvering through space using their sense of hearing as a guide. The visual cortex area of the brains of individuals who are blind is often "repurposed" for touch, or spatial sensing.

What is beauty? There is a body of literature exploring how blind people grow in their ability to explore and understand beauty. Often the textures of an object, the contours of a face, or the scents of nature contain their own innate beauty.

I was sitting with a young adult who was blind. He asked if he could touch my face. As he moved his hand across my face, he was learning about me. It helped him know who I was. Teachers working with children who are blind from birth often use physical objects to explain visual ideas through tactile experiences. Some have even worked on curriculum—using blocks to describe shapes of buildings and space between objects.

The brain adapts and changes as it works to represent reality. Michael Merzenich, one of the founders of research into brain plasticity, points out that sense organs give us information which is translated into a reliable, predictable representation of the world. From this representation, our brains create images. There have been interesting attempts to co-opt this process, having individuals use tactile stimulation to represent sight. Imagine a little strip of buzzers that buzz in a way that represents the visual world. Researchers at the Tactile Communication & Neurorehabilitation Laboratory located at the University of Wisconsin, Madison, have enabled a group of individuals to "see" with their tongues. Noted neuroscientist and physician Paul Bach-y-Rita said, "We don't see with our eyes. We see with our brain." If the brain receives real input, it will translate it into information.

These researchers found that with practice, "buzz vision" improved. Two individuals in this experiment went on for an extra nine hours of practice with the device; their visual acuity doubled.

Other research looked at how blind individuals can utilize their sense of touch. Multiple sources indicate that practice solidifies change and advancement. If practice is what makes the difference; an individual who practices reading Braille will be more sensitive in their fingers than their lips; and an individual who was born blind will have more brain activation in the visual cortex than an individual who became blind in adulthood. Research confirms that this is exactly what happens. Practice matters for our brain.

Touch connects us and deepens us as humans. It allows us to communicate things that are beyond words. It is our tendency to believe that *our* perception of the world is the sole perception and of course, entirely correct. However, by being open to contact with others and experiencing how they "touch" us, we grow our perception of the world, and new vistas open to us. I may never know the elegance of beauty experienced through touch in the same way my blind friends do, but I know that the elegance exists.

The Dance of Understanding

There is a wordless body-to-body communication between people, and in general, this communication builds a sense of being safe and understood. When I am guiding therapy groups, I often ask people to pair up and sit with their chairs back-to-back. One person in the pair has a series of circles and lines on a page; the other has a clipboard, a blank page, and a pencil. The person holding the drawing attempts to describe the images clearly enough for the person behind them to re-create the drawing. It is impossible. At best, the lines have similar shapes but they never materialize to be even close to the original image. This exercise illustrates a clear point: words alone are often not enough. Face-to-face communication is so much deeper. Eye contact, gestures, facial expressions, vocal tones, body postures—these combine to create broader, deeper, richer communication. A mere seven percent of human communication is realized with words; the other ninety-three percent is accomplished through myriad non-verbal signals.

Non-verbal communication is like a dance. It has rhythm, pace, feeling, and tone. Watching this dance in a café, one can see how people feel about each other—no words are necessary. When there is agreement and appreciation, bodies begin to synchronize and mirror one another. When there is conflict, postures and rates of movement differ. Couples who receive a small intranasal spray of oxytocin move more in synchrony with each other. The oxytocin increases their ability to enter into this physiological dance of connection.

Safe, welcomed touches and genuine smiles lead to greater synchrony and capacity for enjoying one another and tolerating conflict. As we have seen in the kangaroo care research, skin-to-skin contact between a parent and child increases synchrony in a family. Synchrony in the family relates to shared positive emotions, happiness, and mutual compliance. Children who grow up in highly synchronous environments are better able to communicate, and display more self-control. A child's level of self-control correlates to the amount of shared positive emotions between father or mother and child.

Feeling Groovy—Touch and Positive Emotion

For years, science explained negative emotions as a mechanism to help keep us safe. However, the role and importance of positive emotions was less clear. In her research of positive emotions, Dr. Fredrickson noted that negative emotions like anger and fear are directed at the removal of threat in the short term; however positive emotions like trust, love, or happiness, do not fill this survival niche. She developed a hypothesis she calls the broaden-and-build theory of positive emotions. In this theory, positive emotions help people build and develop new relationships and long-term goals. As Dr. Fredrickson points out, building a barn, a house, or a farm requires cooperation over the long haul and positive emotions increase cooperation. She also notes that positive emotions build or compound over time, and broaden as individuals focus on them, resulting in increased creativity and innovation.

Touch plays a role in the feeling of safety and connection between family members. It enables people to move from stress, to a state in which they are able to broaden their focus and build love and connection in the long-term. Positive family interactions add up (compound), just as negative interactions do. In any person's life, family will sometimes be a source of stress; however by and large, family is the primary place that individuals can support and encourage each other to develop and thrive. Dr. Fredrickson's research found that people thrived, or excelled, at a ratio of three-positive to one-negative emotion. The amount of safe, supportive contact received through hugs, pats on the back, wrestling matches, and other forms of loving touch may be one factor that enables a family to respond with resilience to difficult situations. Resilience is the highly advantageous ability to consistently recover, or return to baseline, from stress.

Adults Need to Be Touched

Increasing awareness of the importance of touch for healthy child development has brought this issue to the forefront of public-health concerns on several occasions, but the need for touch in adulthood is often ignored. Available literature tends to focus on touch throughout childhood. However, a growing amount of research shows that insufficient touch in adulthood has profound implications for public health, the health of families, and the overall quality of life for adults.

Touch as We Age

Harry has lived alone since his wife died ten years ago. Harry still misses her every day. He takes care of the house, spends time with friends and does his best to enjoy his retirement without her. Since his eightieth birthday five years ago, many of his friends have died, and more and more, he is relying on the care of family and paid caregivers. Harry was never much for relying on others, so this is difficult for him. Since his wife passed, he receives fewer hugs and he has had no romantic contact in years. As his need for more physical support throughout his day increases, Harry most frequently experiences touch when he can't do things for himself. Frustrated by his increasing infirmity, Harry can be grumpy with care providers, putting them on edge, and the hurried care he often receives reflects this. According to the latest U.S. census report, twenty-nine percent of older adults not living in institutions (approximately 8.1-million women and 3.2-million men) are living alone.

The amount of touch we receive declines significantly as we age, and drops precipitously as we enter our elder years. The touch that elders do receive can become more and more mechanical as their need for support increases. Instead of communicating affection and closeness, touch is more often practical help and goal-oriented, creating feelings of isolation and loneliness. Social interactions also change in these older years. In many cultures, elders play a vital role in society—and they are cherished. In western cultures, this is often not the case. Older adults frequently experience stigma and bias, which limits the quality of their relationships and brings about feelings of isolation and loneliness. *Loneliness is a major predictor of untimely death in older adults.* Social connection provides powerful protection against the decrepitudes of aging, and touch is a vital part of social interactions.

Along with social connection, meaning and purpose is vital for long-term health. Having a role and feeling that one is a contributing member of society increase both the length and quality of life for an older adult. Social psychologist Dr. Ellen Langer, in her now classic work on mindfulness, gave some nursing home residents a plant to care for. Most residents responsible for caring for their plant lived longer than most residents with no plant to care for.

Often, touch in nursing facilities can be mechanistic and detached. Family members no longer know how to connect to their loved ones, so rather than inadvertently hurting them, they may stop touching them at all. As the first sense to develop and one of the last senses to depart, touch can link people to meaning and purpose in life. Touch-based therapies for elders in skilled-nursing and assisted-living settings are associated with multiple positive health outcomes. I can vividly recall watching a man in a nursing facility I worked in come back from the brink of death after his family connected him with a massage therapist. Within one month this man regained the weight he hadn't needed to lose, and his skin, once brittle and dry, was plumper, with healthier color.

Elders, Stress, and Touch

It was the first time that Mrs. Johnson had received a massage, and she was nervous. She did not want to take off her clothes, and was most relieved upon learning that it was not necessary. As the massage therapist gently manipulated her hands and shoulders, Mrs. Johnson relaxed. Her shoulders, formerly almost glued to her ears, were now down in their proper place, her breathing was slow and even, and her whole face smiled. Mrs. Johnson reported that she was "in heaven." One study of elders compared relaxation training to massage. The group who received massage showed a healthy reduction in heart rate and blood pressure, as well as a significant lowering of their anxiety levels.

While in general, older adults may seem happier than younger adults because they appear to take more of the difficulties of life in stride; many older adults suffer from depression. Depression in elders is different from depression in younger people, primarily because it can affect overall brain functioning. Elders with depression can become disoriented, and they can even hallucinate; these behaviors can be mistaken for symptoms of a neurological disorder, such as Alzheimer's disease. Neuropsychologists call this condition pseudodementia. For elders, successful treatment of depression can quite often lead to dramatically increased clarity of thinking and a reduction of cognitive challenges.

Depression in elders can lead to dramatic negative physiological effects, increasing the risk of heart attack and early death. Depression can also hasten the development of Alzheimer's disease, a brain disease that leads to degeneration of key parts of memory-forming brain tissue. *Treatment of depression in elders is a vital part of increasing their quality of life and long-term health.*

In a study of the effect of massage on depression in older adults, a randomized, controlled trial compared massage to a well-established technique (visualization) for reducing anxiety. This study found that massage enhanced self-reported well-being, and reduced both anxiety and symptoms of depression. In another study of elders in a skilled-nursing facility, calming music and a brief hand-massage both helped reduce agitation.

Early Life Impacts Later Life

Our stress response is programmed by a combination of genetic, epigenetic, and environmental factors. Early life events can affect the stress response in the adult years. For monkeys, primates, and humans, short-term disruptions in parenting can alter the stress response for a lifetime. What are the impacts of early childhood abuse (damaging touch) on the adult? At least one study implies that early trauma can adversely affect health, even after more than six decades. This study questioned elders about their history of abuse. Researchers found a strong relationship between receiving abuse in early life and developing depression and anxiety in adulthood. Happily, this study also offers hope, as findings show that working to maintain a positive self-image can help mitigate the damage of early abuse.

Aging and Brain Changes

As people age, there are changes in the functioning of their brains. One common (normal) change in cognitive function is decreased processing speed—how quickly an individual can take in and use new information. Stress and anxiety also reduce processing speed. However, as people grow older, their storehouse of knowledge increases. Thus, although many elders may not process information as quickly as they once did, they may still outperform younger adults because of their superior knowledge base. In many cases, wisdom trumps the brash energy of youth.

Another key aging-related change in brain functioning occurs in executive functions—planning, thinking, and organizing complex tasks. These abilities decline with age. However, executive functions are also reduced by very stressful conditions, and by depression.

The Opposite of Stress

The vagus nerve, also known as the 10th cranial nerve, originates in the brainstem and winds its way throughout the entire body. It is responsible for manifesting the opposite of the stress response: the relaxation response—a term first coined by Harvard stress researcher Herbert Benson, who found that we could evoke states of rest and relaxation.

We owe him a debt of gratitude for all his work, which forms the underpinning of much of the stress research that has come since. The relaxation response is often thought of as opposite to the stress response. For example, when we are stressed our heart rate goes up, our breathing rate increases, our blood pressure increases, our mouth gets dry, and our digestion stops. When we are feeling relaxed, or we evoke the relaxation response, we experience the opposite effects— our heart rate slows, breathing slows, blood pressure decreases, and salivation increases.

For adults, evoking the relaxation response can lead to improved cognitive performance. This makes sense, since when we are stressed, it is harder to think. One study examined how changes in vagus nerve functioning changed executive functioning in both young adults and elders. One of the best measures of vagus nerve function is respiratory sinus arrhythmia (RSA). When we breathe in, our heart rate increases, and as we breathe out, it slows. This is because the vagus nerve harmonizes the breath with the heartbeat so the body can most effectively utilize the oxygen it receives. In people who are highly stressed, or suffering from post-traumatic stress disorder, Alzheimer's disease, or depression, RSA is flat. In other words, the heart rate does not change with the breath. This study found that low RSA function related to poor executive functioning (such as ability to solve a maze or a problem) in both young adults and elders. It is compelling to see that elders with decreased RSA had more difficulty solving a maze-puzzle. Our ability to monitor our own success is a vital part of executive functioning. The elders and young adults who experienced the most difficulty monitoring their own success had lower RSA. Many studies of massage and touch-based therapies have found that regular physical touch, when provided in a safe, contained manner, leads to increased RSA. One can make a reasonable guess that increased RSA brought about by increased therapeutic touch could increase executive functions. Imagine the powerful impact of touch-based treatments for adults, whatever their age, with mildly impaired cognition!

Soothing Inflammation

Inflammation is one way the body responds to many types of illnesses or injuries; it is implicated in a wide range of diseases. Redness around a healing wound is an inflammation response. Since inflammation plays a role in pain reaction, many over-the-counter pain medicines contain anti-inflammatory properties. One current theory of complex diseases is that long-term exposure to even low levels of naturally produced protective mechanisms, can lead to the development of diseases. Stress hormones and inflammation response are two of these protective mechanisms. Massage reduces cortisol levels, as we have discussed in detail previously. Swedish massage, as compared to light touch, reduced biomarkers of inflammation. (The markers measured in this research are interleukin (IL) 1ß, IL-2, IL-4, IL-5, IL-6, IL-10, IL-13, and IFN-γ.) Some of these markers are implicated in health challenges that range from depression, to cancer. This study also found that massage increased the activity of immune defense cells in the blood, which has a powerful impact on the body's innate ability to fend off disease. Reduced inflammation lessens the negative impact on the body, and creates a synergistic improvement in its capacity for resisting disease.

This research prompts interesting implications when one considers the reverse of its findings, which imply that a lack of connected touch might adversely affect immune functioning. Given how sterile and isolating medical settings can be for people coping with serious health issues, these are stark implications.

Social Relationships and Touch in Elders

Social relationships are vital for health and increased longevity. One powerful research tool for investigating the impacts of social factors on health is meta-analysis (a research study that systematically examines and pools outcomes of many separate, but similar studies of a single topic). One group of researchers did a meta-analytic study of the effects of social relationships on life span. This meta-analysis looked at one-hundred-forty-eight studies amounting to a total number of 308,849 participants. The findings indicated that likelihood of death increased by fifty percent for people with weak social relationships, while likelihood of living increased by fifty percent for those whose social relationships were strong. The authors (Julianne Holt-Lunstad, Timothy B. Smith, and J. Bradley Layton) state that lack of social relationships is as strong a risk factor for mortality as any physiological risk factors already established! The results of this meta-analysis have powerful implications for how we develop optimal environments for ourselves as we age.

While the number of friendships and work relationships may diminish over the years, not all relationships decrease as people age. In fact, for many older people, the amount of social relationship is either similar to their early adult years or a bit higher. The reasons may be increased contact with neighbors, religious organizations, and other community groups, perhaps due to having more time after retirement. Many elders volunteer, increasing their social contact through service work; this also enhances a sense of purpose and meaning through later years. A pilot study of the program "Experience Corps"—which helps elders engage through meaningful activities, exercise, and social support—found an increase in cognitive functioning resulting from these activities, even in elders with some cognitive impairment.

Elders with Alzheimer's disease or other neurodegenerative disorders experience changes in cognitive function that make building and maintaining good relationships difficult. Some studies indicate that a new concept called "facilitated friendship" can be a powerful tool to increase relationships for elders with changes in cognitive ability. When individuals begin experiencing cognitive challenges, an understandable fear of being rejected if their cognitive impairment is noticed can lead to self-imposed social isolation, which exacerbates cognitive decline. However with the right social support, individuals with dementia can connect to other individuals. Facilitated friendships can range from a clinician communicating with friends and family about methods for connecting with an individual with dementia, to a clinician/facilitator being present during interactions to support connection, and defuse difficulties that may occur because of the cognitive decline.

Another study of loneliness in elders has direct public policy implications. The authors of this study found that loneliness affects blood pressure, and that the effects of loneliness accumulate, or compound over time; thus loneliness is a risk factor in heart disease and myocardial infarctions (heart attacks). Other research indicates that *the perception of being isolated* has a similar effect on long-term cardiac health. This study found that both perceived isolation and negative mental health symptoms adversely affect long-term health, and less social contact leads to higher rates of depression, and suicidal ideations. These findings indicate a great need for programs that support elders (with or without cardiac challenges) living in isolation to develop and maintain solid social support networks.

It is important to note that *perceived social connectedness* is more important for elders than perceived availability of social support. *We want connection.* Support can make people feel dependent. Touch can be a powerful tool to build social connectedness in relationship. Interventions that help isolated individuals branch out and connect to social support groups may be vital for all of our well-being as we inevitably age.

Care Providers and Elders

The quality of the relationship between care providers and the people they support has a strong influence on physical and mental health. Care providers provide support during intimate and embarrassing times, and sensitivity can make the difference between elders feeling angry, hurt, and alone—unable to express their needs, or feeling that they are still maintaining their dignity. However, care giving itself can be stressful. Care providers face a higher risk of suffering stress-related illnesses. Increasing the positive interactions and quality of relationship between care providers and their clients will make a constructive difference for both. Safe, supportive, and nurturing touch is a vital part of effective care. Care providers can learn basic tools of touch for reducing both their own and their clients' stress, and increasing emotional support. Touch in couples and families leads to increased synchrony and emotional connection; nurturing touch should have a similarly beneficial effect on the relationship between care providers and the elders they support.

Touch While Dying

> "At the end of the game, both the king and
> the pawn go back in the box."
>
> ~ ITALIAN PROVERB

He took the hand of his therapist and looked him full in the face, saying, "You are so beautiful." His breath rasped in his chest and he sank to the floor, having lost what remained of his energy on the walk back to his bed. Nursing staff gently helped him to his feet. The therapist walked him back to his room, helped him into the bed, and sat next to him for a moment or two, holding his hand until his breathing settled. The therapist left. His client died in his sleep several hours later.

Touch is a powerful way we communicate emotions and connection. Everyone has one birth and one death. Currently, western culture often ignores the dying process out of a combination of fear and lack of experience. As people enter the dying process, they often experience changes in cognition. Their mind no longer functions in the same way. People can appear to drift in and out of connection. This can be challenging for their families, friends, and loved ones. The fluctuations can make them feel that their loved one is detached, creating a barrier to good connection. Touch is a powerful and accurate communication tool; the immediate impact of wordless connection can deepen a relationship that once felt lost within the fluctuations of consciousness.

In the 70s and 80s, the hospice movement became a part of medical practice. This movement began in order to provide a better quality of life for individuals who were terminally ill. Before the hospice revolution, doctors often felt powerless when confronting their inability to cure their patients, or at least help them get more out of their last stage of life. The hospice program filled this medical void. Palliative care is care that helps us feel better. Supportive, nurturing, and caring touch has become an important part of hospice care, healing both the dying and those who care for them. In the state of Washington, hospice programs include multiple touch-based interventions. Nearly ninety percent of individuals in Washington's hospice programs receive massage therapy (87%). Other individuals receive other forms of touch—

compassionate touch (45%), acupuncture (32%), pet therapy (32%), and reflexology (19%). While each of these interventions has its own treatment goals and impacts, overall, touch therapies have been found to reduce depression, stress, anxiety, pain, and blood pressure, and increase quality of life.

A woman with terminal cancer lies with her back uncovered as the massage therapist slowly works out the tension in her tissue, while soft music plays in the background. The therapist pauses every few moments as the woman takes a deep and restful breath. The therapist exits the room, first covering the client with a blanket so she can dress. The woman's eyes were soft when she emerged from the treatment room; she lingered, smiling quietly as she drank some water in the waiting room. The therapist smiled after the session, reporting that she felt a deep tenderness for her client and that supporting the woman was a powerful experience.

After massage, people often report less pain. The pain from cancer can be intense and at times, unremitting. It is a neurological pain, which doctors call neuropathic pain, because it is caused by nerve-deterioration during the process of the disease. The respite from pain after a massage can be an important reprieve as a person moves through their final days of life.

Another very large, randomized study tested the impacts of massage on pain and quality of life in cancer patients. The patients receiving massage experienced superior symptom reduction. Massage is an effective short-term intervention for pain reduction, which makes it an ideal treatment for flare-ups of acute pain during the dying process.

This result has important implications for improving the quality of touch during care and support of people in hospice; it suggests a need for programs that enhance the quality and amount of simple touch provided by all levels of medical professionals, including doctors, nursing staff, and direct care providers. Teaching family members and friends how to give massage and supportive touch may also have a positive impact on pain and pain management.

The Meaning of Human Contact

She says she feels like she is in a warehouse, put away on the shelf and just waiting to die. People living in assisted care and medical settings often report similar feelings of isolation, loneliness, and lack of meaning and purpose.

People in institutional care frequently state, "I feel like I am no more than an object." Nurses and care providers become frustrated and distant when their patients are verbally and physically aggressive; they may perceive such patients as overly demanding and find it difficult to see their patient as a fellow human being. While there is touch in nurse-patient relationships, it typically relates to care and often does not include emotionally supportive touch. Providing caring, emotionally supportive touch can be a powerful way to transform this dynamic between patient and staff, reminding all of their shared humanity.

When a group of nurses reported on their experience providing therapeutic or emotionally supportive touch, it became apparent that including touch in their work transformed their daily relationship with patients. The research found that giving touch to elders can be an enhancing experience for both. One theme that emerged was that nurses and care staff began to view themselves as a valuable element in the healing process Of course, they were vital elements all along, but it helped them to know it! Nurses reported no longer seeing their patient as just a demanding person with a disease, but as a unique individual, just like themselves. The philosopher Martin Buber described this as moving from a relationship of transaction—"I-it," to a relationship of mutual connection and respect—"I-Thou." This shift is not just emotional. It changes the quality of the working life of professionals and can reduce burnout—also known as caregiver-fatigue.

Another study explored the meaning of touch for elders and nurses. Elders reported that if the touch was safe and invited, it felt "gentle, comforting, and important." Nursing staff reported that touch was not difficult to provide and felt like a natural part of their care. Nurses reported that they often experienced aggressive touch, such as hitting, punching, and pushing, from their patients. Female nurses reported receiving unwanted touch that felt sexual from male patients.

However, the majority of nurses also reported that friendly, grateful touch was very important and made their days better. Touch is an integral part of a good relationship between nurses and their patients. It helps the nurses feel connected and gives meaning to the interactions, while also helping patients feel safer and better cared for.

Touch is integral to physical and mental health throughout our lifespan; however, our culture's overarching reluctance to engage with affectionate or therapeutic touch, and western medicine's lack of awareness of its importance to our physical and emotional health, have created a large deficit in research. Understanding the importance of touch and its best use, will lead to powerful new treatments—and possibly break new ground in research.

Chapter 4

Emotion Regulation:
Touched by a Feeling

In the heady, turbulent decade of the 1960s, a revolution was quietly underfoot: Behaviorism, a basic tenet of psychology, was losing
credibility amongst mainstream psychologists. Behaviorists believed
an understanding of the mind was not necessary in order to understand human psychology. They believed that understanding simple
processes of conditioning explained the entirety of human experience.
Dr. B. F. Skinner, the founder of Behaviorism, argued, "Give me a child
and I'll shape him into anything." To the behaviorist, the mind was a
black box that psychologists did not need to open. A powerful body of
research supported behavioral psychology and it did produce amazing
results. At one point, Dr. Skinner was involved in a program that taught
pigeons to fly bombs accurately into targets. Not bad for a birdbrain!
However, there were some powerful chinks in the armor of behaviorist thinking. While the behaviorists argued that it was unscientific to
study the mind because it could not be directly observed, a new band
of researchers calling themselves cognitive psychologists began studies that would transform the field, lead to effective psychotherapeutic
treatments, and become the new paradigm for modern psychology.

   In mainstream psychology, the mantle of behaviorism finally dropped
due to an unexpected source: Noam Chomsky, a linguist by training,
made a powerful proposal: He posited that the idea of language being
a "purely conditioned" phenomenon does not account for several
aspects of language development. Chomsky argued that conditioning could not account for the fact that the amount of reinforcement

a child gets is insufficient for learning a language. In other words, for reinforcement to be the reason for the learning of language, a child would need constant reinforcement. He also argued that people often put together language in completely new and unique ways. Chomsky proposed that children are born with a language acquisition device (LAD) in their brains. This LAD, evolved through generations of genetic change, is a brain structure primed to learn language.

At the same time, researchers were re-discovering the importance of the "aha!" or "Eureka!" moment. Unlike learning by trial and error, or learning through reinforcement, this is learning through insight. Instead of a behavior slowly being reinforced, a person (or in the case of classic research, an animal) thinks of solutions all at once. In the classic demonstration of this work, a monkey has two sticks, and a piece of food just out of reach of either of those sticks. The monkey looks at the sticks and, apparently all at once with no outside rein-forcement, "thinks" of a solution. The monkey puts the two sticks together and is able to reach the food.

During this same period, Dr. Aaron Beck and Dr. Albert Ellis began developing a new therapy that would also change the Freudian para-digm. Today, this therapy is called cognitive behavioral therapy (CBT). Cognitive behavioral therapy differs from previous forms of psycho-therapy in that it focuses on the here and now with the goal of helping individuals change their thoughts about their experiences. CBT is the most validated and scientifically investigated theory of psychological change to date. More importantly, it works. In trials comparing CBT and medication for treatment of depression, CBT works equally well, or better. It changes the brain too. Studies of brain activity before and after CBT treatment have shown that the brain change is structural. This has led people such as neuropsychiatrist and Nobel Laureate Dr. Eric Kandel to state, "Psychotherapy *is* a biological treatment."

Trauma and an Affective Revolution

Trauma can deeply affect one's life. It is often called the hidden wound of war. Battered by the horrors of war, self-medicating with narcotics and alcohol, war veterans struggled to find a way to rejoin society.

Bessel A. van der Kolk, M.D., along with many others, began research-
ing this phenomenon. They found, unsurprisingly, that experiencing
war changes people's lives, and their stress response. From this
research, they proposed a new diagnosis: post-traumatic stress disorder (PTSD). People who witness intense human suffering, or consistently live in an extreme state of fearing for their life, develop a "normal reaction to abnormal life events." During this PTSD research, a
transformative movement in the field of psychology began, shaping a
revolution that is still underway. Bessel van der Kolk describes what
appears to be "wordless terror" in the people he treated, a state of
mind in which there are no voicable thoughts. Thoughts (the primary
focus of CBT) are not present. The mind is blank. However, the
intense feelings of terror are discernible on the faces of traumatized
people, and the effects are detectable in their brains. By looking at
magnetic resonance imaging (MRI) of the brain of a person in this
state of terror, Van der Kolk found that the language centers were
offline—completely dark, whereas normally they light up. Cognitive
theory would posit that the terror results from perception, or "thought
labels." But wait! If there are no thoughts, what causes the terror? This
was and remains a critical topic for the field of psychology.

   Contemporaneously, neuroscientist Dr. Antonio Damasio began
publishing his foundational work on the limbic system, the emotional
center of the brain. He found that this system has two major circuits:
one circuit is fast, one is slow. The fast circuit sees things somewhat
fuzzily, but assesses them quickly. Fascinatingly, this assessment
seems, at least initially, to bypass the front mind—the thinking mind
of an individual. If you are walking down a forest path and see a snake
out of the corner of your eye, the fast circuit triggers, causing your
body to react (with stress) to the snake before your conscious thinking
mind notices anything. The slower circuit includes the front brain and
the thinking mind in the loop. It makes your perceptions more accurate, but requires more time. The fast circuit is involved in emotional
communication. This has led to what some in the field of psychology
have called "the affect (emotion) regulation model" and others refer
to as interpersonal neurobiology.

Emotion regulation—From Mind to Body

The affect regulation model proposes that we have two major brain systems: one that works explicitly through thoughts and conscious effort and another that works through implicit emotional reactions. Affect regulation theory often refers to cognitive theories as top down systems—cognitive control originating in the front brain affects the emotional systems—whereas emotion or affect-based theories work from the bottom up, offering tools to help change reactions at the level of emotions. These bottom up theories generally allow that changes in thoughts come second, after an individual has a new experience at an emotional level. With the right clinical support and training, people can learn to master emotional reactions to experiences that were previously overwhelming and incomprehensible. Damasio calls his theory of two circuits the "somatic marker hypothesis." The main thrust of this theory is that the body has a physiological reaction to an event, like increased heart rate, change in breathing, or tingling in the stomach, prior to the conscious mind thinking about the experience. These events are labeled by the cognitive, thinking mind as, for example, fear. In Damasio's theory, the body plays a key role in emotional life. Research supports his theory, but controversy still exists as to whether thought, or emotion, comes first, or both occur at the same time.

However, the fact that the body plays a role in one's emotional life is clear and well-documented. Sadness has a somatic marker, joy does as well, and while all individuals have a similar pattern of physiological responses, these patterns are unique in their specifics from person to person. It is not unusual for someone to describe fear as tingling or butterflies in the stomach, while another will describe it as tightness in the chest, and still another reports feeling weakness in their limbs. Learning to read one's interoceptive, or body, cues for emotions can be vital for psychological change. Damasio even famously argues that these body signals are vital in our thought process and decisions. People who have no access to information from their body due to trauma or brain injury can have profound difficulties making choices.

Touch and Trauma

In her research on massage therapy, Tiffany Field, Ph.D., founder and director of the Touch Research Institute in Miami, tested the impact of supportive touch on symptoms of stress and several of the neurochemicals that are affected in post-traumatic stress disorder (PTSD). In 2012, a group of researchers established a new protocol for the treatment of PTSD, combining healing touch and guided imagery in a six-session trial over a three-week period. This randomized control study compared the usual treatments for PTSD (cognitive behavioral therapy or exposure therapy) with this combination of healing touch and guided imagery. The findings clearly indicated a greater amount of significant clinical change (fewer symptoms of PTSD and less depression and cynicism) in the group that received the touch and imagery therapy. The "healing touch/guided imagery" participants also displayed an improved quality of life.

In addition to suffering from post-traumatic stress disorder, people subjected to sexual abuse also experience a difficult relationship with their own bodies. Another study of survivors of sexual abuse found that massage reduced symptoms of depression and anxiety, and increased the participants' positive experience of their bodies. While safe physical contact does not necessarily involve words, it can change the way people experience their feelings, reduce stress, and help activate areas of the brain involved in emotion regulation.

The Brain in the Body and The Body in the Brain

The picture we have worked with for much of the last century is one of a brain that thinks and controls, while a body is just a lump of flesh that acts according to the brain's direction. We see this in science-fiction images of a disembodied brain floating in a jar—connected to the outside world by wires—whereas the image of the body in cartoons and movies is often a mindless jock who can't think very well, but sure can throw a punch. While these images are funny and a deep part of our culture, they are not accurate. The brain is a part of the body and the body is represented in the brain in many different ways.

Wilder Penfield, one of the fathers of modern neurosurgery, mapped the brain by stimulating different areas with a mild electric shock while preparing his patients for surgery. His patients remained awake during this process so that Dr. Penfield could identify the area of the brain to remove, while trying not to remove or damage other areas of the brain that could impact vital functions. He was a methodical doctor and documented his trials, not only for his patients, but also as research for the broader medical community. Dr. Penfield asked his patients to report what they felt just after being stimulated with the electrode. If he stimulated one area, a left foot would twitch—another area and the patient reported a phantom sensation on their hand. Dr. Penfield noted these responses in detail, thus creating the first map of the somatosensory cortex—the area of the brain that coordinates movement and sensations from the body. (This map of the structures of the brain and sensation is often called the homunculus.) At the time of his work, researchers assumed that the brain remained relatively stable after adulthood. However, almost three quarters of a century later, Penfield's careful documentation paved the way for another transformative discovery when neuroscientist Michael Merzenich discovered that the somatosensory cortex was constantly being sculpted by experience. Working with chimpanzees, he found that if an animal had damage to a limb or to nerves, the brain could rewire on a day-to-day basis.

The brain controls how we breathe, our feelings of stress, our movements, our sleep, and even how well we can catch a ball. However, the body changes the brain. Each movement and emotion sculpts the brain. There is a complex dance between the brain, the body, and the environment. The brain's map of the body changes as we move. For example, violinists have profound differences in the density of brain tissue relating to each hand: the hand that holds the bow and is not required to move the fingers with extreme precision has less brain tissue devoted to fingers than the other hand, which requires intricate patterns of finger movement. The signals or experiences of the body literally sculpt the brain.

Touch and the Communication of Emotions

He spent years practicing, learning to make every muscle in his face move independently. Dr. Paul Ekman developed a rigorous research program at the University of California, Berkeley (UC Berkeley). Starting with the theory that human emotions are universal, he developed a tool called the facial action coding system that assigns a number to each movement of the face. In his now classic series of studies, Dr. Ekman looked at the expression of six primary emotions—anger, sadness, happiness, fear, surprise, and disgust, to see if they were universally recognized. He showed photographs of people expressing these emotions to individuals in multiple cultures around the world, including a tribe in Papua, New Guinea that had never been exposed to any media. Dr. Ekman found that people across the world accurately recognize emotions by interpreting facial expressions. Despite the fact that people display emotions according to their cultural rules, facial expressions are remarkably similar. Or in the words of Crosby, Stills, Nash and Young's 1960s song, "Wooden Ships"—"…If you smile at me, I will understand, 'cause that is something everybody everywhere does in the same language."

From his initial research, Ekman developed tools that can predict whether someone is lying with about ninety-five percent accuracy. Even the best poker players and police officers cannot come close. His research was the basis for a prime-time television show called "Lie to Me" in which the protagonist, loosely based on Ekman, helped solve crimes. Ekman's successful research sparked several other lines of research—one fascinating line explored vocal tones and found that people can recognize and identify emotions embedded within tones of voice with a high degree of accuracy.

Not only has Dr. Dacher Keltner worked with the Dalai Lama, he is the founding faculty director of the Greater Good Science Center, and a professor of psychology at the University of California, Berkeley (UC Berkeley). He researched the human ability to read emotions through touch. A reassuring pat on the back and a caress to express romantic love are quite different. To explore this idea, Dr. Keltner placed participants in an experimental condition in which they could touch, but not see, each other. One person sat behind an opaque black cloth and extended an arm under the bottom of the cloth. The person on the other side touched the arm to communicate an emotion. Keltner categorized the types of touch and found that indeed, people can express and understand emotions through touch. Anger might be expressed through brisk movements or abrupt taps, sadness through a despondent, non-committal touch, and happiness through fully engaged contact. Despite the black cloth, people could read the touches just as if they were reading a facial expression.

Emotions in touch are communicated visually as well. Another study asked participants to watch an interaction between two people without being able to hear the interaction. Not surprisingly, they could identify the emotions communicated through touch. You can try this by turning on your television and turning down the volume; while it can be hard to differentiate what you understand through posture as opposed to touch, closely watch the touches and you can see the emotions expressed in simple touch between individuals.

Touch is a vital part of human communication—creating a feeling of togetherness and connection. Touch can be coercive—even without violence. A pat on the back from a principal giving an instruction to a student makes the student aware of the principal's status. Sit at an airport for even a short time and watch the comings and goings of passengers, and you will see tense, forced hugs, and warm, lingering embraces. Touch is a powerfully direct expression of relationship that cannot be captured in words or thoughts, but is nonetheless deeply experienced.

Emotion Regulation and Human Contact

Touch communicates emotions and, like music, it can soothe savage, ragged feelings that at times grip every human heart. The balm of loving human contact helps us tolerate grief in all of its raw profundity. As psychology began to move away from a purely cognitive or thought-based model of human behavior, it offered the concept of emotion regulation as more inclusive of the breadth of human experience. While changing cognitions certainly can and does lead to healing from many forms of emotional anguish, the wordless communication of touch also influences our brains, our bodies, and our emotions.

Emotion regulation is a complex term used in varied ways in the field of psychology. The fundamental concept is that our emotional life works like a thermostat—constantly adjusting to changes in the environment. If someone yells at us, our body mobilizes a defensive strategy by triggering anger, and our cognitions, or thoughts, work to help us understand why the other person is yelling and how to channel our anger effectively. Like any thermostat, there are different settings, and myriad ways for our emotional life to malfunction and get stuck.

The model of emotion regulation is based on two ideas: homeostasis and allostasis. The basic concept of homeostasis is that our bodies and moods need to stay within a functional range. Exceeding that range is unhealthy for the mind and the body. Too much stress for too long damages the body, leading to allostatic load, therefore the body has multiple ways to return itself to that homeostatic range.

Dr. Bruce McEwen, in his book "The End of Stress as We Know It," describes a study in which researchers gave mice a small scrape on the ear and then introduced an infection. (The infection was not deadly and did not make the mice very ill.) In this study, one group of infected mice was subjected to stress, while the other was not. Amazingly, the group under stress healed more quickly. The stress response stimulated the immune system. However, repeating the experiment with mice that had already been under stress for some time did not lead to quicker healing; it lead to slower healing. This is the hallmark of allostasis. In the Greek language, homeostasis means "same state" and allostasis means "different state." The stress response is innate within the body to help it manage threats in the short-term.

As important as it is to turn on the stress response, the body also has to be able to turn it off. If that stress system remains on indefinitely, it erodes the body's basic functions. The longer a system stays in an allostatic state, the more strain there is on the entire body. Now, in our "24/7" news-cycle, coffee-driven, worry-about-work culture, the stress system is asked to perform in a manner that is very different from how it was designed to function. A large body of data indicates that this constant state of stress increases the risk for many diseases—from arthritis, to heart disease, to cancer. Touch is one way we can shift from an extreme state of stress, back to rest. One client I worked with when his relative was very ill, would sit and stroke his pet each day after leaving the hospital. Touch helped him shift from stress back to rest, even in a very difficult situation.

Cognitive Emotion Regulation and Touch

The cognitive revolution revealed that our thoughts determine our moods; hence, by reinterpreting situations, we can change our moods. In a classic study about the impact of "cognitive appraisal," participants viewed an image of a beautiful woman in a white dress standing outside a church; they were asked to talk about their emotional reaction to the picture. One group viewed the picture with a caption that said "wedding" and the other group saw a caption that said "funeral." Not surprisingly, people's emotional reactions to the picture were highly influenced by the caption: people who saw "funeral" reported feeling sad, while people who saw "wedding" reported feeling good. Our thoughts change our feelings. This is the backbone of cognitive behavioral therapy.

Cognitive based coping regulates emotions on two levels: implicit and explicit. The implicit level is a quick and automatic appraisal that happens when people make a conscious interpretation or actively engage cognitively with the world. Implicit or automatic reactions—"automatic thoughts"—can be considered as "mind-burps." Some people have a mind burp whenever they do dishes; perhaps, "I hate this!" The mind burp changes how the individual feels about doing dishes. Automatic thoughts are habitual and happen without intention, yet they do change the way we feel. According to cognitive theorists, automatic thoughts are examples of our fundamental beliefs about the self, others, and the world. In cognitive behavioral therapy, people learn to notice their automatic thoughts and change the underlying beliefs causing those thoughts by challenging them with reality. Someone who is already depressed, when encountering a difficult situation, may have an automatic thought such as "I can never do this."

Like the wedding versus funeral picture study, humans are profoundly influenced by labels. People who label themselves as stupid, incompetent, a failure, will begin to experience the world in this way. The work a client does while in therapy with a cognitive behavior therapist consists of "reality-checking" and, when necessary, modifying the accuracy of their thoughts.

Explicit cognitive emotion regulation uses our thinking mind to change our emotional experiences. Throughout our lives, we develop self-labels by how we perceive others, the world, and ourselves. However, we can and do create inaccurate thoughts, which then become self-imposed limitations. Explicit cognitive regulation is involved when we make an effort to rethink and reexamine our emotional responses to situations.

Groundbreaking though it is, cognitive behavioral therapy does not use touch as a major element of its therapeutic arsenal. Nonetheless, touch plays a role in both explicit and implicit cognitive regulation in everyday life: a group of people waiting for a job interview fidget slightly in their chairs, occasionally rubbing their legs, cracking their knuckles, or running their hands through their hair. Self-touch, while not as effective as soothing touch provided by another person, does help to reduce stress. In therapy sessions, individuals with symptoms of post-traumatic stress disorder often use soothing self-touch like rubbing their legs or squeezing their hands or arms as they begin to shift from a high stress state to a relaxed state. These touches are largely automatic and are part of a person's innate capacity for emotion regulation. This self-touch is like a thermostat—triggered when a stressor or an emotional response is too intense. Self-touch provides a boundary, signaling the body to relax, and supporting the body to shift from stress to rest.

People use touch as an explicit cognitive emotion regulation tool to manage a wide range of feelings. In western cultures, people will seek out their friends or family for a hug and moral support when things are difficult. Others will get a massage when they are feeling stressed. Many people have pets; on a physiological level, holding or petting an animal reduces the stress response. Marsha M. Linehan, the founder of dialectical behavior therapy (DBT), developed a series of tools to help people who were suffering profoundly—particularly those who were frequently attempting suicide, and were not recovering with traditional psychotherapy. She states that one of the basic tools in her treatment is learning to develop "distress tolerance"—an ability to tolerate a range of emotional experiences. When we learn to sit through difficult emotions and see that they come and then pass without killing us, we gain confidence that we can survive the storm of feeling, and that intense emotions do become tolerable. Another tool she teaches is called "soothing in the five senses." Dr. Linehan asks her clients to find things that soothe them through sight, sound, smell, taste, and touch. Choosing to self-soothe when distressed is a form of cognitive regulation of emotion.

Emotion Regulation and Touch

Professor George A Bonanno, a leader in the field of trauma psychology, has written extensively about how even though about sixty percent of Americans have experienced at least one event that would be classified as traumatic, only about eight percent develop post-traumatic stress disorder (PTSD). Why are some people resilient, while others develop PTSD? Most people assessed immediately after experiencing trauma will display some symptoms of PTSD, or another form of PTSD called Acute Stress Disorder. Over time, some people's PTSD symptoms get better even without treatment, others remain about the same, and some people's symptoms get worse.

Dr. Barbara L. Fredrickson, Kenan Distinguished Professor of Psychology at the University of North Carolina, Chapel Hill, measured people's responses to experiencing the traumatic events of 9/11. As predicted by Dr. Bonanno, many people exhibited a stress reaction after the event. Dr. Fredrickson measured the impact of the quantity of a person's positive emotions on the development of PTSD. She describes this as the "granularity" of positive emotions—the tendency to represent experiences of positive emotion with precision and specificity. If you really notice your emotions throughout the day, they change all the time. We have small moments of happiness followed by frustration, then happiness, then stress, and so on. People with higher quantities of small, positive emotions were buffered from the negative effects of stress. Dr. Frederickson's hypothesis is that positive emotions can reverse the impact of stress. In other words, if someone experiences a traumatic event, a high number of positive emotions after that event reduce the period of high stress and help prevent them from developing PTSD. She calls this the "undoing effect." Her findings confirm that those exposed to the trauma of 9/11 who also had a large number of positive emotions afterward, were less likely to develop PTSD than those with a higher number of negative emotions. This is the hallmark of auto-regulation. The positive emotions just automatically happen. This process is much like learning to ride a bicycle. Once you have mastered that skill, you will always know how to ride a bicycle, even if it has been many years since you last rode.

Auto-regulation is an innate capacity to respond well to stress. Some people have a tendency, even in the midst of tragedy, to find meaning and enjoyment in their surroundings—an ability that I call "blue sky" moments: moments when despite their currently challenging situation, they can appreciate the beauty of a blue sky, the elegance of the curve of a tree against a distant mountain, the delicate scent of a flower, or simply notice the kindness in a passerby's face. One tool people use to reduce stress and evoke positive emotions is "cognitive coping strategies"—ways we use our thoughts to help us cope. We all know that if we spend a day ruminating over what a failure we are, we feel abysmal. People who bounce back from stress are more likely to put things into a positive perspective, using their thoughts like a good coach and cheering themselves on to success. There are also tools that help us feel better at the level of the body—taking a deep breath, sighing, walking outside, or doing yoga are some examples.

When Dr. Peter Levine, author of "Waking the Tiger," sits down with a client, he observes their resiliency, determining how well it is functioning and how to best support it. What he is tracking is their ability to auto regulate, in other words how well they are able to shift from stress to rest on their own. He argues that all people do this every day. We shift from minor stresses to minor positive events. Each person has their own basic range of stress response and emotions they can tolerate. For many individuals with PTSD, the stress response system can become sticky and hard to shift.

From this and other insights, Dr. Levine developed a novel approach to treating post-traumatic stress disorder. His therapy does not work directly with cognitions, but with the body's physiological reactions to emotions. There are emotions and stress reactions that feel overwhelming, and even deadly—emotional experiences that seem to go on without end. In his therapy, people receive small, "titrated doses" of negative emotions and then shift to a positive emotion. Initially, the therapist invites and supports the client to shift to the positive emotion, but over time, the therapist allows their client's innate capacity to regulate emotions to initiate the shift, intervening only if the person's stress thermostat remains in one zone for too long.

Dr. Levine argues that as the person gains a new experience of a negative emotion, they *rewrite* their thoughts about the experience. He believes that changes in cognition *follow* changes in experience. According to affect regulation theory, this process is a "bottom-up perspective" on emotional change.

Bodily sensations of emotions can be difficult to tolerate. Some individuals tolerate some emotions better than others do. Some young children can tolerate feeling anger and maintain an even keel, but are overwhelmed by the feeling of sadness with its heavy weight. Happily, people can increase their capacity for tolerating intense emotion.

Dr. Allan N. Schore, a professor in the behavioral sciences and psychiatry department at the University of California, Los Angeles (UCLA), who studies emotion regulation, discusses the rupture-repair cycle and how it relates to early childhood relationships. He argues that while this skill can be enhanced later in life, rupture-repair is formed early in life, by small interactions between children and care providers. The rupture-repair cycle starts with a child's frustration or difficulty in a relationship. Obviously, parents cannot always give children what they want. This creates a rupture. The child feels distress, but by experiencing the repair of relationship with the parent, the child learns to master a wider range of emotional experiences.

This process builds a child's expectancy that the physical sensations of intense emotion will end with a positive outcome, and the child develops an innate capacity to regulate their emotions.

The image below describes how a person can move consistently within a homeostatic range. This range is established in part by genetic, epigenetic, situational, and long-term environmental factors. As the intensity of an emotional experience increases, a person's regulatory capacity kicks in and helps their response return to baseline.

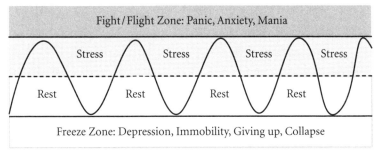

Figure 4.1 **Homeostasis Innate Stress Regulation**

While people remain within the regulatory range most of the time in daily life, they can and do exceed their current ability to tolerate an emotion. It is at this point that people may act in self-destructive ways, or use actively engaged cognitive emotion regulation skills to return to baseline. Figure 4.2 illustrates this process. For the emotion

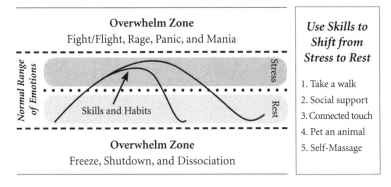

Figure 4.2 **Psychological Skills and Habits Help Shift from Stress to Rest**

of anger, as the intensity of the feeling increases past a range, the front brain or thinking mind shuts down, and the person reacts defensively. Some defensive reactions are helpful in increasing mastery of anger, but others can leave wreckage that may well be irreparable.

Figure 4.3 illustrates how, in the right context, the capacity for emotion regulation can grow over time. As the individual moves into a stretch zone just beyond their innate ability to regulate, they have a choice of adaptations: regulatory support from an outside source, or development of a skill. This helps the emotion return to within a tolerable range. Experiencing being able to return from too much emotional intensity to a tolerable range of emotion develops an increased

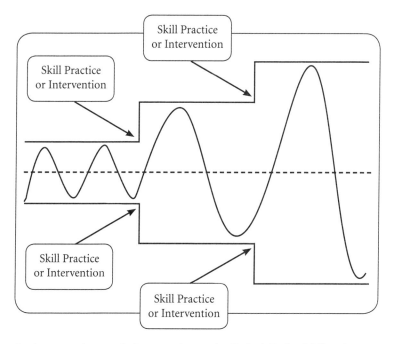

At times emotion regulation capacity can be limited. Early childhood stress, trauma, overwhelm – factors like these can all reduce our regulatory capacity. Learning and practicing skills and interventions through/within relationships can increase our emotion regulation capacity

Figure 4.3 **Emotion Regulation Capacity Develops and Increases**

range of regulation ability. Mastery of this skill is limitless, and people can continue to develop this capacity over the course of a lifetime. In our early childhood, the main way we repair a relationship with our parent or caregiver is through loving or supportive touch. Touch is an effective tool to increase our innate capacity to regulate emotions. Auto-regulation is, ipso facto, automatic and does not require significant effort. It's like riding a bike, once you know how, your body just does it. Nevertheless, it is possible to become an emotion regulation athlete and expand this skill dramatically.

Co-Regulation and Touch

Until recently, the assumption has been that humans live isolated within the bounds of their own skin. The ideal of health in psychology was a fully independent individual who did not need others, but could work, love, and play with ease. However, recent research has begun to point out an entirely new world of "interactive neurobiology" or what Dr. Allan Schore calls "co-regulation."

Sitting in a coffee shop, one can assess the quality of relationships amongst patrons by observing the dance of human body language. Body postures change and mirror one another, people move in a rhythm of eye contact and small touches, leaning toward each other and apart together. Now we are discovering that people mirror each other at an even deeper level. For any new science, there must be new tools of measurement. In interactive neurobiology, scientists have developed tools that enable us to peer into the brain with scans, measure stress response through skin conductance and pulses, and even measure changes in pupil dilation; these tools are revealing the myriad ways two bodies communicate at an emotional level.

To measure pupil-dilation in conversation, a group of researchers focused mini-video cameras on participants' pupils as they contracted and expanded. They found that people's pupils matched one another's faster than the conscious mind's ability to recognize the change. If you were to ask any two people, they would not say, "I know we feel close, because our pupils are dilating in synchrony." Nonetheless, this is in fact the case. When people enter into this dance, they feel more connected and understood by the other person, and the dance, in its entirety, happens below the radar of our thinking mind.

We call this resonance between individuals "somatic empathy." It is automatic empathy at a body-to-body level. Some experts argue that psychopathic individuals have a severe deficit in somatic empathy. The argument is that true psychopaths cannot feel the pain they inflict on others—they are heedless to it. These people have challenges seeing the perspective of another person, thus they do not care about the basic rights and feelings of others. To test this argument, researchers studied a group of individuals with "antisocial personality disorder," the diagnosis applied to people with psychopathic personality traits. They found that people diagnosed with this personality disorder were unable to synchronize pupil-dilation and enter into the dance. This group of individuals received training to develop somatic empathy. When reassessed after this training, not only did the amount of time their pupils dilated in rhythm with their conversation partner increase, they also displayed more empathy than prior to the experiment. The implications here are truly profound.

Neuroception and Touch

Stephen W. Porges, Ph.D., proposes a theory of neuroception: before conscious thought, our neural circuits distinguish whether situations or people are safe, dangerous, or life threatening. "Neuroception explains why a baby coos at a caregiver, but cries at a stranger, or why a toddler enjoys a parent's embrace but views a hug from a stranger as an assault." He describes two primary patterns or systems of behaviors: defensive and social-engagement. Defensive patterns are established to remove or reduce the possible damage of a threat. In a defensive pattern, the brain is primed to defend and not engage socially. Social engagement systems emerge in a safe, contained environment. He argues that when we feel safe, our brain engages the social engagement system, wherein the brain is primed and open to social interactions. Porges believes it is from this state of safety that people enter into the wonderful, unspoken dance of emotional resonance and somatic empathy. The perception of safety becomes the ground for the development of deep social bonds. Dr. Porges argues that people in high states of stress will not be able to access this social engagement system.

Safe touch from a parent to a child soothes the intensity of emotion and triggers the social engagement system. The ability to be in close physical contact and maintain safety is a hallmark of mammals, and is not as present in reptiles and invertebrate species. Unless violent or aggressive, most human touch occurs in a state of safety. People allow those they feel safe with to come close and offer supportive touch. Supportive touch amplifies the reduction of stress response and increases the activation of neurological systems involved in emotion regulation. Touch can therefore be a medium for increasing closeness and regulating emotions at a non-verbal, or implicit, level. While Dr. Porges' theory of neuroception is still under debate in the field of psychology, it does explain many aspects of human interaction.

In describing a series of behaviors that occur when people are in social engagement, Dr. Porges states that people make increased eye contact and have a wide range of musicality in their voice; in addition, their inner ear tunes to the human voice. One way a clinician can assess which brain-system (defensive or social engagement) a person is in at a given moment, is listening for prosody, or the musicality of the voice. When people are stressed, their voices become monotone and do not modulate. When people are socially engaged, the voice has a wide range of tone, and changes along with the emotional tone of others. This is one difference between a powerful speech, and a boring or uninspiring speech that lacks enough emotional impact.

Regulation—Increasing and Decreasing Emotions

Touch can be a conscious, explicit tool to regulate emotion. Touch can amplify emotional closeness. The experience of increased closeness and excitement—of being recognized and accepted as one is, is an important aspect of relationship development. The ability to regulate emotion is not simply reducing the intensity of a negative experience, but also being able to heighten an emotional experience. An individual who plays a competitive team sport does not need to relax; they need to get their mind into an optimal state. Before a game or after a big play, football players are seen exchanging high-fives, bunching-up in huddles, giving fist or chest bumps, and shoving one another. Touch can increase the intensity of emotions people feel. Touch can also be a part of a person's repertoire for calming emotions in any relationship. A hug after a difficult day, a kiss on the top of the head of a two-year-old child after a meltdown, reduces the intensity of the emotion, and communicates safety.

Self-Regulation and Touch

Self-regulation is the integration of auto-regulation, patterns of co-regulation, and one's cognitive-regulation skills. This is the entire package of behaviors, skills, and innate abilities that help a person manage their inner emotional life. For the routine vicissitudes of daily life, we use our innate emotion regulation, or our capacity for-auto-regulation. Consider how a small argument over lunch can leave one feeling grumpy for thirty minutes. Sometimes just waiting it out and distracting oneself enables the body to calm down and feel better. When a stress is greater, people naturally start to use some of their cognitive-emotion regulation skills. In a moderately stressful situation, one might put the situation into another perspective by calling a friend to talk it out, going for a run, asking for a hug, or taking a walk, to help diffuse the attached emotion.

In highly intense situations, or if our usual skills are unavailable and we don't have a burst of creativity, we go on overwhelm. In this state, most people are in a pattern of action and reaction. The front brain that we normally use to analyze a situation is offline and we just act. While some of these actions are helpful, many are not, and can prolong the amount of time spent in difficult emotional states. Some actions or habits can even lead to depression or other mental health challenges. Consider figure 4.4 below:

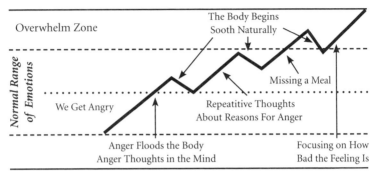

Figure 4.4 **Psychological Habits can Lead to Overwhelm and Explosions**

Sally—Touch and Reconnection to Life

Sally had experienced what most would consider a tough year. There were difficulties at work. Her marriage was rocky, and to top it all off, her eldest child was struggling in school. Sally was stressed. At first, she attempted to reduce her stress by talking with friends, attempting to fix the problems, and eating chocolate.

As time passed, Sally began watching television from in her bed as soon as she got home. When stressed at work, Sally would long to retreat to her bed. When tasks needed doing at home, she did them, and then got right back into bed. Sally was sleeping much of the day, which is a normal response to a high level of stress. She was attempting to limit the amount of time she was in stressful situations, whilst seeking a place of solace. However, sleeping all the time had a negative impact that Sally was not aware of—it can make someone even more depressed. It also severely limited her social life, and she literally lost contact with her world. Sally was no longer getting small hugs from friends after an outing, or from her younger children as they sat on her lap; moreover she was not feeling successful at work.

Sally was having fewer good periods of connection and success in her life, and evermore frequent bad periods of stress and isolation. Over time, Sally went from knowing how strong and capable she was, to believing that she was weak and worthless. This all took a toll, and eventually Sally developed major depression. Sally's situation describes a very common pathway to depression. A person exceeds their *innate* capacity to regulate their emotions and their current *learned* emotion regulation skills are not sufficient to solve their problems, so they seek a way to cope. Some people (like Sally) withdraw, while others cope by using drugs or alcohol, by excessive shopping, or even by infidelity. In therapy, Sally learned to increase her emotion regulation skills, to fight the pull of her bed, and to find a more true and accurate belief about herself. One tool she used was a monthly massage. While Sally could not afford a highly priced massage every week, she could afford one from a student at the local massage school. Sally found the contact deeply healing and left the massage feeling relaxed in a way she had not experienced in a long while. Although the difficult circumstances in her life continued for some time, her emotion regulation capacity and skills increased to a point where she could manage her difficult emotions effectively.

Growing Our Limits

Everyone has limits. To paraphrase the words of Dr. Judith L. Herman, everyone has a breaking point—some level of stress that is overwhelming. However, many people can bounce back from extremely stressful events without significant long-term impact. According to emotion regulation theory, a person who can bounce back has resiliency. All of us have the possibility of increasing our innate capacity to develop more skills to regulate our emotions. All of us can grow our resiliency.

A Tibetan teacher, Chögyam Trungpa Rinpoche, spoke about an experience he called confidence. In his writing Trungpa Rinpoche often said one cannot avoid the ups and downs of life, but over time and with practice, one can develop "confidence." This is one of the two "meta-skills" of self-regulation. While at times all of us exceed our current capacity of emotion regulation, after working through difficult times and coming back to our homeostatic range on multiple occasions, we gain trust in our ability to endure difficulty and learn from challenge. In the practice of meditation, people learn to watch their thoughts, their feelings, and their reactions. As they develop this skill, they learn to trust that, in the beautiful words of the German poet Rainer Maria Rilke, "… Let everything happen to you: beauty and terror. Just keep going. No feeling is final. …" A person who has developed this capacity and trust, rather than moving towards a choice that would ultimately be self-destructive, learns instead to tolerate troublesome feelings—developing their emotion regulation skills in the process.

The second major meta-emotion regulation skill is awareness of our limits. While we can and do develop trust in our ability to tolerate a range of emotional experiences, even when we feel temporarily knocked off-center; there is a time to seek support. When one's capacity is exceeded for too long, seeking out the right form of support to develop more skills, think through solutions, and strengthen one's innate capacity for resilience is vital. This skill takes two highly developed human abilities, of which the first is the ability to accurately self-reflect. This, in and of itself, is one of the most difficult skills to develop; it is also an ability that few other creatures in the animal kingdom appear to display. Second is the ability to admit one's difficulties openly. People who do both can develop through difficulty. In trauma-related literature, this is "post-traumatic growth"—the increase in inner strength one gains through learning how to live well, both during and after a profoundly difficult experience.

Co-Regulation—Connecting to Ourselves through Animals

Young George's grin stretched across his face as he sat tall atop an easygoing, brown horse. Since birth, George had struggled with cerebral palsy and brain damage; he was participating in a summer program at a camp in the south. The program supported children, both with and without developmental disabilities, to work together and learn from one another. Today he was learning to groom the horse, care for the horse and finally, much to his excitement, ride the horse. This was his first ride. George rode the horse around the yard while a guide helped him master sitting up and holding the reins.

Dr. Rebecca Cohen did her dissertation work on Equine Facilitated Psycho-therapy. She discusses how people can learn to be in relationship with other people through being with horses. Dr. Cohen works with children with reactive attachment and severe relationship traumas; she posits that as the children she works with gain relationship with the horse, they gain relationship with themselves and other people. Through learning how to care for horses, children start learning how to care for themselves.

She describes a group-exercise wherein a group of teens—struggling because of abuse they had each experienced—gathered together with a herd of horses. She told the teenagers that in this exercise the horse would choose them. The teens were learning to wait and watch. She helped them learn how to watch for non-verbal signals in their relationship with the horse. The children learned to notice eye contact, body-gestures, and other signs of relationship. As he or she began recognizing signals the horses were offering, a horse chose each teen. At the end of the exercise, the teens stood beside their horses and discussed the impact of being in touch and relationship with their horse. In a study of children given classroom counseling rather than equine-assisted counseling, all the students improved, but the equine-assisted group had markedly greater improvement in significantly more domains.

In relationship with any animal, but particularly horses, the physical contact is beyond words. Although only television's "Mr. Ed" could actually speak, children and adults alike can learn "who" a horse is. Some horses are shy. Some are bold. Some will respond to simple instructions. Some need a firm guide. From learning "who" the horse is, children can learn to trust others again, and learn to trust themselves. In Dr. Cohen's studies of children with early-life abuse, these children showed significant improvement in their ability to be in relationship with themselves and other humans through their contact with horses. Dr. Cohen describes how she often will walk a child who is new to horses out to the field where the horses graze, and just watch. She says from the moment a child walks into the therapy session, she is watching how they enter into connection. As she and the child watch the horses play and move, she adroitly supports the child to explore fears, anxieties, and their longing for connection.

Dr. Cohen says that it is not uncommon for an abused child to burst
into tears when they are grooming a horse for the first time, as they
grieve their realization of how lacking the care they received in their
early life really was.

How we approach relationship matters deeply. Children in equine-
assisted therapy learn to approach the horse with care. They learn
where to stand and how to enter into a non-verbal dialogue. The horse
has to learn to listen to them, and they have to learn to listen to the
horse. Often, a child who has been required to be too independent too
early in their development, will step into the role of caretaker for the
horse—a role this child knows all too well. Through gentle support,
Dr. Cohen helps them learn to feel the support the horse is giving back
to them. As a personal example, one patient I worked with described a
horse on the property where she lived as a child that "…would let me
cry into his shoulder when I was upset." She went on to say, "Jake, the
other horse, would not let me, but Don would." This image became a
source of strength for her even years later.

Riding horses has also helped people who live with one of the more
challenging mental health conditions people face. Living with symptoms of psychosis can be difficult. Many individuals with symptoms
of psychosis hear things that others do not (auditory hallucinations),
have anhedonia (the inability to feel pleasure), and at times the difference between their personal reality and consensual reality is not clear.
A study of equine assisted therapy for individuals with symptoms of
psychosis found a strong improvement in their ability to feel pleasure!
Their anhedonia was reduced. More research is needed to clarify this,
however, one might make an educated guess that their connection
with the horses helped reduce cortisol and increase oxytocin levels,
and gave these individuals a sense of meaning and purpose.

Loneliness is a painful state of existence for anyone, but it can be
deadly in older people—as can believing that one's life lacks purpose or meaning. Increased purpose and social contact can increase
an individual's long-term health. There is a large body of research
showing that connection with animals increases both of these highly
important factors. As another personal example, I was in a nursing

home with a client who was quite ill. This home kept rabbits in a hutch outside, and once each week, staff members brought a rabbit inside to visit with each patient. My client shifted from slumping in her chair, to being alive and engaged, when the rabbit was brought into her room. She would pet the rabbit for some time, smiling and making small talk. This connection mattered. I would watch stress drain out of her body as she spent time with the rabbit. Connection with another being is real and important. Often, elders living in nursing homes can feel isolated, alone—completely unimportant. Caring for an animal helps change that: it brings connection, purpose, even joy, back into their lives.

In another controlled study, one group of elders diagnosed with dementia received regular visits from an animal. The individuals who received the animal visits had fewer behavioral challenges than those who did not. When an individual develops dementia, they may feel dehumanized and very isolated. The individual suffers fundamental changes in their ability to be in relationship. Spending time with an animal gives them a clear pathway to connection.

Given the choice between a pill and a dolphin, many will choose dolphins. A group of depressed individuals participated in a very interesting experiment exploring how a relationship with dolphins might help lift their depression. One group of depressed individuals swam with dolphins and another group did not. The group who swam with the dolphins had a significant reduction in symptoms of depression compared to the group who did not. Two weeks of swimming, feeling the warm water on their skin, occasionally touching a dolphin, or being touched by a dolphin who chose them, connecting and being emotionally touched as they built group-bonds, and also inter-species bonds—this helped people connect to themselves past their symptoms of depression. It is hardly surprising that positive emotional impacts come about from exercising in the sun. Nonetheless, I have talked with many people who, when in the grip of depression, could not enjoy the beauty of a sunset— even in the Caribbean. For some of these people, the fact that they did not feel pleasure witnessing a Caribbean sunset was amplified by their perception that they *should* enjoy it in such a beautiful place.

Chronic pain impacts an individual's life at a profound level. People living with chronic pain are frequently misunderstood, particularly when their pain is caused by an invisible wound or condition. Sometimes, even family members do not understand; they may become impatient and make comments like, "Just get over it." However, pain is not just a physical experience; chronic pain has an emotional component. Increased stress brings increased pain. In the lobby of a pain clinic, the atmosphere can be quite tense. People feel desperate, doctors are often running behind, and just being in one position for any length of time can exacerbate discomfort. Staff at one pain clinic had a wild idea, and they put it to the test with a study wherein staff members provided some patients with a dog to sit beside them in the waiting room. Other patients did not have a canine companion. Staff surveyed each individual to measure his or her pain. Over the course of this study, two-hundred-thirty-five patients participated in the research. This study showed a twenty-three percent reduction in pain levels for those who sat with a dog, compared to a four percent reduction in the group that did not. This is a clinically meaningful impact, achieved with a simple intervention!

Contact with animals has a powerful effect on people, thus animals play a part in many treatments. Often, soldiers with PTSD have a therapy dog as part of their healing. It is entirely possible to build connection across species, and one of the most powerful languages for this connection is touch. Touch plays a role in our ability to regulate emotions. Therefore, it is important to get beneath the skin and see how touch affects the biology underneath the psychology.

Chapter 5

The Neurobiology of Touch and Emotion Regulation

The Neurobiology of Touch and Emotion Regulation

If you have ever hit your thumb with a hammer, you know how intense the sense of touch can be. There are four types of nerves for communicating touch; these nerves are classified as slow communicators and fast communicators. The fast nerves are wrapped in a protective covering of non-conductive glial cells that form the myelin sheath, which is like coating on a wire that stops it from losing signal, thus helping it rapidly transmit information to the other end. Other nerves, or axons, do not have such a coating. The signals in unmyelinated axons travel much more slowly. If we could run between five and twenty-five meters-per-second, we would be breaking world records. This is the rate of transmission of the "slow" unmyelinated cells. Myelinated cells transmit at one-hundred-twenty meters per second! Fibers that transmit pain to the brain use slower, unmyelinated nerves.

Studies in the last ten years have begun to change our thinking about some of the information carried to the brain by unmyelinated neurons. Until recently, slower, unmyelinated cells were believed to carry information from the skin relating only to pain and temperature. When you put your hand under the faucet to check the water temperature, your hand registers this feeling, and sends it via the slow fibers to the brain. However, new research indicates that a section of these unmyelinated fibers also carries sensations of soothing touch to the emotion regulation centers of the brain.

The faster myelinated cells carry information about deep pressure, joint position, muscle tension, vibration, hair movement, and proprioception (sense of where your body-parts are in relationship to each other and how you move through space). Since these cells transmit faster and have a thicker "highway" to travel, they are able to override pain signals. Imagine you have stubbed your toe. It hurts and you are hopping around the house holding your foot. Grabbing one's foot makes sense, but why do we move around so much? Why do we shake our hand after we smash our thumb with a hammer? Recent research indicates that shaking and rubbing activates these faster cells and overrides the pain signals for a moment. This is one component of the "gate-control" theory of pain.

So let us slow down the process of hitting our thumb with a hammer. It feels like the pain is in our thumb, but it's a bit more complicated than that. First those slightly slower, but still too fast for comfort, unmyelinated cells shoot up to the emotional centers of the brain. They send an intense signal saying, in essence, "Pain!" It's not a subtle message about what happened and where, it's simply an alarm ringing to alert us. Because it hits our emotional centers, it grabs our full attention! If our pain pathway stopped there, we would not know where we were hurting and the pain would go on indefinitely. Fortunately, the next cells to fire localize the pain by signaling that the throbbing is coming from our thumb. This is vital, because if we cannot find the threat, we cannot remove it or learn from it. After registering the origin of the pain and the level of danger, we make sure we are currently safe. If we are safe, an area deep in the brainstem related to stress reactivity signals the body to reduce the nerve impulses carrying the pain signal. This area sends out neurochemicals, some of which we have already discussed such as oxytocin and serotonin, and endogenous opioids (these are natural chemicals produced within the brain, similar to opium, heroin, and painkillers like methadone). The three cell types relay, in this order, "Pain!" then, "My thumb hurts!" and finally, "I am feeling better."

In recent years there has been a new addition to this map: a group of unmyelinated cells thought to transmit pain and pain alone, actually carries a type of information that forms the bedrock of safe emotional touch. We live in exciting times; research about the brain is exploding! Scientists are finally able to peer into the brain as it functions, and have begun to test theories in the way biologists did when they first developed the microscope. Researchers place people in a functional magnetic resonance imaging machine (fMRI) that illustrates the brain as it functions. Participants in one such study received four types of touch: static (unmoving) skin-to-skin contact on a limb (e.g., arm); skin-to-skin massage; static contact with gloves on; massage-like touch while the researcher wore gloves. Not surprisingly, people reported that the massage-like skin-to-skin contact was the most pleasant. The contact with the glove on did not feel as good as the contact skin-to-skin. This is more than just a subjective comparison, there is biology driving these feelings. In the images provided by the fMRI, one area of the brain was highly activated during the massage-like skin-to-skin touch. This area is the pregenual anterior cingulate cortex (pgACC) and relates to reward and pleasure; it is also activated by opioid medicines such as morphine (the activation of the pleasure centers by opiate medications is one reason opiates are so addictive), that reduce pain.

Light touch stimulates what we call C-tactile, or CT cells. These cells signal safe, connected emotional contact. In this study, research participants sat in an fMRI machine. They were touched lightly on the arm, the leg, and the face. The participants in this study were able to identify where they had been touched ninety-seven percent of the time. Deep in each hemisphere of the mammalian brain is a structure called the insula (also called the insular cortex, insulary cortex, or insular lobe). Like many structures in the brain, scientists are still studying the insula; however, research has begun to develop a theory of the function of this area. One of the known functions of the insular cortex is to be a relay station for CT cells. When we cuddle a baby, or run our hands through our spouse's hair, we stimulate their CT cells. These cells then signal their insular cortex. This area is involved in emotion regulation, and receives information about both positive and negative sensations from the body. Areas in the insular cortex are organized "somatotropically."

In other words, specific regions of the cortex are responsible for different areas of the body, just as Wilder Penfield found when he mapped the somatosensory cortex. In addition to its involvement in painful touch, the insular cortex plays a powerful role in emotion regulation and the regulation of bodily homeostasis. It is our insular cortex that gives us the nuance of emotional information rising up from our bodies. When we look in the face of our lover and our heart seems to swell with tenderness, the bodily sensations rush up to the insula, which mixes, or pairs, these visceral sensations with the intense emotion. Again, touch and emotions are woven together in the fundamental brain systems that support both processes.

Touch and Emotion Regulation—The Triune Brain

Her mom was not angry; she was worried. Julie, a teenager, yelled at her mother anyway. After Julie had calmed down, her mom asked, "Why did you yell?" In a matter-of-fact manner, Julie replied, "You were so angry at me. I just got mad back." Julie's mother replied, "No, honey. I was not angry. I was worried about you." Teenagers who experience traumatic events in their lives tend to misperceive fear as anger. Teenagers in general tend to perceive an emotion and react. When they read emotions on faces, different parts of the teen-brain fire (compared to adult-brains). When teenagers see a face with emotion expressed on it, they have a strong reaction in their amygdalae. (Technically, there are two amygdalas, one in each brain hemisphere, collectively known as amygdalae.) Several theories about the function of amygdalae point to their role in the fight-flight response. Comparing brain scans of teens and adults shows that different areas activate when they see emotions. When adults see an emotion expressed on a face, they engage their front brain or thinking mind. Their mind assesses the emotion and considers it, rather than immediately reacting. However, as any parent knows, there are times when a teenager's front brain goes offline and there is just raw, emotional reaction. This reaction is exactly what brain scans show.

Touch affects so many of the brain structures involved in emotion regulation. There are important implications about how touch can play key roles—not only in helping people feel better, but also in helping people develop consistently better emotion regulation, and in helping people heal, both physically and emotionally, from overwhelming life events.

In 1964, renowned neuroscientist and physician Dr. Paul D. MacLean put forward a concept still in use today. Calling his model the "triune brain," MacLean observed three major functional regions of the human brain. The lower section of the brain—the brainstem—is evolutionarily older, which means it is also present in lizards and other reptiles. This area regulates life-sustaining body functions such as sleep, wakefulness, stress levels, pain, and breathing. However, in mammals another structure develops—the limbic system, sometimes referred to as the emotional center of the brain. In complex animals (primates) a third structure develops—the neocortex (which is the major part of the cortex) consisting of up to six horizontal layers covering the outer portion of the cerebrum. The neocortex area of the brain is highly related to complex thinking, planning, and emotional reasoning. When we are hugged and we like it, we engage an area of the brainstem—the periaqueductal-gray (PAG)—that can trigger stress, but also triggers a relaxation response called the parasympathetic response. This response tells your body to relax and come to rest. In response to the hug, your breathing slows and you begin breathing from your diaphragm, your heart rate slows, your pupils begin constricting, and your stomach starts preparing to digest.

The second area of the brain in the triune theory is the limbic system, or emotional brain. The limbic brain structures—deep in the center of the brain—are believed to have evolved after the development of the brainstem. This system is present in many mammalian animals and humans. In Charles Darwin's "The Expression of the Emotions in Man and Animals," he explores biological reactions in other animal species that appear to mimic human emotions. Snarls of anger are present in both human and animal expression, as are demonstrations of affection and safety. While genetic processes play a large role in mapping the limbic system, much of the development of the limbic system occurs through experience-dependent mechanisms.

If you are communicating with someone who is angry, you are communicating with his or her limbic brain; if you are trying to communicate with someone who is absolutely enraged, you are talking to a walking brainstem! This is important, because if an individual cannot access their thinking mind, they may make impulsive and potentially destructive decisions.

Now, more than fifty years after Dr. MacLean proposed his triune brain model, therapists are still working to translate this understanding of the brain into practical tools for their clients.

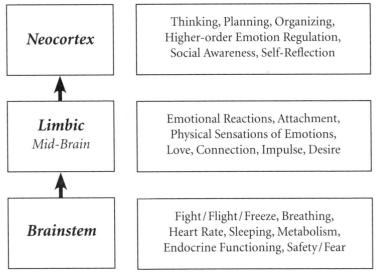

Figure 5.1 **Triune Brain**

Some areas of the limbic system are primed for certain experiences, and these experiences play a vital role in the developmental process. In young mice, being licked and nuzzled by their mothers tunes key aspects of the limbic and social brain. Mice, particularly males, who lack this type of nurturing, do not develop well socially and exhibit increased aggression in peer relationships.

The amygdalae have many functions, some known, and others still awaiting identification. These almond-shaped structures have become well known in recent years because of their role in the decision-making emotions: anger and fear—two of the most difficult emotions for people to tolerate in themselves or in others. When the amygdalae fire (particularly the areas related to fight-flight), the body mobilizes a strategy to defend itself with one of these two emotions—anger (fight) or fear (flight).

Let us consider a common human interaction between a parent and child. Joseph, two years old, does not want to put down his toy, but it is time to go. He feels conflicted because he wants the toy, but he likes his mother and wants to please her. Therefore, he does what many children do: he protests. As Joseph's grip on the toy tightens, his amygdalae fire and send a signal to his hypothalamus—a very important structure for stress response regulation. The hypothalamus secretes a neural chemical called corticotrophin-releasing hormone (CRH). As this hormone enters the bloodstream, it travels to the adrenal gland at the top of the kidney, signaling the adrenal gland to send out a burst of cortisol. Joseph grips the toy harder, his body becomes tight, his face gets a little red, and his breathing becomes deeper and more rapid. The front brain, responsible for making good decisions, starts to shut down. Joseph is ready for a fight. This ancient physiology is in all people, even his mother. If Joseph's behavior persists, it will not be long before her stress physiology fires and she has a similar cascade of events. However, she will have one thing her son does not: a more mature emotion regulation system. In other words, for most adults it takes more fight-flight elevation to start shutting down the functions of the front brain. However, everyone has his or her limits.

The good news is that with practice, the emotion regulation structures develop and grow stronger. This is in fact what Joseph's mother teaches him when she has him put down the toy and take a time out. After he calms, she asks him to apologize, reminding him that she will always love him, but that it not okay to talk to his mommy like that. She gives him a hug, and the tears of frustration in his eyes stop as she holds him. His body begins to relax and his breathing slows. This type of neurobiological training has been going on for all of human history and it continues to this day. Knowing how important touch is to the development of this system can help doctors, psychologists, and families become more effective facilitators of emotional development.

Two other key brain structures are helpful in understanding the impacts of touch: the insular cortex and the cingulate cortex. The insular cortex is a very interesting area of the brain. Like the amygdalae, researchers are still developing theories of its functions, but it does aid in interpreting cues from the body, and from touch. When Joseph becomes upset, that physiological cascade activates the thalamus (a relay station for most sensory information in the brain), and then the insular cortex, which sends that information to the front brain and thinking mind. Receiving too much information from the insular cortex is theorized to be the reason the front brain can be overwhelmed. In essence, too much insular information is as if the emotion regulation system, accustomed to drinking from a water fountain, is now trying to drink from a fire hose. The insular cortex is also involved in interpreting safe, supportive touch; it reads that hug of reconciliation, as well as harsher touch.

Before considering the cingulate cortex, let's look at the third major area of this triune brain—the cortex. When you look at the outside of a brain, all of the folds are called the neocortex. It has a six-layered structure that may play a role in how it processes information. The neocortex probably develops by interaction between genetic, epigenetic, and environmental factors. The front brain (the frontal part of the cortex) is believed to be the last structure to develop; many consider it one of the main differences between humans and other mammals. The functions attributed to this area of the brain are thinking, thinking about thinking, planning, organizing, problem solving, and emotion recognition and regulation.

Many people suffering symptoms of post-traumatic stress disorder (PTSD) have experienced the most horrible and difficult things that can befall us; some have witnessed the most horrible atrocities we humans can produce. Those who solely *witness* violence may experience "survivor" guilt at the senselessness of the violence and their inability to prevent it. This can be a profound catalyst for change and growth. It often pushes people with traumatic experiences to give back to society—perhaps working to prevent similar traumatic situations from occurring, or helping traumatized people deal with their experiences so they can resume a more normal life.

Dr. Ruth Lanius (current holder of the Harris-Woodman Chair in Mind-Body Medicine at the Schulich School of Medicine & Dentistry at the University of Western Ontario), a neuroscientist who investigates emotion regulation in trauma survivors, worked with a group of soldiers suffering from PTSD. The soldiers entered an fMRI machine and listened to scripts of the events they had experienced during the traumatic event(s). (Repeated exposure is also a part of certain treatments for PTSD). She found that about seventy percent of the participants' brains displayed a similar pattern of over-activation of the insular cortex, which registers the sensations from their body. They also displayed under-activation in the cingulate cortex. The cingulate cortex is vital to emotion regulation, and plays an intermediary role between the sensations from the body, and the front brain. The soldiers also displayed under-activation in the orbital medial pre-frontal cortex (the very tip of the brain right under the eye sockets). This area is vital to regulating emotions. In other words, their emotion regulation system was offline, but their emotions were on maximum-high; this gives new meaning to drinking from a fire hose! These individuals are flooded with intense experiences of emotion, but their regulation system is not functioning. Many veterans find that being with an animal companion is helpful in decreasing the impact such experiences have on them. As discussed earlier, petting an animal (touch), massage, and safe, supportive touch have multiple beneficial impacts on the emotion regulation system.

Touch first reduces activation in the amygdalae, thus allowing the stress system to begin to soothe. Touch also reduces the stress response initiated by the brainstem, which reduces sensations flowing from the body into the insular cortex. Additionally, touch influences functioning of the front brain. In fMRI research, touch increases activation in the frontal cortex, particularly the orbital medial pre-frontal cortex (OMPFC). It also helps makes higher-order emotion regulation systems more effective at regulating emotional response. In short, touch brings the flow of emotion in the "fire hose" down to a more manageable level.

Dr. Lanius also observed an opposite pattern: rather than too much activation in the frontal cortex, about thirty percent of the traumatized soldiers had too little. These individuals displayed a mere trickle of information coming to the insula. They also displayed highly increased activation in the cingulate and frontal cortex. This implies that these soldiers had very little signal reaching their insula, and what was received was quickly squelched. The soldiers in this study once again did humanity a great service as scientists attempted to develop ways to help other soldiers heal from this difficult combat wound. Through their willingness to participate in research, they also gave many people experiencing PTSD from other traumas a chance to heal. One of the most difficult symptoms people suffering from PTSD face is numbness. These veterans had difficulty feeling emotions at all, and some would seek out intense and even dangerous situations trying to feel something. People with trauma report feeling numb, flat, disconnected—as if they don't care about anything. This can be very difficult for an individual who before experiencing the trauma, loved his or her spouse and children deeply, but, after returning home from war, feels nothing upon seeing their family. Simple, light touch can help people begin to have feelings again. The safety of felt contact can wake up the emotional systems, allowing them to come back online.

One of the terms used in research about cognitive function and aging is "cognitive reserve." It refers to people who have a very active mental life, average to above-average intelligence, and a college education; these appear to be neuroprotective factors against cognitive decline in aging. It may also be that such people have a limbic reserve—a store of positive mastery of socially or emotionally challenging situations. It seems this storehouse of experience becomes a neural protector against the many stresses of life—i.e., that limbic reserve is a partial explanation of resilience. Safe touches from a parent or caregiver during early attachment may play a significant role in building limbic reserve.

Barbara Fredrickson's broaden-and-build theory of positive emotions seems to come to a similar conclusion. She notes that difficult or protective emotions like anger and fear take aim at just one goal: the removal of a threat in the short-term. She argues that these emotions are not aimed at long-term plans or development of relationships. They are intended to flare up for a moment, dissipating after the threat is removed. Dr. Fredrickson posits that the social emotions are directed toward building in the long-term. We cannot build anything beyond a small cabin without lots of cooperation. Positive emotions, like love, happiness, joy, or gratitude, aim at the development of long-term relationships, enabling people to accomplish complex tasks. Positive emotions broaden people's thinking, focusing on the big picture and long-term goals. One does not have to strain very hard to imagine our distant ancestors gathering around a fire after a successful hunt, slapping each other on the back and laughing as they discuss how they will construct an even better spear for the next hunt.

Fredrickson has also explored the ratio of positive-to-negative emotions we require to thrive. Most people who are able to weather difficulty and thrive—who are resilient—have a ratio of 3:1. While we are born with our genetic code and cannot control the childhood we experience, we can develop our minds. Practicing positive emotions may in fact lead to an increased resilience and ability to bounce back from stress. Monks and nuns who regularly practice experiencing positive emotions have a thicker orbital medial prefrontal cortex, which is responsible for regulating emotions. Through self-directed neuroplasticity people are able to sculpt the brain of tomorrow with their choices today. While no research at this time has explored the long-term impact of increasing the amount of hugs, massage, and loving social touch on brain tissue, one can posit that a steady increase in positive, safe touch will help emotion regulation process in the short-term, *and* lead to long-term changes in brain architecture.

Chapter 6

Touch and Psychotherapy: Connection to Healing

Psychotherapy came of age in the Victorian era. This was a period when one of the top parenting experts advised parents not to touch their children more than once per day, and then only with a pat on the head or a firm handshake. Considered abusive today, this type of parenting was common practice when psychotherapy first developed.

It is hardly surprising that since psychotherapy first developed in the Victorian era, it included strong prohibitions against touch as a therapeutic technique. This prohibition has continued to the present, despite increasing evidence that touch is a powerful and useful clinical tool. Sigmund Freud founded his "talking cure" in Vienna in the Victorian era. As psychoanalysis developed, Freud argued for a distant stance between therapist and client, thus Freud sat behind his patients so that they could not see him. They talked and he listened, with the intention of producing a neutral and objective stance. This practice looks archaic to most of today's clinicians, who practice face-to-face, sitting across from their clients and using, in many cases, a highly collaborative therapeutic style.

Therapeutic Touch

In a very real way, the human brain is a mirror for the body; in the words of the pre-eminent stress researcher Dr. Bruce McEwen, the brain is the "master organ of the body." Our brain puts us to sleep and our brain wakes us up. Structures in the brainstem regulate breathing and heart rate. Structures in the limbic brain modulate emotion, metabolism, growth-hormone production, and thyroid function. Human touch and physical contact affect the systems of the body at a fundamental level. Many psychological theories focus on human development as the root of psychological functioning, yet ignore the impact of touch. Other psychological theories focus on the here and now, but ignore the powerful influence human contact can have on mood, emotions, and stress for a client in the present. This has led Dr. Ofer Zur, a prominent member of the American Psychological Association who has worked diligently on ethics in psychology, to say in his foundational paper on the topic of touch in therapy, "Practicing risk management by rigidly avoiding touch is unethical." Zur goes on to state, "We must remember that the therapeutic effect of touch has been scientifically and clinically proven. We must also remember that we are hired to help rather than being hired to practice risk management. Therefore we must touch clients when appropriate in a way that will help them grow and heal."

A Case of Stress and Contact

She sits in the office shaking like a leaf. The psychologist knows that her stress response is firing, causing her to shake and feel deep panic, although she is, in fact, in a safe environment. The psychologist uses a soothing voice, knowing the impact of vocal tone on the stress response, and that this can normalize the symptoms. (Normalizing means helping the individual understand that the feelings she is having are a common physiological reaction and that there are tools that can help shift it.) The woman sits across from her therapist, deciding if she believes what the therapist is saying. The clinician also points out that these feelings will stop, and that most panic attacks don't last much longer than ten minutes. She agrees they usually do calm down, but states in a shaky voice, "It takes me the rest of the day to recover." She takes her first deep breath in a while. The therapist watches this, noting that she is already shifting, and then asks if she would feel comfortable putting her own hands on her stomach and chest, lightly pressing into her chest and inhaling deeply, with a pause at the top of her breath where it naturally changes from inhale to exhale.

During the first few breaths, she misses the top, but her face is already less tense and she makes eye contact with the clinician. Over the next few minutes, the panic diminishes. The clinician asks how the contact with her own hand on her upper chest helped, or did not help. She replies that it felt "containing" and reports that she feels calmer after the contact. The clinician and the client then make a list of tools she can use to reduce the panic the next time it occurs. Clinician and client also collaborate on creating a list of signs that can help her recognize the feeling, and implement her tools before the anxiety reaches a disabling level.

This is a rudimentary use of touch as a clinical tool. The clinician knew several things that helped him choose how to use touch: that a hand on the stomach can make it easier for a person to breathe into their belly, and that a good "diaphragmatic" or belly breath can help someone shift from high stress back to rest. The clinician also knew that self-touch on the upper chest can feel safe and containing. The clinician used touch as a part of a bigger treatment intervention with a clear plan and goal. While touch-based work is used in more complex ways than described in the above intervention, this example illustrates how touch can easily be woven into clinical work.

Clinical touch-based interventions can fit into many types of therapeutic practices, and, once the principles are understood, be adapted for a wide range of symptoms. These tools are also powerful for individual clients to learn and use on themselves. Psychotherapeutic touch can have a powerful impact on psychological and physical health, particularly in reducing precursors to diseases such as stress and inflammation.

As with any treatment, to use psychotherapeutic touch effectively, clinicians need good training in ethics, risk factors, indications and contraindications, and supervision as they are learning. Touch can feel safe and supportive, or it can feel invasive; often the only differences are a very subtle shift in the quality of the contact, and in how the client and the therapist talk about touch. It is vital that therapists who use touch work obtain informed consent from their clients prior to starting touch-based therapy. A person seeking psychotherapy can ask if the prospective clinician has training in, and uses psychotherapeutic touch.

Psychotherapeutic Touch and Clinical Applications

Dr. Eric Kandel, Nobel-Prize-winning psychologist and researcher stated, "Psychotherapy *is* a biological treatment." Interventions used in psychotherapy change the fundamental biological functioning of the brain and endocrine system. Like prescription medication, interventions in psychotherapy have purpose and methodology. How one understands an intervention and its application guides how it is used and how helpful it is. Many psychological difficulties are successfully treated with psychotherapy. In fact, for several mental health challenges, psychotherapy provides better treatment than available pharmacological interventions; especially considering that medication can lose efficacy due to non-compliance (not taking the medication, or using an incorrect dosage and/or frequency) or increasing tolerance from long-term use, whereas the skills and knowledge gained in psychotherapy remain with clients for the remainder of their lives.

Touched by Depression

Depression, according the World Health Organization, is the leading cause of disability on our planet. It affects seventeen percent of Americans at any given time, and over the course of a lifespan, this percentage is much higher. Depression is corrosive, not just on the psyche, but also on the brain and body. It erodes physical health, causing loss of brain cells, and increased risk of stress-based diseases such as heart attacks or stroke, and autoimmune-diseases such as diabetes. Touch interventions offer significant promise for reducing symptoms of depression, serving as the basis for novel clinical interventions, and helping many individuals heal. Nevertheless, despite the growing body of evidence demonstrating how touch is an important part of many treatments, psychotherapy clings to the Victorian-era taboo against physical contact.

Cognitive Behavioral Therapy and Touch Interventions

Dr. Aaron Beck is a kind man with a quick smile. When he and others developed cognitive behavior therapy (CBT), they had a large battle ahead of them. However, solid research proves CBT is a medical intervention that can effectively relieve or reduce symptoms of myriad health conditions. When Dr. Beck initially developed CBT, he was influenced by the Stoics—ancient Greek philosophers who believed how we *think* about our life changes how we *feel* about our life. CBT practitioners set out to do just this: change thoughts in order to change feelings. Indeed, this is what transpires.

Cognitive behavior theory involves three elements: thoughts, emotions, and behaviors. The theory is an ever-growing and adapting set of tools to help people change their thoughts, engage effectively with their emotions, and shift their behaviors.

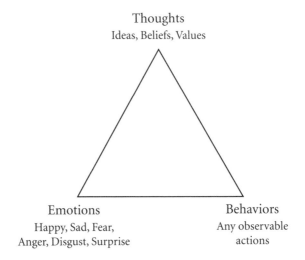

Figure 6.1 **Cognitive Behavioral Triad**

Cognitive behavior theory does not sift through the past with a fine-toothed comb searching for the roots of psychological difficulties. It works in the here and now, focusing on challenging and then changing unhelpful thoughts, and developing skills to manage emotions and act more effectively. CBT has been highly effective in treating conditions ranging from anxiety to sleep disorders, and the body of research on CBT is growing.

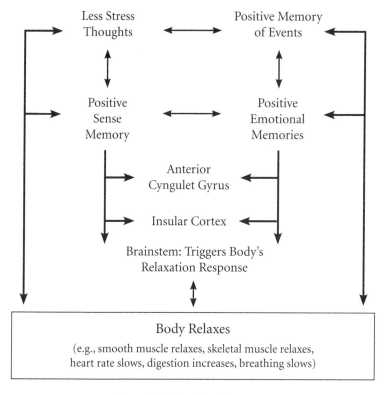

Figure 6.2 **Relaxation Response**

Touch has distinct and predictable impacts on human physiology and psychology, which can aid clinicians in making the best use of touch in a clinical setting. Touch affects stress levels—heightening the activation of regions of the brain involved in emotion regulation, and altering levels of neurochemicals involved with exacerbating multiple mental-health conditions. Safe, supportive touch has been successful in altering an individual's thoughts or cognitions about a disease-process, a client, or a work environment. Offering a sense of safety, touch has increased medication compliance in multiple health settings, as well as increasing client trust in doctor-patient relationships.

While massage and bodywork can be excellent adjunct treatment referrals for any cognitive behavior therapist, touch work can be woven into multiple aspects of their own clinical treatment. Below are several touch-interventions a clinician can add to their practice.

Supportive Self-Touch

Supportive self-touch is a powerful technique can lead to increased relaxation response and help increase tolerance of intense emotional states. This technique asks the client to do two things: be aware of changes in their emotional state, and use self-touch to increase their ability to tolerate the feeling or reduce its intensity. Tapping lightly on the outsides of the shoulders can distract an individual from the physical sensations of their emotions and pull their mind away from unhealthy thought-patterns. Squeezing the outside of opposite shoulders can increase the relaxation response, helping a person shift from an intense emotional experience to a more manageable one. A neck, foot, or hand massage reduces muscle tension and increases the relaxation response. Supportive self-touch is already incorporated into a highly effective treatment developed by Marsha Linehan called dialectical behavioral therapy (DBT).

Dialectical behavioral therapy was the first therapy to effectively help individuals with a diagnosis of emotional dysregulation, symptoms of which include chronic suicidality and other severely dysfunctional behaviors. Using DBT has helped such individuals find peace, or in Linehan's words, build a "life worth living." Linehan incorporated mindfulness skills with several branches of the field of psychology, creating a comprehensive approach that supported people to have access to their own innate strengths and capacity. Her therapy includes a skills training group focused on developing emotion regulation skills (self-touch and contact with animals are often used as soothing or relaxation techniques), and individual therapy focused on developing skills and integrating those skills into life. DBT also makes skills coaching available twenty-four hours per day, so a person can call for support and self-management to practice skills. Dialectical behavioral therapy is now used all over the globe; it has helped thousands of people previously abandoned by the fields of psychiatry and psychology.

Client Homework

Cognitive behavioral therapy solves the problem of helping therapy transition from the clinical office to real life through homework practice. Clients monitor their mood and thoughts and use skills they have developed to help manage their mood. A depressed client may establish an exercise plan and other tools to manage the intense feelings of depression; these tools include learning to notice negative, inaccurate thoughts and challenging those thoughts with reality. However, this is particularly difficult for individuals suffering with depression because their depression creates a tendency to recognize only negative information. Depression makes people more likely to ignore or discount positive moods, effective actions they have taken, and their own unique personal strengths. Therapist and clients can include self-massage, contact with animals, and other touch-based interventions to build emotion regulation capacity. Depressed people start detaching themselves from the things that previously brought them joy and happiness. CBT homework asks clients to practice increasing the amount of "pleasurable activities" in their lives. Touch is a powerful way to connect to soothing, safety and pleasure. One of my group members recently announced, "I am getting a massage this week." This willingness to give himself safe, nurturing touch is a powerful shift— from giving up—to investing in his own wellbeing.

Animals are good companions for individuals who are depressed, as petting or caring for an animal can help them tolerate the intense feelings, and build an ability to manage their mood. Contact with the animal changes not only the way an individual feels, but puts in motion that wonderful neurobiological cascade of decreasing cortisol levels and increasing brain chemicals involved in enjoyment (serotonin, dopamine and norepinephrine). For an individual with high anxiety, contact with an animal can be a powerful intervention. When people become highly anxious, it can feel like the entire world is a threat. While anxiety does pass on its own, because given enough time the cortisol system (stress) shuts itself off, having safe physical contact with a pet or a loved one can distract from negative feelings and worried thoughts long enough for the individual to return to rest.

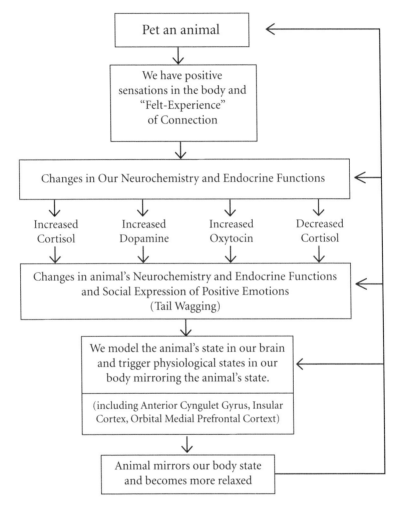

Figure 6.3 **Physiological Impacts of Petting an Animal**

Clinical Interventions

At this time, many clinicians are not trained to provide effective touch interventions. For touch to be successful in treatment, a clinician needs adequate supervision and training about creating safety, developing treatment plans, and applying touch within the treatment hour. Clinicians need to include information on touch treatment in their informed consent. Clinicians also need to develop skills to track any impact of touch intervention on their client, as well as to observe their client's ever-changing comfort level with the contact. Touch can be a powerful tool in a cognitive behavioral therapy session, as long as it is safe, within the clinician's scope of practice, and the clinician is aware of why they are using touch as an intervention.

Cognitive Behavioral Therapy-Based Touch—an Example

The client was in session, her chest heaving. She had just started talking about a previous panic attack, and boom! She was in the middle of one. The clinician had previously discussed the use of touch with the client and she was open to it. The clinician asked if he could sit near her and place his foot lightly on the top of her foot, and she agreed. The clinician provided steady pressure to her foot as he guided her to use another relaxation technique. She began calming: her breathing slowed down, and her eyes softened. The clinician used the opportunity to help his client realize that the panic did lessen and end, and to identify what she did to begin that shift. Clinician and client discussed how she could use the tools she'd just practiced at home in the event of another attack. One item on her list of home-practice was petting her dog when she felt anxious. She also learned to challenge thoughts telling her that the anxiety meant she would die. Combining methods to increase relaxation and challenge negative thoughts enabled this client to master her panic.

Touch can be used in very subtle, non-invasive ways, as illustrated in the above intervention. Touch can also be used in more focused, direct ways. Some clinicians keep a bodywork table in their office so they can quickly access it when they deem touch will benefit their client.

Touch Based Tools for Exposure Treatment Extinction of Anxiety Symptoms

Tapping: After exposure to a triggering event, one can tap their upper chest and the outsides of their shoulders, arms, and legs

Treatment Objectives:
- Distraction from adverse sensations of stress/anxiety reaction
- Supports mastery and confidence in the ability to reduce stress and return to rest after experiencing a triggering event
- Repeated sensations of tapping provide soothing, regular distraction, pulling focus off the stress sensations which often monopolize attention during an anxiety reaction

Why This Tool? After a practice of facing the fear reaction associated with a trigger, tapping can help prevent a person from being pulled back into residual sensations of anxiety

Touch Based Tools for Exposure Treatment Extinction of Anxiety Symptoms

Self-Contact During Breath: A significant portion of the parasympathetic nervous system (PSNS) involves feedback from the body. Putting hands on stomach and upper chest allows one to evoke the relaxation response and sense the movement of breath

Treatment Objectives:
- Distraction from adverse sensations of stress/anxiety reaction
- Supports mastery and confidence in one's ability to reduce stress and return to rest after experiencing a triggering event
- Repeated sensations of tapping provide soothing distraction, pulling focus off stress sensations which often monopolize attention during an anxiety reaction

Why This Tool? This skill supports awareness of sensations of breathing and safety. It can increase activation of the brain's frontal lobes and reduce stress response

Touch Based Tools for Exposure Treatment Extinction of Anxiety Symptoms

Self-Contact During Breath: A significant portion of the PSNS involves feedback from the body. Putting hands on stomach and upper chest allows one to evoke relaxation response and sense the movement of breath

Treatment Objectives:
- Distraction from adverse sensations of stress/anxiety reaction
- Supports mastery and confidence in the ability to reduce stress and return to rest after experiencing a triggering event
- Repeated sensations of tapping provide soothing, rhythmic distraction, pulling focus off stress sensations which often monopolize attention during an anxiety reaction

Why This Tool? This skill supports awareness of sensations of breathing and safety. It can increase activation of the brain's frontal lobes and reduce stress response

Touch Based Tools for Exposure Treatment Extinction of Anxiety Symptoms

Deep Pressure Through Holding Joints: Clinician or other individual can provide pressure through feet or hands into joints by providing resistance as individual pushes with moderate pressure using their hands or feet against clinician's hands

Treatment Objectives:
- Increases proprioception into joints (increases relaxation response)
- Deep pressure may have increased efficacy over light pressure for reducing stress response, and increasing relaxation

Why This Tool? This skill activates deep proprioceptive receptors which increase relaxation response

Touch Based Tools for Exposure Treatment Extinction of Anxiety Symptoms

Containing Contact: Provided either by clinician or by self-touch. Contact is applied on outsides of shoulders with steady, moderate pressure

Treatment Objectives:

- Provide increased relaxation response to support stress reduction during a session of practicing exposure to a triggering cue
- Increased frontal lobe activation augments ability to regulate stress reaction and ability for the body to shift from stress to rest

Why This Tool? This skill supports individuals to reduce triggers, increase mastery when facing triggering situations and increase the extinction rate of stress reactions to external events

Mindfulness-Based Touch Interventions

Jon Kabat-Zinn, Ph.D., founding Executive Director of the Center for Mindfulness in Medicine, Health Care, and Society at the University of Massachusetts Medical School (UMMS), is very present as he talks directly to a person (in an audience of more than four-hundred people) who just asked him a question. He speaks clearly, with a focused, deliberate, and engaging manner. Unlike many question and answer sessions between a famous speaker and an audience member, there is direct communication going back and forth between the two people who are speaking. Jon Kabat-Zinn, who is also the founding director of UMMS's renowned Stress Reduction Clinic, and Professor of Medicine emeritus at UMMS, seems quiet and steady—well-grounded. There is an almost tangible hush as he speaks. While CBT works to change the way people think, feel and act, mindfulness techniques, though working toward the same outcome, have a fundamentally different starting point. Mindfulness techniques start with observing what is happening right here, right now, and *accepting* it without judgment. The assumption is that the more aware people are of what is going on around them, the more beneficial change will naturally occur. For some, the change may be simply accepting difficult feelings; for others, it may be a profound change in lifestyle. He is quick to point out that *everyone* has to work at this, even trained medical professionals. Along with many others, Jon Kabat-Zinn has spearheaded a radical shift in how psychotherapy is practiced, and how the tools of mindfulness are used in treatment.

Jon Kabat-Zinn has influenced many individual's lives with books he has written. He has also worked diligently to develop a body of peer-reviewed studies of his work. It is because of this that mindfulness based stress reduction (MBSR) is practiced in many of the best medical settings around the world. Classes are offered for medical providers and their patients alike. Studies have addressed its efficacy in the treatment of depression, anxiety, and living with cancer and chronic pain. A hallmark of mindfulness techniques is that there is an inherent compassion and appreciation for human experience woven into them. The title of another form of mindfulness-based therapy states this very clearly: ACT—acceptance and commitment therapy. The first step of this therapy is accepting one's reality; then one determines one's values and develops commitments geared toward living within them.

Mindfulness, while it seems like an intellectual act, is really a process of directly experiencing life *as it is.* It is connecting with a reality too often obscured by judgments, fears and false beliefs, which we will call "habits of mind." The tools of mindfulness support people to recognize these things for what they are: creations—habits of their own mind. Mindfulness points out that *the past does not exist* (except in our imaginations) *and the future is a fantasy.* Learning to *live in contact with one's body and in the actual moment* helps one begin seeing through the intense feelings conjured by memories of the past, and fantasies about the future. Touch is one of the fundamental ways that people connect with their world. (Remember, touch is the first and foremost sense neonates and infants use!) Many mindfulness techniques include touch. In a "walking mindfulness," individuals breathe in rhythm with their walking, while paying exquisite attention to the contact of each foot with the ground. As a person practices walking mindfulness, all of their habits of mind come up. The individual can then return again and again to their feet contacting the ground. Over time, this process of returning to the present allows the individual to see the habits of mind for what they are, thus seeing that they themselves are not the habits. This allows the individual to begin ceasing or changing destructive behaviors and beliefs, thus entering into a new relationship with self. Once painful emotions soften, the individual's reaction to them becomes less intense. People can learn to watch anxiety come and go. Through this process, they build confidence in their own ability to tolerate and bear witness to a much wider range of emotional experiences.

Touch can aid a mindfulness-based practice in many ways. Understanding the impact of touch on the brain, mind, and experience of self, can help clinicians and individuals develop tools to engage more fully with their experiences, reduce the intensity of their emotions, and tolerate their emotional life with increased equanimity.

Self-Touch and Mindfulness

He sat in session—depressed—his body heavy, the intensity of his despair palpable in the room. In a soothing tone, the therapist asked his client to breathe into his stomach and make a pause at the top of his breath, but his client continued breathing shallowly and with no pause. The depression was so severe, his ability to observe himself was simply not present, and he had difficulty following instructions. The therapist then asked if he could place his hands on the outsides of the client's shoulders. The client agreed. As soon as there was contact, the client unconsciously took a breath that was naturally deeper than before. The clinician then asked his client if he was aware of the change that had just manifested in his breathing. The client answered, "Yes, I can breathe a bit easier. But I still feel like crap!" The therapist stayed present and replied, "Yes, sometimes we all feel like that. Feelings do change—let's pay attention to the change." The therapist's touch and confidence seemed to help his client feel steadier and he took another deep breath. The therapist continued giving his client more supporting information, saying, "When we are depressed our body feels heavy and our breathing can become very shallow—we breathe more from our chest. When we are relaxed we tend to breathe more from our stomach." As that statement settled in the client began to breathe more naturally into his stomach, and as his stomach rose and fell, the client's skin tone changed from pasty white to a rosier hue. The clinician then asked his client to put his own hands on his stomach and the top of his chest (pressing into his chest with his own hand) and ignore the feeling of depression, instead putting his attention completely on the rising and falling of his hand on his stomach. As they sat together in the present, the depressed feeling shifted. Then the clinician and the client were able to develop a plan to work with both accepting the feelings of depression, and learning skills to shift the feeling more quickly.

In this intervention, the clinician combines two techniques that increase mindful awareness: understanding of the problem (psycho-education), and touch interventions to support a shift. The deep pressure on the chest works by triggering a relaxation response through accessing proprioception receptors that send information to specific brain areas about where the body is in relation to space. This is the type of pressure used in massage and is associated with evoking a relaxation response. In the brain, touch increases activation in the orbital medial prefrontal cortex (OMPFC), an area associated with emotion regulation. While brain research is still in its infancy and assumptions about the impact of any brain structure on behavior should be taken with a grain of salt, one might assume that this type of touch supports, or scaffolds, the client's emotion regulation circuits to come back online. Another function of the OMPFC is self-awareness. In people who have practiced meditation for long periods, the OMPFC is thicker than in those who have not. This self-awareness is one of the healing factors in mindfulness techniques. Similarly, the contact of the hand on the stomach brings awareness to the breath by providing increased sensory feedback. This makes it easier for the client to continue to breathe deeply into their stomach and helps them become aware of their own ability to effect a change in their anxiety levels.

Listed below are tools for touch in a mindfulness-based approach:

Mindfulness Touch Based Tools

Hand Over Heart: Put one's hand over one's heart. Bring attention to the feeling in the heart. Alternate attention between the feeling of the heart and the feeling of the breath (noticing all the differences between them)

Treatment Objectives:
- Increase mindful awareness of positive sensations/emotions and breath
- Increase ability to shift attention
- Reduce stress
- Regulation of heart rate variability

Why This Tool? This skill supports individuals to shift from a negative to a positive affect, and can increase self-compassion. It bolsters capacity to trust one's ability to shift from states of overwhelm to compassion

Mindfulness Touch Based Tools

Hands Over Eyes: Ask client to let eyes rest into their head as though they are reclining on two soft pillows. After a few moments, have client put the base of their palms over their eyes. Have client bring their attention to the supportive contact

Treatment Objectives:
- Increase relaxation response
- Increase mindful awareness of resting

Why This Tool? This skill supports individuals to shift from negative to positive affect and can increase self-compassion. It allows an individual to develop confidence in their own ability to shift from a state of overwhelm to a state of rest/relaxation

Mindfulness Touch Based Tools

Alternating Attention: Put hands on outside of legs. Bring attention to hands. Press legs into hands. Alternate attention between the sensations of pressing and sensations of difficult emotions in the body

Treatment Objectives:
- Build the ability to have dual awareness of body and difficult emotions
- Attention often gets stuck on negative sensations. Builds the ability to shift attention

Why This Tool? This skill supports the felt experience of containment and draws attention to the periphery of the body. This supports an individual to access the present and shift attention away from internal patterns of thoughts and emotions unrelated to current context

Homework and Mindful Touch

Touch—contact with the world, can be a powerful tool for increasing mindful awareness. A client can learn to pay attention to the coldness of the water they drink, the feeling of a frying pan in their hand, the contact of their clothes against their skin. All individuals have feelings that are intense—at times more intense than they are able to tolerate. Intense emotions have powerful urges to act associated with them, but distraction is a powerful tool. The practice of mindful touch can help clinicians and clients alike come back into connection with the here and now. When one practices mindfulness, one learns to witness emotions without acting upon them; physical contact with the ground, the computer keys, or one's own breath, can create small breaks in the ongoing intensity of a feeling. This not only gives an individual relief, it also allows one to develop an experience of mastery over an intense emotional experience. Mastery in emotion regulation has two major aspects— acceptance and empowerment: acceptance is the ability to tolerate, understand, and accept an experience just as it is. As the old twelve-step adage says, "What we resist persists." The very act of acceptance shifts the relationship between an individual and their experience, reducing the stress brought about by fear of the experience. Fear or hatred of our experience adds to the already difficult sensations and amplifies them.

The second major aspect of mastery of emotion regulation—empowerment, is being able to affect that experience by increasing or decreasing the experience. We can gain the ability to shift our inner states. This helps us choose skills and tools to help us feel as good as possible in spite of difficult circumstances, and grow trust in our ability to naturally move through inner states—from deeply uncomfortable—to states of mind and heart that are much easier to enjoy.

Touch homework can also increase the quantity and quality of touch we receive from and give to others. A couple whose relationship has lost the spark of connection can rekindle it by increasing the quality of their touch and contact. This improves their sexual intimacy, and the quality of their relationship overall. Studies of rate and quality of touch in couples indicate that touch has a profound impact on relationship health. Touch is a primary way of displaying affection, and it increases trust of and empathy for others. Increasing rates of positive touch is healing for a difficult and tense relationship.

Homework interventions for mindful touch are listed below.

Mindfulness Homework Tools

Contact with Ground: Walk (outside is best). As you walk, put your entire attention on the sensations of the contact of your feet with the ground, clothes on your body, and air on your face. Find a connection between the rhythm of your steps and your breath

Treatment Objectives:
- Increase relaxation
- Reduce stress
- Increase ability to tolerate difficult emotional responses

Why This Tool? This skill pulls awareness to contact with the here and now. It allows an individual to develop confidence in their own ability to be present in difficult sensations. Movement provides constant new information to the senses that pulls attention back to here and now. It can strengthen and grow attention capacity

Mindfulness Homework Tools

Contact with Partner: With a significant other or friend, sit back-to-back, pressing into the back of your friend or partner. Notice sensations

Alternative: With significant other, one partner requests a type of contact and where on their body they want contact. Partner follows direction and shift.

Treatment Objectives:
• Awareness of impact of touch on stress and health
• Reduce stress response
• Increase awareness of safety and contact with others

Why This Tool? Brings attention into the here and now. Develops contact with another being, providing physiological and psychological support. Reduces stress response

Mindfulness Homework Tools

Imagining Contact: Let your imagination begin creating a picture of yourself being cradled by someone who loves you (if no one comes to mind visualize an animal or a historical figure, or use an icon, e. g., spiritual figure of love like Mother Teresa, Virgin Mary, Christ, Mohammad, the Buddha, and so on). Make the image real through imagining sensations

Treatment Objectives:
• Increase self-regulation of emotions
• Increase ability to accept and receive love
• Increase self-compassion

Why This Tool? Creates a new experience of self and grounds this experience in sensory processes that help deepen the impact of the experience. Some data indicate that grounding imagination—practice in sensation experiences, has a stronger impact on changing brain structures than does practice without sensations or imagining of real felt-experience of the event. This skill practices self-acceptance and safety in relationships

Mindful Clinical Touch

The client sits on the couch and reports feeling deeply depressed; the miasma of grief in the room is palpable. This client and therapist have used touch interventions before. The client asks if they can "do some table work" in this session. The clinician sets up the table and the client reclines on it, covered by a blanket and with a soft pillow under their head. The therapist asks the client where they need contact saying, "Where would it feel most supportive today for contact?" The client replies, "The outsides of my shoulders." Getting into position behind the client and providing light, steady contact on the outsides of the shoulders, the therapist asks, "How does this contact feel? Is it in the right place? How is the pressure?" The client requests that the contact to be slightly lighter and a little further down, near the biceps. As the clinician touches this area, the client takes a deeper breath. The clinician asks if this is a better position, or if another adjustment is needed. The client replies, "Yes it is better, but could your right hand be a little lower, closer to the table?" The clinician moves the hand. The client takes another breath, tears well up, and the client is able to cry. The clinician bears witness to the tears, murmuring encouragement and supporting their client to tolerate the experience. As the tears subside, breathing becomes more even, and client and therapist begin discussing a recent loss.

In this interaction, the client understands touch, and has practiced touch work in the past. Throughout this negotiation, mindful attention is given to the client's experience; the client learns to read and trust his or her own reactions, and to ask for the support that is right for them. This powerful ability can translate to a greater acceptance of one's emotional experiences, and more effective communication in relationship. Along with these factors, the support the therapist gives with touch helps the client tolerate the difficult emotion. The contact increases neurochemicals related to safety (oxytocin and serotonin) and decreases the intensity of the stress response. The client is the director of what type of contact they receive. The client's guidance regarding the quality of touch they receive brings about a feeling of safety, and a respect for their body. Pressure on the outside of the arms can often feel containing and safe—this may be what enabled the client to allow the sadness to come forward, thus shifting from feeling shut down and stuck, to a very sad, but also vibrant emotional experience. This is one example of using mindful touch in a clinical setting.

Healing Attachment Wounds through Touch Interventions

Attachment is something that hides in plain sight. It is a set of patterns of emotions, beliefs, and experiences developed over a lifetime about what it is like to be in relationship with others, and how we are in relationship with ourselves. There is no language when an infant is born, but a wordless connection of heart begins developing between parents and their children. As a father pays attention to the subtle expressions on his child's face and attends to his child's needs, the child begins to experience self, others, and the world. In a secure attachment style, the message communicated about self, other, and world is one of predictability, appreciation and safety. Attachment researchers and theorists are quick to point out that this learning is not purely intellectual. Rather, it is a combination of emotional experiences, intellectual knowledge, and sense memories.

A secure attachment style gives a feeling of safety with others, and a basic sense of being comfortable in one's own skin. On the other side of the attachment spectrum are children with what is called reactive attachment disorder. These children have difficulty feeling empathy for others and have often spent their first years in highly neglectful environments. From their earliest awareness, their bodily needs were not met. They might lie for hours, cold and isolated in a soiled diaper, while loneliness stretches into an endless horizon of blank walls. One shudders, imagining what touch children receive in such environments; at best, it may be intermittent and unpredictable.

The attachment theories point out that an understanding of one's mind and feelings develops in relationships. As parents attune to their child's experience, anticipate their child's needs, and give words to the wash of confusing sensations—words like sad or angry, a child's understandings about the mind of another ("My mom is upset because I did not follow directions.") begin manifesting. Without these experiences, a child does not learn to develop awareness of his or her own feelings, let alone awareness of another person's often-subtle cues about their own feelings.

In psychology, the term for the ability to make accurate guesses about another's mind is called theory of mind (ToM). Most creatures in the animal kingdom have a very limited ability to understand and predict the mind of another. Recently some evolutionary biologists have posited that the demands of living in a highly social community, which requires understanding the minds of others, is the factor that led to developing the complex brain we humans enjoy today.

As explored in previous chapters, touch is a deep and vital aspect of attachment. The first paternal tosses into the air and the first loving strokes of maternal contact are part of the ecology of a family, the environment in which a child develops attachment. The attachment between two parents, and between parents and child, sculpts not just the feelings and thoughts a child has about the world, others, and self, but also fundamentally sculpts their brain. Children with reactive attachment disorder demonstrate a profound physiological difference in their brains. Children who grew up in those bleak Romanian orphanages have brains up to thirty percent smaller than the brains of children growing up in a more normal environment. Children raised in abusive homes have profound alterations in brain areas relating to memory, reward, and stress. Some studies have found a "dose response curve" between the number of adverse childhood events and changes in brain development. In other words, the higher the "dose" of abuse a child receives, the greater the adverse changes in their brain structure.

British psychologist, psychiatrist, psychoanalyst, and founder of attachment theory, John Bowlby (1907 – 1990), described ideal conditions that lead to a secure attachment. He pointed out that if a child has vastly different life experiences, their development will begin to veer off course. Now, years after his initial predictions, the biological data appear to support his theory. In one lecture, Bowlby drew a dot right in the middle of a chalkboard. He then drew a two lines extending out from that dot in the shape of a "V." In his inimical way, Bowlby explained that the dot is the beginning of a child's life, and the two lines of the "V" represent typical development. Most children develop within that V, but significant adverse life events will push a child beyond the V. Bowlby went on to say that many ways exist to help a child whose development has been pushed off-course return to the normal developmental range. John Bowlby taught methods to help children move from disorganized, avoidant, and ambivalent styles of attachment, to a secure attachment style—even in adulthood.

Dr. Allan Schore is sometimes called the American Bowlby. He is a passionate speaker, as quick with dense, neuroanatomical terminology as he is perceptive about the profound and difficult feelings people face. Dr. Schore is animated as he describes what he calls "right-brain to right-brain communication." He argues that there is non-verbal, direct communication that occurs between individuals and he describes how two individuals' physiology will match up: as people are talking, not only does their body language match and synchronize, but their brains do as well. Dr. Schore believes this synchrony happens before people are conscious of it, and that people don't recognize it happening. The pupils of two individuals who are having a moment of emotional communication will begin to match. As one person's pupils expand the other person's open wide, as one person's shrink the other person's pupil-size contracts. Breathing rates can match each other or fall out of synchrony, depending on each individual's reaction to the conversation or the felt emotional content of the interaction. This, he argues, happens before the brain can even register it. Dr. Schore believes that this direct communication is the experience-dependent context supporting the development of healthy attachment, and that this direct communication and ability to enter into emotional synchrony is lost in unhealthy attachment styles.

One line of research that seems to support Dr. Schore's theory is that individuals who lack empathy for others also do not demonstrate any ability in their own physiology to mirror the emotional state of another. In other words, it may be the ability at a physiological level to "feel" the pain of another that enables us to have empathy for each other. A hallmark of children with reactive attachment disorder is a fundamental lack of innate empathy.

Dr. Schore describes what he calls experience-dependent environments that create the conditions for psychological change. In their work, therapists develop a relationship with their client and support interactions that lead to their client's development of a healthy attachment style. Schore calls these interactions "corrective experiences," and the conditions it takes to develop healthy attachment "experience dependent maturation processes." In his book "Affect Regulation and the Repair of the Self," Dr. Schore discusses how clinicians develop the clinical context for change. Within this context, the self, the brain, and biological systems begin changing as the client experiences direct examples of healthy emotion regulation in their relationship with the clinician.

While he does not discuss psychotherapeutic touch directly, Dr. Schore's work implies that human contact through wordless emotional interaction is vital for the development of emotion regulation. It is through human contact that emotion regulation first develops. A therapist who is able to demonstrate non-verbal emotional empathy while also providing safe, supportive touch, can nurture their clients to have profoundly different experiences of themselves and their relationship with others and the world.

Joan, a spunky, sharp, fifty-five year-old woman, visits a therapist—not a psychotherapist—but her body-based trauma therapist. Joan has had with difficulty forming good and safe relationships. She experiences even small disagreements as deeply painful; they leave her wanting to cut herself or destroy things. Her body-based trauma therapist has been working with her for three months. (Joan is also seeing a psychotherapist on alternating weeks.) When she arrives for this session, Joan reports feeling angry, but she cannot say why. Joan says she has not been sleeping and asks brusquely, "Can we just get to work?" The clinician supports her to lie (fully clothed) on the massage table, gets a pillow for her head and puts a blanket over her. When asked where she needs contact today Joan replies, "I don't know. I am too angry!" The clinician asks her to locate where in her body she feels the anger and Joan grudgingly reports feeling tightness and heat in her stomach-area.

The clinician asks Joan what would make her anger even a little bit more tolerable and she replies, "Scream and destroy things." The clinician asks her if she would rather destroy things with her hands or her feet, and Joan says emphatically, "FEET!" The clinician then places another pillow at her feet and Joan presses into it with her feet. As Joan does this, the clinician reminds her to go very slowly. Joan complies and within moments, Joan takes her first deep breath since she entered the room. The clinician notes the change, but doesn't comment yet. Joan pushes her feet against the pillow a few more times and as she does this, the skin-tone in her cheeks, once deeply flushed with red, becomes softer and rosy. Then Joan makes eye contact with her therapist for the first time. The therapist meets the gaze and says, "It is good to see you; it looks like things have shifted a little." "Yes." Joan says, "But now I feel terribly sad."

The therapist asks, "Where can I put my hands to support that sadness?" and Joan replies, "Under my back." The therapist maneuvers to find the correct hand placement and as she does, Joan's eyes fill and she bursts into sobs. The therapist increases the pressure of her hand for reassurance, saying, "Easy, easy, good, just let the feeling move, I am right here." Over the next few minutes, the tears become softer and the therapist continues reassuring, "I am right here." Joan's breathing becomes more even and she sits up. Sitting on the edge of the table, Joan talks with the clinician about how she has never felt that people were there for her when she was upset. Joan describes always feeling like she is alone; but today that feeling is gone—she is not alone. Working together with her body-based trauma therapist and her psychotherapist, Joan is building a new relationship with her emotions, and a new "relationship" with relationship.

Affect Regulation Theory: Building Emotion Regulation through Touch

"I should not be anxious. There is nothing to worry about; my life is good; but I still feel terrible." His body is rigid with tension as he perches on the edge of the couch. Intellectually, he knows he is okay, but inside, he feels what he describes as a dull terror. He has tried talking himself out of the feeling, but it has not worked. The therapist asks, "If I shouted at someone to relax, would it work? Would they relax?" The client laughs and says, "No." The clinician nods and says, "While we cannot just "think" that we need to relax, we can learn to trigger our relaxation system."

Our stress system can be stuck at "ON." When the stress response system is stuck, it is as if a heating system in a house stays on all the time, no matter the outside temperature. One goal of affect regulation therapy is resetting the thermostat, or if there was none to begin with, building one.

Top Down versus Bottom Up Processing

One powerful metaphor proposed in the last decade for understanding treatment methods is the concept of top down versus bottom up approaches. This model follows the insights of MacLean (and others) and attempts to help people understand which brain system might be most helpful in creating more ease, comfort, and success. Top down approaches, such as cognitive behavior therapy, work by attempting to change the way people think and then, with top down interventions, change the way they feel. Bottom up approaches work from the other direction. Bottom up processes can affect the brainstem structures that provide the deeper foundations on which emotions are built. The brainstem changes the state of stress and affects the bodily aspects of emotions. Without these deeper aspects of emotions, it would not be possible for the limbic structures to build complex experiences like love, longing, and tenderness. Other bottom up interventions affect the limbic structures. These interventions are aimed at connection to emotional life and relational drives for connection. Limbic structures do not follow the same linear pathway of logic and thought that the higher-order structures do, but they have a logic and insight of their own. Clinicians can learn the languages of these structures, thus connecting to transformative processes that support the meaning and thought-making systems of the cortex. In essence, bottom up processes change feelings by affecting limbic structures and the way the brainstem functions to change stress, arousal levels, and automatic functions such as breathing or sleeping. To make the relationship between limbic structures and brainstem structures more clear, imagine that the brainstem provides the electricity, and tunes the intensity of the emotional expression mobilized by the limbic system. If my brainstem process—fight or flight—is tuned high due to a previous argument, and then a friend offers a small criticism, I am more likely to react negatively than if my brainstem had not been "primed" for stress. Through changing the lower, or older, systems of the brain, a person can rewrite their story and create more realistic and helpful ideas about themselves, others, and the world.

Affect regulation theory is an integrated theory that combines top down and bottom up interventions. However, affect regulation theory typically considers that for many of the common challenges that people face, change begins from the bottom up.

Touch interventions are bottom up tools. In other words, they change the way we feel in order to change the way we think. The concept holds that if a person feels lousy—stressed or overwhelmed, they will select thoughts and behaviors that are appropriate for those feelings. It is as if the cognitive mind is a chest of tools, and it tries to choose a tool that fits the situation at hand. If a person feels overwhelmed, it selects thoughts that match that feeling. If a person is anxious, the cognitive, or top, layer of the triune brain chooses anxious thoughts. Therefore, if an individual learns to tolerate the sensations of anxiety, or gets a massage and feels better in their body, their mind chooses a different set of tools or thoughts. A good way to think of this is that if you are having one of "those" days—a day when you are grumpy and tired, you will respond to even small challenges in a different way than if you are feeling excited or confident that all is well. When we are excited, the mind brings up thoughts that match the way our body feels. The same thing happens when we are grumpy.

This theory, first proposed by William James (1842-1910), one of the founding American psychologists responsible for psychology taking root in the United States, and by Danish physiologist Carl Lange, is known in the field as the James-Lange theory of emotion. His proposal? First, *the body* has a physiological reaction to an event, and second, *the mind* interprets that reaction. For instance, if you see a tiger prowling in your direction, you probably perceive that as a threat, triggering a physiological reaction that bypasses your thinking mind; then you are running away slightly before you realize you are afraid. In other words, the fear and the impulse to take action (e.g., run), tell your thinking brain how to interpret the bodily sensation. Perhaps this seems counterintuitive, but if you engage your cerebral cortex to think about it, there is an elegant logic to the James-Lange theory of emotion: when our ancestors were living in the savannah, most threats (like seeing a tiger) required an immediate reaction. If a person stopped to think about which reaction to choose—well, they would very quickly become another animal's meal. This immediate "gut-level" response enables a person to reach safety (provided they are a fast runner!) before they initiate complex thinking, such as analyzing how they reached safety. In intense, high-stress situations, the physiological response includes a narrowing of the visual field, and in extreme cases, reduced activation in the frontal lobes (measured by blood flow to the front brain in a functional magnetic resonance imaging machine). The frontal lobes are the most complex aspect of the top part of the triune brain. Touch supports us to feel at rest by changing our sense of safety from the bottom up. Touch changes our feelings to change our cognitive processes.

Polyvagal Theory—Stress, Rest and Beyond

Dr. Stephen Porges, professor of psychiatry and director of the Brain-Body Center in the College of Medicine at the University of Illinois, Chicago, points out that one function of touch for children is creating a sense of safety and emotional connection. Dr. Porges says that because human infants have such a long period of dependence on their parents, they must have an ability to be at rest while in close physical contact. Touch is one factor that stimulates the social engagement system—the system that brings about feelings of safety, connection, and relaxation.

Dr. Porges' polyvagal theory (gr. 'polus', i.e., "many" + 'vagal', i.e., "vagus" nerve) proposes a biological basis for social behavior, and an intervention strategy for enhancing such behavior. His theory speci-fies two functionally distinct branches of the vagus nerve: the more primitive branch elicits immobilization behaviors (freezing, or feign-ing death); the more evolved branch relates to self-soothing behaviors and social communication. The primitive systems activate only if the more evolved systems fail. Dr. Porges posits that the neural regulation of the autonomic nervous system moves through three stages; each stage has an associated behavioral strategy. The first stage involves the parasympathetic nervous system (PSNS), which consists of nerves that connect internal organs to the 10th cranial nerve—the vagus nerve—and the sacral region of the spinal cord. The first stage responds to a threat by depressing metabolic activity, such as digestion. Behavior-ally, this first stage involves immobilization—"freeze" responses.

The freeze response happens when an animal is in life-threatening danger. It leads to a shutting down of consciousness and rigid body posture. While the freeze response is present in most, if not all, animals, some animals use this response more than other defenses. One well-known creature whose first response is to freeze is the opossum. (If the deer is a good "poster-child" for the flight response, managing danger not by fighting, but by running faster than predators; and the lion is a good will ambassador for the fight response, solving survival demands with fighting, then the opossum is a perfect poster-child for the freeze response.)

When a predator animal is ready to attack, there are behaviors that trigger it to follow through with the attack. Both running and fight-ing back indicate good health, which triggers many predators to con-tinue to bite and attack. But some predators will not eat dead animals unless they are extremely hungry, preferring meat they have killed themselves. If an animal is limp and does not respond to an attack, a predator will often leave the "dead" meat, giving the prey animal a chance to lick its wounds, escape, and live to fight another day. When under threat, an opossum (while at times quite fierce) uses the freeze response to make predators believe that it is dead.

Another animal known for its freeze state ("tonic immobility" in physiology literature) is the eastern hognose snake. This snake looks terrifying, but it has perfected the art of the bluff. When it is threatened, it bobs and weaves, feigning strikes. As it strikes, it appears to bite, but instead head-butts the animal with an intensity that stuns. However, if the animal is not deterred by the snake's assault and continues its attack, the snake's body will enter into the physiological state of freeze. It will become limp and flaccid, appearing dead. This could indicate to the attacking animal that the snake is unhealthy, and might make a meal it would live to regret eating. Adding to the effect, as the snake's body enters the freeze state it excretes a noxious smell (musk) that mimics the smell of a rotting animal. The combination of these factors can put the attacking animal off its appetite, prompting it to hunt for a safer meal. When the attacking animal leaves, the snake can rouse from the state (freeze is a time-limited response) and go on its way—none the worse for wear.

There is a large body of science about how the freeze response affects chickens and lizards. (Much of the data about chickens comes from research into the farming industry and livestock housing.) Dr. Porges points out that a number of situations trigger the freeze response, but one of the largest is a life-threatening event in which an animal believes it will die if it fights or flees.

In studies of freeze response in lizards from 1928, researcher Hudson Hoagland could easily invoke the freeze response, and measure the impact of freezing on their physiology. One interesting finding was that a lizard put into freeze and given a shot of adrenalin (triggering the fight-flight response), stayed in the freeze response indefinitely if the researcher kept injecting it with adrenalin. However, if the researcher stopped injecting adrenalin, the lizard would come out of the freeze state as its body metabolized the adrenalin. This finding has some strong implications for humans regarding how reducing the fight-flight response can allow the completion of the behavioral action sequence of the freeze response. Measuring the freeze state in humans is more challenging. It is a heightened state of self-protection and would thus be unethical to induce in an individual. Due to this, the literature on freeze, or tonic immobility, in humans is sparse—however, literature on rape survivors indicates the presence of this state as a defensive coping mechanism for surviving the attack.

Touch has a transformative effect on the fight-flight response—triggering what Dr. Porges would call the social engagement system.

To clarify with an example of the social engagement system: at birth, a baby doesn't have all of the complex brain structures that adults enjoy for reducing stress and regulating emotions. When an infant of six-months lies in its mother's arms, the physical contact and feeling of safety engage the infant's ventral vagal brake. This aspect of the nervous system triggers social engagement by applying a finely tuned brake to the fight-flight response. While the baby is cooing and making eye contact with its mother, their physical interactions help that brake effectively inhibit the fight-flight reaction. However, if a loud noise nearby causes the mother to startle, the baby reacts to this change by crying. According to Dr. Porges, this is when the ventral vagal brake (V.V.C.—known in medical literature as the ventral [forward], vagal [part of the vagus nerve/parasympathetic/rest system], complex [group of neurons]) releases, allowing the fight-flight system to engage. In other words, our rest system is consistently inhibiting our stress system. When the rest system is told to release, it allows the fight-flight system to activate, increasing levels of cortisol and affecting many body systems, including breathing, heart rate, digestion, and muscle tension. When the mother relaxes and soothes her baby, the baby's stress system slowly calms down and when it calms enough, the vagal brake engages again. This is when the baby reinitiates eye contact with its mother, takes slower, deeper breaths, and returns to rest, re-engaging the social engagement system.

The social engagement system is a system that—when activated—pushes us towards safety, social connection, and trust. Porges argues that we have a subconscious threat detection system that leads to activating the mind state best suited to the situation. As discussed in Chapter 4, he calls this subconscious threat detection system "neuroception." In other words, the lower structures of the brainstem set the stage for which higher-order emotional and cognitive state the person enters. The social engagement system is "engaged" or "on" when we are in a state of rest or ease. This has an intuitiveness to it. We all know how it feels when we are relaxed and safe with people we know well.

We find that talking and engaging is easy. Now if we are in a more stressful situation like a job interview, it is much easier to be awkward, and difficult to be fluid. I have personally developed a friendship with someone who interviewed me. Once I felt safe with them (after the interview), it was easy for me to engage. The powerful implication for us is that if we can trigger a socially engaged state, it can pull us out of stress—helping us be more effective in our relationships—and in job interviews!

However under more intense threat, as the vagal brake disengages, the fight-flight response rises until the freeze response kicks in, shutting down consciousness and leading to the same action sequence seen in opossums. Dr. Porges argues that this response is mediated by another older, unmyelinated part of the parasympathetic (rest) system originating in the dorsal motor nucleus (DMNX) of the brainstem. (It is called the dorsal motor nucleus because it is in the back—dorsal—of the brainstem and has motor effects—movement effects, and nucleus is a term for a cluster of neurons.) One finding appearing to support this theory is that in Parkinson's disease, which is characterized by postural freezing, abnormalities manifest in the DMNX of the brainstem about ten years before the first external symptoms become apparent.

To put this all together, according to polyvagal theory, along with the fight/flight system, we have not one, but two systems aimed at rest. The first system is newer and helps establish social engagement. It helps us remain at rest even around other animals and may be one reason that mammals (who share this system with us) tend to prefer living in packs or groups. Interestingly, current thinking is that our brains are as complex as they are due to the need to understand social interactions. It may be that learning how to determine whether we are safe with others, and deciding whom to trust in a social group, were the drivers for developing all the higher-order brain processes. The second, older rest system is the DMNX. This system does not create rest in the same manner, that is, by increased social engagement, but by shutting down consciousness, which leads to inhibited movement. This older system, present many species, creates the defensive state of freeze, or tonic immobility.

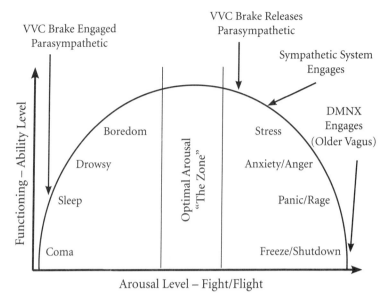

Figure 6.4 **Overview of Polyvagal Theory**

Interactive Neurobiology

When we smile at another person, it changes our own physiology, triggering warm feelings and changing our stress response. This is probably why meditative traditions encourage sitting with a half-smile on one's face, and many depictions of the Buddha meditating show a small, enigmatic smile on his face. However, the impact of our emotions does not stop there. When we smile at, or even just "hang around" other people, we change their physiology as well. Their brains begin to model our own moods, albeit they will have a smaller experience of the emotion we are experiencing. In the anterior cingulate cortex (the brain area we explored for its role in emotion regulation), we create a model of the moods of other people. We evoke a series of bodily sensations similar to those relating to the emotions that other people are feeling, which explains why seeing someone else cry can bring tears to our own eyes. This change appears to happen in a preconscious manner. Like the subtle matching in pupil dilation when people are in synchrony, the physiological aspects of emotions are also wordlessly communicated between people.

Touch and Psychodynamic Theory

Dr. Daniel N. Stern (1934-2012) was a psychodynamic theorist who worked on understanding the impact of early childhood experience on the brain and functioning of a child. He discussed how for an abused infant, the feelings of being wet, cold, and hungry, along with receiving aggressive touch from parents, all added-up to form a child's experience of themselves and others. Object relations theory holds that our experiences of all of our previous relationships (and in particular our first relationships) shape how we act in relationships throughout our lives. The "object" in this theory is the internal representation of the early parental figure. Dr. Stern described how an infant of nine-months would lie in its crib and replay images of the interactions it had with care providers. The infant is in an interaction with these internalized representations of its parents (a.k.a. objects). Dr. Stern pointed out that touch is a vital aspect of the early relationship, noting that an infant first experiences its world through physical contact.

While the importance of early touch to successful bonding is not in dispute, psychodynamic psychologists often are unable to allow even small amounts of touch into treatment. Understanding touch and using it safely and supportively, can lead to developing effective touch interventions within a psychodynamic model of treatment.

Psychodynamic theory is one of the oldest theories in psychology. While it has been through multiple formulations over the years, it dates back to Freud. Its name comes from the idea that there is a "dynamic" relationship between parts of the psyche. Psychodynamics is the study of "energy exchanges" between parts of the psyche. This concept also has a strong intuitive basis. Imagine for a moment that there is a part of reality we do not like (sadly, this is not difficult to imagine). Dealing with the fact that we don't like it by repressing the experience (an early defensive strategy) takes energy, or effort. In other words, we have to use our "psychic energy" to push the experience out of our thoughts. Thus, the thinking is that if we have an intense grief reaction and deny it, we will expend a lot of energy pushing it away, and eventually become drained and depressed. Later psychodynamic theories focus on the drive for connection and relationship as an impulse that can be inhibited, leading to the buildup of excess psychic energy. When there is an excess of certain psychic energies, symptoms come out as an expression of the system being out of balance.

In some forms of psychodynamic theory, the idea is that our early relationships form how we learn about our inner world and the inner world of others, and how we live with our emotional states. According to psychodynamic theory there is a balance between three factors (all of which form in early relationship)—initially mistranslated as the *Id* (actually in German the *"It"*—which represents our drives and impulses), the *ego* (in German it is closer to the *"I"*—which is our sense of self and mediates a balance between impulses and our ideas of right), and the *super-ego* (in German the *"over I"* which is the part of us that holds our ideas about socially appropriate behaviors). These three systems can get out of balance. The *ego* can, at times, gratify every impulse of the *Id* (sex, drugs, and rock and roll, are examples of impulses the *Id* likes). This leads to self-destructive behaviors and poor long-term functioning. Alternatively, the *super-ego* can be out of balance, leading to an inability to allow love, play, or joy into one's life. When Freud developed his theory, he envisioned the idea of health as being the ability to work, play, and love. In this theory, when we are out of balance between these systems, the "psychic energy" builds, leading to release of pressure on the system through symptoms that leak the energy out, but do not transform the deeper processes that initially caused the challenge. Health happens when a person can move through and integrate the processes that are causing the system to be out of balance. Typically, in psychodynamic theory, these disruptions in psychic energy come from disruptions in early relationships between a child and their parent.

Freud himself originally included touch in his work. However, more and more throughout his career, he began to pull back to a more distant relationship with his patients. When he was in his prime, Freud's style of clinical relationship was to sit behind the patient. This allowed what he called a blank slate, so that any expression his patient made related to the patient's own experience—not to their reaction to the therapist. We now know that this stance in and of itself can cause stress and most clinicians—even psychodynamic clinicians—work face-to-face.

Freud began making strong injunctions against touch. It may in fact be that psychology's resistance to recognizing the power of touch in early bonding and healing is due to Freud's personal clinical style. Freud's original theory of what drives people—the core psychic energy—is all about libido or sexuality. This may also have led him and others to avoid touch out of fear of the impact of such contact on the patient. No one can deny that sexuality is a part of human life; however, it is not the sole drive we humans have. The fact that touch is a vital part of early childhood development is unquestionable; as is the fact that touch can influence psychological functioning at a profound level. Hence, it is quite curious that the field of psychology continues to react with such disquiet to the concept that touch is a vital part of the healing process in therapy.

Reconnecting to Self

Bob has a tendency to be overly controlled. His movements are tight, precise and sharp. Everything in Bob's life is on time. When things are not clear and precise, he quickly becomes frustrated and over-whelmed. After many sessions with Bob, it becomes clear that his parents rarely held him. Most of the touch he received from his family was gruff—directed at getting him to comply with his parents' wishes. Over time, Bob became gruff with himself. His father, an emotionally distant engineer, and his mother, a researcher, expected a lot from him and did not tolerate his difficulties. One of Bob's earliest memories was falling from a high place after feeling powerful and strong for being able to make the climb. He lay on the ground, shocked, bruised, and with a skinned knee. His father yanked him up by the arm and told him to stop fooling around, and young Bob quickly stifled his tears. In relationship with his partner, he reported that he did not enjoy contact and very infrequently gave her hugs or affection. This was creating considerable tension in their relationship. Over the course of his sessions, Bob explored how he expected touch to be gruff and coercive and did not connect touch with love and affection.

Bob's therapist prescribed a touch intervention for the couple: on several occasions before their next session, Bob's wife would give him a shoulder massage, and then Bob would give her a shoulder massage. When Bob returned to treatment the next week he reported that he had felt anger when his wife gave him the massage. Bob also reported feeling shame and despair. This result of the touch intervention prompted the clinician to explore how Bob connected touch and support with being weak and never having his needs met. As the therapist pointed this out, he asked if Bob would allow him to support him through contact on his shoulders. Bob looked angry at first, but nonetheless agreed. The clinician allowed Bob to find the right type of touch for him and they explored the feelings of anger and fear that came up. Bob feared closeness, believing it meant that he was in danger. As time passed, Bob started experiencing the therapist's contact on his shoulders as kind, rather than coercive; it was at this point that Bob began softly crying. The clinician maintained supportive contact and reassurance as Bob sobbed. This intervention gave Bob another experience of touch in relationship. The homework of reciprocal massage continued and Bob and his wife were able to have more comfort and enjoyment from touch in their relationship.

Humanistic Psychology and Touch Applications

She was ninety years old and experiencing symptoms of dementia. She was terrified of losing her mind. The psychologist sat with the elder woman and her family, and asked the daughter to hold her mother's hand as they talked. The psychologist then asked that the daughter express words she felt were true and authentic for her mom. The daughter, all the while holding her mother's hand, told her mother that she loved her, that she was scared, but that she was not leaving, and that even if the situation was difficult, they would get through it together. Her mother sobbed, and her breathing relaxed. The mother then said to her daughter, "This is scary and difficult but you know honey, we've been through a lot of crap in life and we will get through this too." The mother then expressed her fear about what it meant to have dementia, and her fear of being alone, of not having a life. The daughter was able to express that her mother was still deeply valuable, and no matter what her diagnosis, she was still loved. The clinician supported the family to explore ways to live well with dementia, and to just sit with and accept the grief that would inevitably occur.

When we touch one another, we validate each other's existence and focus the relationship on our connection in the here and now. Process-oriented psychotherapy uses touch to express emotions. It is not uncommon for a clinician to stand face-to-face with their client and ask the client to push into the therapist's hand to express the intensity of an emotional experience. Touch is a fundamental aspect of human connection, so it is hardly surprising that many humanistic therapists have incorporated touch interventions into treatment.

The Impact of Cultural Differences on Touch Interventions

We are all part of a culture. Our culture gives us our perspective, our worldview, and our beliefs about how life in general is supposed to be. Culture also impacts how often people are touched, when touch is appropriate, and how people communicate through physical contact. *All therapy happens across lines of differences.* Even when it seems that someone is just like us, differences in age, economic status, and education, all influence how we relate with each other; this has a profound impact on all therapeutic interactions—touch included.

Therapists need four skills to work effectively across cultural lines of differences. First, therapists need a basic respect for differences. Therapists must recognize and internalize that differences do not make people good or bad, but if misunderstood, they can lead to damage and disconnection.

Second is learning about the other individual's culture. It is vital that a client is not placed into a role of representing their culture in its entirety. In order to do this effectively, it is important to discern what culture a client grew up in. Some individuals identify very strongly with their cultural history, while others have adopted most of the norms of their new culture; it is important for a therapist to be open to these possibilities.

The third important skill for working across cultural differences is having a clear understanding of your own beliefs, values, and cultural norms. An individual who grew up in England may expect much less touch than would an individual who grew up in France. Our expectations can lead to assumptions about how we will be received by our client. Another difficulty in working across cultural differences is navigating a new course if we find that our impact has not matched our intent. Full understanding of our own beliefs, including our beliefs about touch and touch interventions, give us clues about how we "expect" others to behave.

The fourth factor in cross-cultural work with touch is recognizing how much cultural and gender differences impact power dynamics in the relationship. If this is not recognized, it can lead to clients feeling silenced—unable to speak up and express their needs. Different cultures have different beliefs about the roles of health professionals and how to speak with them. An understanding and appreciation of this can help both clients and therapists navigate these differences, thus avoiding the pitfalls of miscommunication and unspoken needs.

Ethics and Touch Interventions

Hippocrates, the father of western medicine, recognized that at one dosage a medication can heal, while at another it can kill. Touch is no different. Human contact is one way that we can be at our best, our most heroic, our kindest, our most loving and inspiring. The firefighter risking his or her own life to pull a child from a burning building, or the father holding his family after a tragedy, are powerful images of the positive impact of touch. It makes sense that human touch can just as easily be damaging and violating.

Psychotherapeutic touch can be a powerful and vital aspect of treatment—when it is used ethically. It also carries the risk of damaging clients if performed in an unethical manner.

There are five important aspects about ethical use of psychotherapeutic touch. People need to know the risks and impacts of any treatment they receive: informed consent is a crucial part of all therapy, and is an absolute for ethical therapeutic relationships. Touch work needs discussion before its implementation—preferably at the start of treatment, rather than at the beginning of any one session. The training a clinician has in touch work and their limits in current training should also be discussed. Therapists need to provide information about the use of touch on the informed consent forms that their clients sign at the beginning of treatment.

The second aspect is that if a therapist plans to use psychotherapeutic touch, with its far-reaching and profound impact on a clinical relationship, they must have training and supervision as they learn to implement touch in their practice.

The third and very important aspect of psychotherapeutic touch is developing healthy clinical boundaries. Clinicians must provide safe touch. In order to do this they need to learn how to connect with their clients, develop the clinical skill to listen with that connection, and recognize when the impact of their intervention does not match their intent.

Psychotherapeutic touch is always aimed at a treatment goal: a psychotherapist using touch needs to understand why they are using the intervention, and how they expect it to improve the life of the client they are supporting. A hand on the shoulder has very different meanings in different contexts. Touch is not a tool to use when a therapist feels they have run out of other techniques. Touch is a powerful part of healing, and must link directly to a treatment goal. If a client is in the throes of a panic attack, the simple intervention of putting your foot over their foot and providing steady pressure can be a powerful adjunct to other interventions. It changes the stress response and helps the individual experiencing panic make a shift. Using the same touch intervention on an angry client could have profoundly different results.

Finally, psychotherapy never includes sexual contact. Psychotherapeutic touch is focused and supportive, but completely non-sexual. Clinicians must be able to provide healthy, non-sexual contact that is safe and supportive. By following these principles, psychotherapeutic touch can be administered in an ethical and safe way, leading to profound healing and healthy relationships.

Touch can be both supportive and threatening. The difference between a safe, supportive touch and a threatening touch often lies in how touch is discussed with a client before its use, and whether a client feels safe discussing how touch work is affecting them. If a client has power and autonomy to tell a clinician what they need, to negotiate how and when touch interventions are used, and feels empowered to tell a clinician when they do not like a certain type or timing of touch, then the psychotherapeutic touch has more probability of having a positive impact on treatment. It is important for anyone who gives or receives touch as a part of treatment to know that *human boundaries are always changing.* What is good and supportive in one moment is not supportive in another. A client receiving touch interventions needs ample support to express and recognize these changes. Therapists can help their clients recognize their own signals of safety, thus augmenting the development of healthy boundaries. Through this process, people who receive psychotherapeutic touch *can learn to negotiate safe touch in other relationships* in their lives, and recognize healthy touch when in contact with friends and loved ones.

Touch Treatment—Integrating Touch into Treatment and Treatment Teams

Touch is a fundamental part of the ecology of human life. From our birth to the last breath we draw, touch and human contact are essential. Touch also can have a powerful role in changing and treating psychological symptoms. Understanding key impacts of touch, and how to develop touch interventions for a treatment team, will lead to treatments that are more effective, and address issues that psychology has often ignored.

Touch in Health—Treatment Team

Many individuals with health and mental health challenges have less touch and physical support than they need. Increasing safe touch in friendships and romantic relationships is an important treatment goal. The physiological impact of loneliness is measurable! In hospital or skilled-nursing settings, touch often becomes purely mechanical. Patients report feeling as if they are merely an object. Often people report that their doctors do not seem to care about them, and push their bodies around. Doctors and nursing providers do care, but most are not trained in providing supportive and emotionally connected touch to their patients. Working with a treatment team, health providers and families can support an individual to feel safe, whole, and respected.

Touch-Based Treatment Goals

Psychotherapeutic touch affects multiple aspects of human psychology. From a biopsychosocial perspective, one can see profound biological, psychological and social impacts of psychotherapeutic touch. Due to the field of psychology's ignorance or avoidance of touch as a key aspect of treatment since the Victorian era, many touch interventions have yet to be developed. Nonetheless, psychotherapeutic touch produces a positive effect on stress levels, helps in emotion regulation and supports the development of healthy boundaries.

Chapter 7

Different Minds:
Mental Health Challenges and Touch

They knew that Katelyn was different. She was as smart as other children, and her verbal communication skills were comparable to those of her peers, but she did not like being touched. Tags on clothing were unbearable to her. Her mother said Katelyn did not like to look her in the eyes, and when she tried to hold her, Katelyn would attempt to squirm away within seconds. Like many children with high-functioning autism, Katelyn has differences in how she processes her sensory world. For some, it can be as if a sensory channel has its volume turned up painfully loud. For others with high-functioning autism (formerly called Asperger's Disorder), a sensation that would make most people shrink away feels like nothing out of the ordinary. Katelyn is hypersensitive to touch—not deep touch—but light touch. It took some time for her parents to recognize this. However, when her mother held her tightly, squeezing her in a way that would feel terrible to most children, Katelyn calmed down immediately; her body relaxed and she was able to sit still. But if her mother wanted her to sit on her lap and read a book, or give her a light caress, Katelyn would startle as if she had just been sharply pinched.

Not all children and adults with autism spectrum disorder contend with touch sensitivities. Many people on the autism spectrum have differences processing signals from their other senses, or differences in how they integrate their senses. The autism spectrum ranges from a mild state (high-functioning) to far more profound levels of challenge. Katelyn is a child with normal to above-normal intelligence, and she will do well in life. Nevertheless, Katelyn has a different mind. It is not a bad mind. It is a different mind, filled with unique and powerful gifts and perspectives on life. In the autism-rights movement that has developed over the last twenty years, the terms for mind differences are "non-neurotypical" and "neurotypical" minds. Non-neurotypical minds process touch (and/or other senses) differently. Understanding these differences—understanding how touch impacts brain/body physiology and psychology, will help us determine how to incorporate touch-based interventions into care for people with mental health challenges. While it no longer makes sense to differentiate mental health from physical health, these are distinctions that the medical field still uses to understand processes. All psychological challenges also have biological impacts, and all biological illnesses also impact psychological and social functioning. The brain is an organ of the body—even things like the amount and type of bacteria in the gut change our mood and sense of self. Eventually a language will develop that does not keep recreating this split, but until then we must keep reminding ourselves that the language is inaccurate—that the split between mind and body does not exist.

Psychosis

Researchers showed videos of adolescents to people trained in mental health diagnoses. Some adolescents in the videos would develop profoundly different minds. They would develop symptoms of psychosis later in life. Researchers found that the adolescents' style of movement could predict who would develop psychosis; differences in facial movements and upper body movements were the best predictors. A study on brain development (Penn State, 2014) found that early differences in the trajectory of neurocognitive development can be detected. The study authors indicate that with early interventions such as targeted neurocognitive skills development, the developing non-neurotypical brain might develop in a more neurotypical manner. These new early detection skills may be vital in understanding and supporting people with psychosis to lead their best lives.

Psychosis is a difference in mental functioning that is difficult to live with. For some, it can bring about ongoing auditory hallucinations—voices that are difficult to discern from reality. Others suffer deep paranoia about perceived dangers in their world. Psychosis symptoms are grouped into two classes: the first is "positive" symptoms, and includes hallucinations and paranoia; the second is classified as "negative" symptoms; these include difficulty with social relationships and challenges with certain types of memory. While medications and treatments can help reduce positive symptoms like hallucinations, they generally have little impact on negative symptoms. The research is clear; better social skills and cognitive function give an individual with psychosis a better chance of living a life with connection, meaning and purpose. It may be that touch and human contact are factors that will help people with symptoms of psychosis enhance their social skills and connect to a meaningful life.

Children who develop psychoses exhibit differences in movement and socialization. Some recent research has found that children at risk for developing psychoses have differences in the neurocognitive skill called theory of mind (ToM). We all make ongoing guesses about what is happening in the mind of another person. This ability to make guesses about another's inner experience and change our behavior to match a situation is vital for having friends, and success in school, work, and life-partnerships. Children and adults with psychoses experience great challenges with utilizing theory of mind. Interestingly, the ability to make accurate guesses about another person's mental state is one of the best predictors for enabling someone with psychosis to have more quality of life. Several studies have examined whether giving oxytocin to an individual with psychosis helps increase their ToM ability. Preliminary data is unequivocally positive, although more research is needed. Touch is a powerful method of stimulating expression of oxytocin. No studies to date have examined increasing safe touch through referrals for massage or the development of healthy, safe touch interventions; however one can posit such research would show that touch interventions significantly increase both oxytocin levels and theory of mind for individuals suffering symptoms of psychosis.

For most individuals with different minds, life is challenging. Psychosis is one of the most stigmatized mental health conditions at both individual and societal levels. While the situation has improved since the age when Britain allowed people—for a fee—to enter asylums and poke the residents with sticks; bigotry against people with mental health conditions is still alive and well. Social isolation of individuals with psychosis is not one-sided. Those who enjoy neurotypical minds, including employers, often lack a basic awareness of how to form relationship with someone who has a different mind. However, this awareness can be developed—a worthy goal—because people with psychoses who are receiving appropriate treatment have a lot to offer as intelligent and capable employees.

Adjustment between a person and society is always a two-way street. Often however, people with psychoses are expected to make the entire adjustment. While adjusting to societal-norms is a vital part of the equation, society and its institutions also can make adjustments for people with differences in mental and emotional functioning. We need to work together against the tyranny of a narrow-minded and under-informed majority. Not all minds are the same. In truth, *no* minds are the same, and different is not bad.

The stigma and isolation that people diagnosed with psychosis often experience in relationships and work adversely affects their mental health, making the symptoms worse. For most people (with or without psychosis) being socially isolated and feeling judged increases stress and hence cortisol levels—and cortisol makes symptoms of psychosis worse. People with psychosis exhibit changes in brain structures associated with emotion regulation—the amygdalae and the pre-frontal cortex; they also show elevated levels of cortisol and dopamine, and reduced oxytocin levels. Elevated cortisol levels often make people with psychosis hypersensitive to social cues implying rejection—a miniscule expression of anger across a face may be perceived as an intense expression of rage. Individuals with psychosis often feel intense anxiety—another condition that can be reduced or alleviated by touch. A vast body of research indicates that elevated stress response and cortisol secretion can trigger hallucinations and delusional thinking. Since safe and supportive touch reduces cortisol secretion, it is likely that regular supportive touch can improve development of theory of mind, thus heightening the probability of lessening social isolation; this happy circumstance could reduce rates of relapse, or non-compliance with medications.

Early theories (now defunct) of causes of psychosis posited that "refrigerator parents"—parents unresponsive to their children's needs, were the culprits. Such parents tend to put their children into double-bind situations: a child receives conflicting messages, so failure is inevitable. Poor parenting does not cause psychosis, but reducing expression of emotion within a family can help reduce symptoms. Intense expression of emotion can lead to increased cortisol expression, which escalates the risk of individuals developing more intense symptoms. Small, safe, supportive touches help a person feel safe, and are thus a good therapy goal for families that include individuals with psychosis.

Mood Disorders and Touch

Joe has not left his bed for more than a week. Since the dissolution of his marriage three months ago, he is increasingly isolated. He has stopped calling friends or going out, and more than a week ago Joe called in sick and stopped reporting to work. On top of feeling deeply sad about the loss of his marriage and what that will mean for himself and his family, Joe has also quite literally "lost touch." Since separating from his family, he is not receiving touch often, if at all. Like many Americans, Joe does not receive much touch at work or often exchange hugs with his friends, and while he loves his children, they are not living with him. The occasional kiss-in-passing from his wife, times when she would put her hand on his shoulder and say something about dinner or what was happening the next day, hugs from his children in the morning; these little touches improved the functioning of Joe's mind; they reduced the stress of his work-day, they increased his body's secretion of oxytocin and helped Joe feel loved and happy.

Joe has severe reactive depression, a depression that can occur after a difficult life event. His work is suffering, and he feels that his life has become small and useless. Without the right support, Joe could lose his job and his home—perhaps even his family.

Depression affects nearly one-billion people worldwide. Touch is one of the most understudied and misunderstood factors influencing depression. Touch work such as massage is proven to reduce symptoms of depression, as well as changing some of the neurochemicals involved by reducing cortisol, and increasing dopamine (a neurochemical that increases motivation and pleasure) and serotonin (a neurochemical targeted by many antidepressant medications).

After a divorce, men often have more difficulty adjusting to their new reality and suffer more health problems than divorced women do. This result may be in part because the stereotypical male role in American culture leads to a profound lack of physical contact after a divorce. Reduced physical contact leads to increased stress and health problems. While not yet confirmed by data, it is probable that lack of touch after divorce plays a role in men's difficulty with adjusting; however, such research is not yet occurring, due to the tendency among most psychological scientists to ignore or discount the importance of touch.

Along with other interventions for Joe, touch interventions such as making regular dates to play with his children, increasing physical contact—perhaps via a company softball team or some other team sport, or spending time with a pet, would help Joe shift out of his depression.

Depression has multiple aspects: biological (changes in neurochemical levels, and patterns of sleeping and eating), social (isolation), and psychological (negative thoughts and feelings). Effective treatments for depression include interventions aimed at all three aspects. Moreover, touch interventions can be directed at all three aspects. Medications and exercise will change neurochemistry. Increasing healthy social contact could include touch interventions such as sports, massage and bodywork. Touch helps people tolerate feelings; it even reduces the intensity of difficult feelings. Touch can alter people's thoughts about others, themselves, and their future. Our current methods of treatment are effective for eighty percent of depressed individuals; however it is possible, even probable, that adding touch-based treatments would provide a lifeline for the remaining twenty percent—or *two-million* persons!

Bipolar Disorder

Individuals with bipolar disorder can have distinct difficulties with touch. Frequently, when people are depressed, their bodies ache. One study found that individuals with depression have more muscle trigger-points (knots) than do non-depressed individuals. In the grip of depression, a person can feel isolated, even unworthy, with painful emotions and sometimes even excruciating physical sensations. During these periods, it would be helpful for individuals to develop supportive touch interactions, perhaps visiting a massage therapist, walking with a close friend, or spending good physical time with an animal. When people are depressed even simple actions like getting dressed can take a tremendous amount of effort and will. Individuals suffering under depression often need loving coaching to be able to take the steps needed to heal. However, feelings of connection with people or animals will help individuals who have depression feel less isolated, and help them experience more positive emotions.

When a bipolar individual is in a manic state, they can feel invincible. In this state an individual may spend money they don't have, or invite everyone in the local phone book over to their place for a party, oblivious to the certainty that they are making choices they will later regret. An individual in a manic state may override indications that the touch they are experiencing is not healthy; they may have sexual encounters they would not even countenance were they in a different mind-state. Learning to read one's signals, and recognize when one is in the "danger-zone" for these types of missteps is very helpful for individuals with manic symptoms. Learning to monitor their own social rhythms can help an individual with bipolar disorder be more effective, and experience fewer and less severe manic episodes. Monitoring how often they eat and how much they sleep provides bipolar individuals with clues about their state of mind. Touch-based interventions, possibly in combination with medication, can help an

individual in a manic episode shift to a more restful state, thus allowing more sleep, which can lead to less cycling between mania and
depression.

Many individuals (and animals), when kept awake long into the
night, experience changes in their dopamine systems. Most teenagers
have experienced this at one time or another. A term that is often used
for this state is "slap-happy" or "punch-drunk." People laugh about
nothing and stay up very late, just talking. It can even become difficult
to fall asleep. As one teen I worked with at a summer camp said (while
camping under the stars with other teens), "But I am too tired to sleep."
Social rhythms therapy proposes that during the onset of the manic
state, a similar change in dopamine levels occurs, and that if people
can learn to help themselves get good food, good rest, good exercise,
and healthy relationships, they can reduce the rate of cycling through
manic and depressive episodes. Along with training in recognizing
indicators of changes in mood states, building healthy touch interventions would aid individuals with bipolar disorder in this process.

Co-regulation Tools for Bipolar Disorder

Partner Massage for Rest: Set up boundaries such that touch is focused
towards relaxation and reset. Massage feet, hands or back with lotion. Pay
attention to any small hints of relaxation

Treatment Objectives:
• Increase positive healthy touch
• Increase quantity and quality of sleep when falling asleep is difficult or
  awakening during the night is a recurring problem
• Increase relaxation response

Why This Tool? This skill helps create rest and aids an individual in
shifting from overwhelm states to more regulated states. Challenges
with sleep and self-regulation processes increase risk of both manic and
depressive episodes. Improving ability to attain sleep and manage sleep
effectively improves quality of life and long-term functioning

Co-regulation Tools for Bipolar Disorder

Quiet Together: Find a shared activity that is not activating or stressful, e.g., movie, television or reading. Make physical contact while doing the activity

Treatment Objectives:
• Reduce stress response
• Increase safe social bonding and healthy boundaries with touch
• Reduce feelings of aloneness or isolation

Why This Tool? This skill can create the habit of rest and improve the ability to shift away from stress states

Co-regulation Tools for Bipolar Disorder

Soothing Contact: Set up a type of contact with a friend that helps after an overwhelming event, e.g., hugging, hand holding, sitting closely together. When an overwhelming event occurs ask partner or friend to use the skill. For this to be effective both parties must be safe to say "no" and be respected.

Treatment Objectives:
• Increase self-regulation by pairing overwhelm with safe contact
• Increase ability to use safe emotional and social support
• Increase healthy touch
• Increase bonding and health in relationship

Why This Tool? This skill can increase the relaxation response. Stress and overwhelm are each major risk factors for both mania and depression. Supportive contact from a close friend or a loved one can reduce stress-load, reducing risk of experiencing depressive or manic episodes

Self-Touch Tools for Bipolar Disorder

Self-Massage: Rub shoulders with hands or massage tool, find "knots" in muscles in body and work them out, rub sore body parts, use a nice lotion to rub one's feet or hands

Treatment Objectives:
- Increase ease falling asleep as part of a social rhythms protocol
- Increase emotion regulation, distress tolerance and impulse control
- Increase bonding and health in relationship

Why This Tool? This skill can increase self-care, the relaxation response and the ability to shift difficult affective states

Self-Touch Tools for Bipolar Disorder

Containing Self-Touch: Put one's own hands on the top of head, or outsides of shoulders or legs. Squeeze shoulders like self-hug, press into outsides of legs or press lightly into top of head.

Treatment Objectives:
- Reduce feelings of overwhelm
- Increase emotion regulation, distress tolerance and impulse control
- Use ten minutes prior to bed to facilitate ease of sleeping

Why This Tool? This skill can create the ability to shift difficult emotional states

Self-Touch Tools for Bipolar Disorder

Body Tapping: Tap the body from head to toe with the tips of one's fingers. Tap lightly over eyes and face. Make sure to tap feet and back

Treatment Objectives:
- Reduce stress response
- Pulls attention to periphery away from uncomfortable sensations and breaks cycle of under-regulated affect
- Increased proprioceptive awareness of body leading to increased felt-experience of being "grounded"

Why This Tool? This skill draws attention away from internal processes and shifts the focus from sensations of overwhelming emotions to "here and now" processes

Anxiety Disorders and Touch

Fear and anxiety are emotions that help us avoid danger. However, in modern society we do not encounter the same dangers that concerned our ancestors. Very few of us encounter "lions, tigers, and bears" on a regular basis. The current stressors we face are different in that they are frequently more prolonged. If we encounter a bear, we can get away quickly (at least, we hope we can!). If we have a difficult boss or an overwhelming project at work, that stress can last for months. Our stress system did not evolve to manage long-term stress. Our ancestors experienced stress within a different cultural context. Throughout our early evolution, we mostly lived in groups of about twenty people and generally did not form groups of more than one-hundred persons; because of this, we knew all the other people living amongst us. For most cultures in these smaller group contexts, there was more contact and connection as people worked together toward a community goal. This physical contact created a buffer against our stress-systems running wild, and it helped develop a strong community. The community itself played a role in each individual's resilience in the face of stress.

Our stress-system is supposed to fire-up rapidly and then shut down quickly. Lack of community support, touch, and other social factors, make it more likely for people experiencing anxiety and worry to have difficulty shutting their stress system down.

The feelings people have when they are anxious are intense. They are also internal. A cut, bruise, or broken bone can be shown to other people, thus garnering sympathy and support. When an individual is feeling intense anxiety it is not always apparent to others, except perhaps by a worried expression, or a clenched jaw; it is theirs to suffer alone. This can make people feel disconnected from their friends and family. Individuals who feel highly anxious can sometimes also be highly irritable, increasing the likelihood of anxiety becoming a deeply isolating experience. All emotions give us motivation to act. Fear or anxiety provides motivation to "get away," which is a prudent thing to do if we are facing a bear. However, this appropriate and natural response is counterproductive to enjoying a good life in today's society. Extreme anxiety causes people to avoid stressful situations that they can conquer, such as taking tests, public speaking, or trying new activities. For some, even activities like being with friends or going to work can trigger intense feelings of fear or anxiety, making it challenging for them to enjoy very much in their lives.

Extreme anxiety has myriad symptoms that decrease quality of life. These include panic attacks (intense feelings of panic and physical symptoms of anxiety), post-traumatic stress disorder, obsessive-compulsive disorder, or generalized anxiety disorder (excessive worry), to name a few. Each of these challenges can be mitigated with touch-based interventions, thus reducing suffering on a daily basis. Anxiety and stress systems are profoundly affected by touch and human contact, yet professionals who treat anxiety rarely use touch-based interventions. Touch-based tools to help therapists reduce stress and anxiety have not been adequately developed, because the medical field has too often ignored touch as a powerful intervention for healing and creating psychological health.

Eating Disorders and Touch

Joann hated her body. When she looked in the mirror, Joann saw herself as "fat." If asked, she would even say she thought that she was "disgustingly overweight." Joann believed her body was completely undesirable, and that she could fix it if she just worked hard enough. By the time Joann entered treatment, she was nearing death. Her overwhelming need to "fix" her body by controlling her caloric intake and subjecting her body to constant excessive exercise had left her emaciated, and vital physiological functions, including her menstrual cycle, were shutting down. She also had severe tooth decay. Even as Joann entered the treatment program, she did not truly believe she was underweight. She saw herself as fat, bloated, and disgusting.

A false self-image is common for individuals with eating disorders. Nearly eight-million Americans have eating disorders, including more than one-million men. Symptoms include overeating to the point where movement becomes difficult; severely restricting caloric intake; binging and purging (overeating and then ingesting laxatives or inducing vomiting to purge the food from the body); and exercising until the body shuts down.

Dr. Tiffany Field studied the effects of massage on people with eating disorders. She offered a group of nineteen women diagnosed with anorexia either standard treatment alone, or standard treatment and twice-weekly massages for five weeks. Individuals with eating disorders often have high levels of anxiety and elevated stress hormones, and massage has a well-documented effect on neurochemicals. Dr. Field found that massage reduced cortisol levels, and increased dopamine and norepinephrine levels in individuals with anorexia. In addition and perhaps even more significantly, the group receiving massage had significantly lower body-dissatisfaction then the control (no massage) group.

One challenge that individuals with eating disorders face is profound body dissatisfaction. Women with anorexia or other eating disorders often report a history of touch-deprivation. Mice (females more so than males) that experience touch-deprivation tend to exhibit abnormal feeding habits. People (and mice) need to be touched—it is part of the primary environment for human development. Lack of enough appropriate touch can have a powerful impact on body image. Touch-deprived children have a difficult time building a positive body image. Studies from the University of Michigan Medical School support the relationship between touch-deprivation and poor body image. One study surveyed a group of shoppers about their touch history, body image, and tendency to develop eating disorders. Individuals who reported touch-deprivation in childhood had a negative attitude towards their bodies and an increased drive towards thinness and perfectionism. Another study from the Michigan Medical School indicates that woman treated for eating disorders reported more touch-deprivation in childhood, compared with a random sample of women with no history of eating disorders.

Eating disorders are among the most damaging and deadly of all mental health conditions, because complete abstinence from food causes death, whereas abstinence from alcohol, or tobacco, or other addictive substances, does not. The impact of touch-based therapy on body image highlights the importance of clinicians being able to refer clients to well-trained bodywork therapists. Psychotherapists have ignored the powerful impacts of touch on mental health for too long. The role of the body-based psychotherapist will be very important in developing touch-based treatments. A psychologist who understands the psychological and biological roots of eating disorders will be in a powerful position to develop effective interventions.

Touch and Pain Disorders

Pain is in between worlds. It is not just the reaction of body tissue to an injury, or the creation of psychological reactions to sensation: it is both. At home, when we turn on the television, the television turns on—this illustrates how most of us think about pain. A common view of pain is that we have nerves connecting, for instance, our hand to our brain. If these nerves send a signal, we are in pain. If they send no signal, we are not. However, the real process is far more complex. The human brain is not simply a collection of wires installed once, and unchanging forever after. It is vital to remember that our brain is not like a computer in an extremely important way: the structure of the brain is changed by human experience, but no matter how many times you open a file on your computer; it is still the same computer chip. This is really important when understanding how pain works!

The human brain can rewire the pain reaction. Imagine turning on a television and simultaneously the smoke detector begins to blare. You hasten to turn off that alarm and as you do, all the lights start switching off and on. The brain rewires itself constantly. In complex regional pain syndrome even light sensations, such as the brush of a feather against the skin, can feel like fire burning the flesh, due in part to a rewiring of the brain causing a misreading of signals. Current pain treatments include antidepressants, psychotherapy, physical therapy, medication-management, and training in biofeedback. Pain treatments are still evolving—many people suffering chronic pain have to search extensively to find them—but there are effective treatments. The best treatments combine multiple techniques in programs tailored to each individual.

Some receptors of sensory neurons—nociceptors—are designed to carry pain signals to the brain. Other neurons carry sensations like pleasant touch, muscle tension, temperature, vibration, and pressure. In the 1860s, researcher Wilhelm Heinrich Erb proposed that pain could be generated by any neuron if the sensation was intense enough. While this is certainly the case, it is not the whole story when we discuss pain. Think about listening to your favorite music at a comfortable volume in your home. If you increase the volume, you may feel discomfort as the music approaches concert-level volume. If you were attending a live concert, you might not experience discomfort at this volume because you are mentally prepared for that; nonetheless, if the music gets loud enough (another effective form of torture!), it will begin causing physical pain. Both of these routes for signaling pain to the brain—intense sensation from any sensory nerve or nociception from a pain-carrying nerve can be modulated by brain state, stress, and other biopsychosocial factors.

Many brain systems can modify pain reactions. One relay station involved in the flow of pain to the brain is the dorsal horn of the spinal cord. This area functions like a gate, regulating the reception of pain. The same area in the brain also closes the gate while we sleep, so we do not physically act out our dreams. When we are in rapid-eye-movement (REM) sleep, our brainstem tells the dorsal horn of the spinal cord to shut down, stopping sensory information from our body from reaching our brain, and conversely, preventing signals for action from the brain, from reaching our body. There are parasomnias (sleep disorders) wherein disruption of this process causes people to act out their dreams. In animal studies, inhibiting this area of the brain from functioning will, under most circumstances, cause sleeping animals to act out their dreams. I have seen amusing videos of cats with this challenge stalking their dream prey in real time.

Stress and the resulting increased cortisol levels make the "pain gate" harder to close, so pain signals reach the brain more easily. Hence, one can posit that touch-deprived people are more vulnerable to chronic pain. Other factors that make it harder for the pain gate to close and thus may amplify pain include: lack of sleep, poor diet, negative thoughts, unprocessed emotions, lack of exercise, and lack of good social support. Focused effectively, touch-interventions help reduce the impact of stress and make the pain gate easier to close. For some individuals, increased positive touch would be a powerful treatment to address pain disorders.

The dorsal horn (pain gate) of the spinal cord is one structure that modulates pain; the insular cortex is another structure, deeper in the brain, that can increase or decrease pain signals. The insular cortex is involved in distinguishing physical pain from emotional sensations, and important survival emotions such as disgust, or craving. Craving is an intense desire for a substance, an action, or a need to be met. It is different from hunger because hunger can be satisfied by food, whereas in general, cravings can only be satisfied in very specific ways.

The cingulate gyrus is another area disrupted by pain disorders. This area is involved in emotion regulation and anxiety, and is implicated in depression, which may be one reason that some antidepressant medications help reduce physical pain. Neurochemicals activated by antidepressants also assist in signaling the body to stop or reduce pain, thus these medications act as another mechanism for pain-reduction.

Individuals with burns on large areas of their body suffer excruciating pain. Regular debriding (washing) of burn wounds feels like being burned all over again and changing bandages is torturous. The exposed nerve endings make the pain almost unbearable. People report that their skin itches, but they cannot scratch it, and even tiny movements bring about intense pain. Anything that can reduce the intensity of pain that burn victims experience during these procedures would be a welcome reprieve. Touch interventions can reduce, albeit not stop, pain. Dr. Field measured the impact of regular massage on people healing from burns. In one of her studies, individuals received ten thirty-minute massages over the course of five weeks (of course, none of the massage was performed too near to burned areas). A comparison group received relaxation training over the same period. The burn victims receiving regular massage reported less itching and anxiety, improvement in depression symptoms, and a significant reduction of pain. These are reasons to believe that touch-based treatments can be developed and implemented to reduce the terrible impact of chronic or extreme pain on people's lives.

Not all touch has the same effect. Deep pressure has a different impact on the nervous system than light pressure. Safe touch has a different effect than touch that feels invasive. As it develops, research needs to become more nuanced in how it organizes treatment programs. In an article by Dr. Field in the *International Journal of Neuroscience,* she reviews research indicating that light pressure is not as effective as deep, steady touch for improving growth and development in infants, and stress reduction in adults. It may be that deep touch stimulates proprioceptive neurons in a way that triggers novel (new) learning, while light pressure does not, because it is too similar to other forms of contact a person experiences. Many studies on touch do not use highly-trained clinicians, nor do they focus on the depth of pressure; rather they lump all touch from light, or unskilled, to deep-tissue massage into one group; this dilutes the veracity of such studies' findings.

It is more and more apparent that a body-based biopsychosocial perspective is vital for successful treatment of pain. Since therapeutic touch is able to affect biological, social, and psychological factors in a person's life, it is an ideal intervention for pain management. Astute clinicians and psychologists could develop highly effective touch-based treatment programs. Psychologists have already developed effective cognitive-behavioral programs to help reduce pain, and these programs are incorporated into most of the best pain-management programs around the world. However, if the beneficial impacts of therapeutic touch on pain remain unaddressed, many people will continue suffering from extreme or chronic pain unnecessarily.

Substance Abuse Disorders and Touch

Substance abuse rips apart communities and families. Early childhood adversity makes substance abuse more likely. According to the Adverse Childhood Experience (ACE) study at Kaiser Permanente, a person who experienced more than four types of childhood adversity had close to a five-hundred percent greater likelihood of taking up smoking, and a forty-six-hundred percent greater chance of using intravenous drugs! Such profoundly disturbing results indicate a great need for our society to provide easy access to education and support for parents and prospective parents. After all, we are required to pass two separate tests before we are licensed to operate a motorized vehicle; this protects us and society from potentially disastrous mistakes. Consider how similar requirements for parenting could support and protect current generations of children—and all generations to come— enriching our society immeasurably in the present and forever after.

While there is not enough good research on using touch and massage as part of addiction treatment, there are good indications that these are powerful treatment tools. One recent finding in addiction research shows that just before a person uses their substance of choice, they experience intense craving and increased activation of the insular cortex (reads body signals and relates to feelings of satiation) and the amygdalae (related primarily to defensive actions like fight-flight reaction). This craving is not "regulated" or brought back to rest, hence the person often resumes drug-seeking behavior. This finding may show a link between trauma and addiction. The elevated stress levels a person with trauma and early childhood adversity experiences may, in essence, flood the individual's capacity to regulate this emotion. To analogize, for a person without adverse childhood experiences, craving is like a garden hose of water-pressure that can be stopped with a thumb or by bending the hose, but for someone who has experienced too much childhood adversity, the craving is like a fire hose of water-pressure—practically impossible to stop.

Touch can reduce emotional spikes in other disorders (e.g., anxiety, depression, and post-traumatic stress disorder). Weekly massage reduces cortisol and can activate areas of the brain, such as the orbital medial prefrontal cortex (OMPFC), that help regulate difficult emotions. If their OMPFC is inactive, it is more probable that a person will act impulsively. According to most research, when the OMPFC activates, a person is able to reason without too much interference from their emotions, thus reaching decisions that are more objective. How wonderful that a simple hand on the shoulder can call the OMPFC into action.

There are indications that touch-based interventions tailored to individuals with addiction issues could be powerful aids in helping them move toward a life of wholeness. Current addiction treatments work, but not very well. For any given attempt at quitting an addiction, only about one third of people will succeed, on the next attempt another third, and so on. If people keep trying, they will eventually succeed; but current treatments require multiple failures and far too much suffering before most individuals achieve success. Remember the results from anorexia research demonstrating how touch-based therapies increase positive body image, thus supporting people's willingness to implement good self-care? Improving body image and self-esteem via touch would complement and augment current addiction therapies.

Self-Touch for Addiction Treatment

Mindful Contact: Find an activity you enjoy and do it, putting your full (100%) attention on the way your body is moving and your contact with the ground or objects. If negative sensations distract you, pull your attention back to the sensations generated by the activity

Treatment Objectives:
- Short-term survival strategy to tolerate a craving
- Regular practice reduces overall stress levels in life
- Increase body awareness

Why This Tool? Sensations of craving or urges to use (substances) happen just before a relapse. Touch can reduce stress reaction and help draw the emotional regulation centers of the brain online. Reduction of stress response can reduce the risk of giving into cravings

Self-Touch for Addiction Treatment

Tapping: Tap the entire body from head to foot lightly with the tips of fingers
Slapping: Lightly slap the outside of the body from head to foot

Treatment Objectives:
- Short-term survival strategy to tolerate a craving
- Increase overall body awareness which allows an individual to have negative sensations associated with craving without reacting
- Increase attention if mind is foggy and experiencing trouble waking up

Why This Tool? Tapping lightly with finger-tips can distract the mind from the sensations of cravings. It can increase body awareness and increase the ability to tolerate difficult sensations

Self-Touch for Addiction Treatment

Holding a Weighted Exercise Ball: Hold a weighted exercise ball on your lap as you work or when experiencing a difficult emotion or craving

Treatment Objectives:
- Reduce length of craving
- Reduce stress response

Why This Tool? Weight increases input to c-fibers and can reduce stress

Family Mental Health and Touch

Life had become too busy. She felt like she was always cleaning up messes the kids had left, and she was always tired. He felt like it had been years since they'd had a good time together. He worked until he came home. Then it was time to make dinner, get the kids to bed, work some more, and pass out for the night, only to wake up and do it all again. Sitting next to each other on the therapist's couch, their bodies were tense. They faced the therapist, and throughout the first session, there was no physical contact between them.

People touch each other when they feel affection and safety. For this couple, the conflicts and the business aspects of their relationship had taken over. They were tired, and even somewhat burnt-out. Although affection prompts touch, touch also increases affection, which can be the glue that connects people to one another. It helps a couple tolerate the frustrations of living closely with each other. Affection can turn one's perception of the other person's habit from "downright annoying" into a "moderately endearing quirk." And as anyone who has lived for any length of time with another person knows—all people have quirks.

This was not a toxic couple. However, the myriad demands and stress of daily living made it difficult for them to keep the habits of affection and connection going, which was undermining the health of their relationship. The lack of affection had adversely impacted their sexual intimacy, and their enjoyment of time spent together, as well as their connection with their children. Family is full of conflicts.

Small affections and connections encourage us to find reasons to work through conflict and strengthen our relationship, rather than undermine it. This couple attended a weekend-workshop to learn couples' massage. The workshop taught the couple new ways of touching and connecting, and increased the sense of closeness between them.

Dr. John Gottman has conducted extensive studies of relationship health. He brings couples into his lab. He hooks up cameras and asks them to discuss a conflict in their relationship. The couple is recorded for fifteen minutes, capturing all of their gestures, facial expressions, and exchanges. Dr. Gottman painstakingly reviews the video. Using a coding system for facial emotion—the system developed by Dr. Paul Ekman at UC Berkeley—Dr. Gottman can predict with better than ninety-five percent accuracy the likelihood that a couple will stay together. One of the best predictors of relationship health is the ratio of negative to positive emotions.

Research on touch in couples is clear: small, safe, connected touch makes a relationship healthier. It increases the sense of connection, safety, and synchrony—the non-verbal, physiological dance of human interaction. I can remember watching a brilliant storyteller captivate an entire crowd. People in the crowd would touch their cheeks, gasp and even laugh as if they were one body! If two or more people are feeling understood, connected, and safe, their bodies naturally begin to mirror each other. When we feel stressed or lack a sense of safety, we cannot enter into synchrony. People are often out of synchrony when they are in conflict with one another. Of course, a healthy relationship does not mean things are always rosy. Transitioning through conflict to resolution and back into connection is a vital skill that every relationship should develop and practice.

How a family or a couple tolerates conflict and finds resolution largely defines how the family will function. There are other important domains of family functioning, such as how a family tolerates distance and closeness in relationship, healthy boundaries, and problem solving: being able to work through conflict successfully is vital for all of these aspects. Safe, supportive touch has a powerful impact on the resolution of conflict. Although it is best not to touch some individuals when they are angry, safe touch can increase the likelihood that people will use constructive strategies in conflict resolution. We know that safe touch increases the positive emotions in a relationship, which makes it easier for people to be willing to resolve conflict when it arises.

Families are not just parents and children, but a wider web of connections. Jody is four years old. She sits next to her mother on the couch and wants the book read to her for the umpteenth time. The book contains no surprises for Jody or her mother—they can recite it by heart. As Jody sits next to her mom, she feels loved and connected. Jody's mother feels the same (with occasional bouts of boredom due to reading the same book repeatedly). The touch between Jody and her mother is wiring Jody's brain for learning, safety, and connection. The contact is bathing her young brain in oxytocin and reducing her stress. The excitement Jody feels about mastering the words leads to small dopamine spikes in her brain that increase connection between neurons. The oxytocin generated by the contact between them increases their sense of closeness, connection and safety, and sets the foundation for resolving inevitable conflicts.

It will not be long before Jody is up and about, and her mother will need to help her stay safe (and convince her to tidy her room). These moments of connection are what help Jody know that even when she makes a mistake and her mother becomes angry with her, she will always be loved. Children who know that their relationship will survive even when they make mistakes are better able to solve problems, take appropriate risks, and tolerate difficult feedback. Children who do not know this often make one of two very unhealthy choices; they externalize problems, blaming their mistakes on everyone and everything else, or they internalize problems, filled with so much shame that they cannot make good choices.

Even our nearest cousins, non-human primates like chimpanzees, monkeys, and gorillas, reconcile conflict with safe, supportive touch. One can watch two rival chimps extend their hands towards one another in a gesture of peacemaking. This is relationship repair. We do not repair relationships that we do not value. Receiving the message that there is no repair after conflict can evoke intense feelings of being unsafe—even feelings that one's very existence is threatened! In a family, touch plays an important role in conflict resolution. After resolution of a conflict between father and son, the father commonly pats his son's shoulder, or gives him a brief hug. This contact helps the son know their relationship survived the difficulty, and he may work harder to avoid making the same mistake in the future.

Going through stressful times and transitions, such as adding a new member to the family, or moving to a different area, can lead to the cessation of many positive habits within a family. When stressed, people may stop the supportive touches, nurturing comments, playfulness, and other activities that they formerly enjoyed as a family. Our stress system often works by prompting us toward more practical actions. While this may be good in the short-term, not making the shift from stress programs back to safety programs can lead to erosion of the family relationship. Our stress system is designed to function in the short-term to help us avoid a threat or face a challenge. If it fires too often for too long, it can lead us to abandon many healthy and effective behaviors. For individuals, this can lead to isolation and depression; for families, it can lead to increased conflict and lack of resolution. To an individual or a family in stress, the idea of increased play, safe touch, and relaxation time can seem frivolous, perhaps even dangerous. However, if a family does not work to maintain the habits that built their sense of safety and connection, the family unit will be threatened by increased internal conflict.

In chimpanzee communities, the leader, a powerful alpha male, regularly grooms his troops. The grooming bolsters the relationship so that when they need to defend their community or leader against a threat, they are more likely to be willing to do so. The safe, supportive touch they experience when being groomed increases their loyalty. This is not surprising. Oxytocin, a hormone stimulated by touch, is associated with building strong pair bonds and increasing the strength of friendships.

Humans, like other primates, are innately social. A recent theory proposes that the human brain is so much larger than other species because it developed to solve complex social problems. When we cooperate, we can produce marvels like the Eiffel Tower or the iPhone, but we also can be a great danger to each other. Our ancestors needed to discern whether a member of their group or family unit was safe or dangerous, and if they deemed a member dangerous, what solution they could implement. While humans are primed for social connection with their families, they are also primed to defend themselves against threat from their closest confidants. Two aspects of the social-emotional system that help us determine if we are safe or in danger are the emotional synchrony we have with other people, and safe, connected touch. A child's social and emotional system is developed by interaction with family members, peers, and adults in their life. This system involves key structures in the brain that govern the ability to read emotions, regulate feelings, understand the minds of others, and interact in a socially acceptable manner. For example, emotional intelligence has a profoundly positive impact on how successful an individual is in their work environment. If a family is struggling such that conflicts are not reaching resolution, learning skills that facilitate more constructive conflict is vital. Just as vital is establishing times to connect with each other, play together, and remember the value of the relationship. Touch plays a crucial role in the family system. Clinicians helping families successfully transition through challenging periods can increase the beneficial effect of their work by helping families increase safe, supportive, and connected touch.

There are myriad forms of touch within relationship. Some are casual, like taps on shoulder, small hugs, or a brush of contact in passing. Some touches are more intentional, like wrestling play, hugs in the morning before school, or romantic contact between parents. Some touch is mechanical—aimed at providing care. A clinician can do an evaluation of family touch to determine whether touch within the family is largely mechanical, or whether there are healthy amounts of casual and intentional touch.

Touch can feel threatening to the giver—not just the recipient. When daughters enter their teen years, fathers often stop hugging them because they fear the contact will be misperceived. Children who have experienced aggressive touch may feel anxious and afraid of any touch, leading to more acting-out and aggression when they receive nurturing touch. A father with a history of abuse in his childhood may not be abusive to his children, but he probably was not exposed to a good model of how to offer safe and caring touch to his children. Touch is woven into the fabric of a family. Clinicians who ignore or are unaware of its impact on family functioning cannot fully assess problems; hence they will not be able to offer the most effective tools for helping a family heal.

Touch-Based Tools for Families

Loving Daily Contact: Teach family members to provide daily supportive contact through hugs, playful gestures, pats on the back, caresses and other forms of brief contact. Teaching safe supportive touch can have a powerful impact on family health. This requires healthy boundaries, i.e., the ability to respect a "no" from any person

Treatment Objectives:
- Increase family resilience
- Increase positive emotions within family
- Support healthy connection between parents and provide a buffer for inevitable conflicts

Why This Tool? Increased hugs and contact can increase family health and resiliency

Touch-Based Tools for Families

Playful Contact: Supportive play via wrestling, tug of war, patty cake or other play

Treatment Objectives:
- Increase play, reduce conflict
- Increase family resilience

Why This Tool? Human relationships thrive when there are more positive than negative experiences in the relationship. Often, simply increasing play and enjoyment in a couple or family will reduce conflict

Touch Interventions for Children with Non-Neurotypical Minds

There are ways for people with vastly different brains to learn from one another and live a good life. Temple Grandin, Ph.D. stood on the stage of the TED conference (Technology, Education, and Design) and stated that people with different minds offer unique value to this world. Temple was diagnosed with autism when she was a young girl. Her parents encouraged her to find ways to thrive. Temple, with her unique mind, did just that; among many other notable accomplishments, she has transformed the cattle industry with her humane innovations. When we have many individuals around us with minds similar to ours, we learn how to understand our own mind through talking with others, watching others, and having others help us make sense of our experience. Temple Grandin often plays this role for people with autism. She talks about her inner experience, and methods she's devised to cope with autism. Autism and Asperger's support groups can be invaluable to anyone trying to live well with a different mind. People in such support groups feel understood, perhaps for the first time.

In a number of her presentations, Dr. Temple Grandin has stated that it would be good for children with autism to find ways to enjoy being held, because the feeling of being loved and cared for is worth that effort. However, Temple never advocates forcing any child. One famous Temple Grandin story concerns the squeeze-machine she invented when she was eighteen years old. Visiting a relative who was a rancher, she saw cattle herded into a machine that squeezed their bodies. Before the squeezing they fought and bucked, but once inside the machine, the cattle quieted, becoming calmer and more relaxed. Young Temple saw this as an intervention that could possibly help her, so she constructed a machine she could crawl into that squeezed her body tightly. She reported that it helped her feel more relaxed and safe after an overwhelming event. Today, parents can easily buy weighted blankets for children's beds or jackets that have weights in them. These provide a deep, calming, proprioceptive input, helping children feel calmer and more relaxed.

From Temple Grandin's Journal of Child and Adolescent Psychopharmacology:

> As a child, I craved to feel the comfort of being held, but I would pull away when people hugged me. When hugged, an overwhelming tidal wave of sensation flowed through me. At times, I preferred such intense stimulation to the point of pain, rather than accept ordinary hugs. On the Ayres Checklist for Tactile Defensiveness (1979) I had 9 out of 15 symptoms by age 10 years. Whenever anyone touched me, I stiffened, flinched, and pulled away. This approach- avoidance characteristic endured for years during my childhood.

> At puberty, anxiety and nervousness made me feel as though I was constantly in a state of "stage fright." While the nature of this anxiety was not diagnosed at the time, they have been retrospectively diagnosed as panic attacks, and would fulfill the *DSM-III-R* criteria.

> At age 18, I constructed the squeeze machine to help calm down the anxiety and panic attacks. Using the machine for 15 minutes would reduce my anxiety for up to 45-60 minutes (Grandin and Scariano–1986). The relaxing effect was maximized if the machine was used twice a day.

> Gradually, my tolerance of being held by the squeeze machine grew. Knowing that I could initiate the pressure, and stop it if the stimulation became too intense, helped me to reduce the oversensitivity of my "nervous system." A once overwhelming stimulus was now a pleasurable experience.

> Using the machine enabled me to learn to tolerate being touched by another person. By age 25, I was able to relax in the machine without pulling away from it. It also made me feel less aggressive and less tense.

All people on this planet are learning to deal with their minds; some of us have more help than others. Because our minds color how we view each other, relationships, and the world, it can be very difficult to see past the basic assumptions of our brain and understand the way another's brain organizes the world. Despite the level of difficulty, this is a worthy undertaking that would positively impact our entire society.

"Nothing in the world is worth having or worth doing unless it means effort, pain, difficulty… I have never in my life envied a human being who led an easy life. I have envied a great many people who led difficult lives and led them well."

~ THEODORE ROOSEVELT

"Nothing worth doing is completed in our lifetime; therefore, we must be saved by hope. Nothing true or beautiful or good makes complete sense in any immediate context of history; therefore, we must be saved by faith. Nothing we do, however virtuous, can be accomplished alone; therefore, we are saved by love."

~ REINHOLD NIEBUHR

Touch and Learning Challenges

A third-grade teacher burst into the room I had set up for games and an after-school program and asked, "Can I borrow your mats?" Intrigued, I agreed. She brought in a young boy from her class who was unable to stay in his seat and had been acting up more and more over the course of the day. She pulled out the mats and asked him to roll up and down on the mat like a log. The child, mildly annoyed and moderately amused, agreed. He rolled up and down the mat a few times. She also had him do a series of exercises, and then they left. Later that afternoon, I asked her what had happened during the rest of the day. She said that before she had done the "mat-exercise" with him, he was verging on being sent to the principal's office, but instead he calmed down for the rest of the day and was a good class participant. She said the young child needed to "feel something," and when he felt his body again, he began settling down. This was a touch-based intervention. It took all of eight minutes. It made her day easier, and the child was able to avoid disciplinary action. It also helped this young boy learn a huge and important lesson; when he was feeling overwhelmed he could reduce the negative feelings by changing his behaviors.

For children with learning challenges, school is often much more stressful than it is for other children. I have personally witnessed children intentionally get themselves kicked out of a class, rather than face the embarrassment of admitting how hard a subject was for them. High stress levels have a very negative impact on learning because they can shut down the front brain—the area involved in regulating behavior and learning new information. I have listened to many children in treatment talking about their minds going blank before a test, or having an anxious day that led to them getting into trouble with their teacher. Not many students have access to floor mats, let alone such a perceptive teacher; however, there are many touch-based interventions that can help children reduce their stress. Holding a stress ball and squeezing it increases proprioceptive input. I have had children press their feet into the ground when they are anxious in class, or rest their hands on their stomach so they can feel their breath going in and out. These interventions change a child's stress levels, and when their stress is lowered, children act more appropriately and learn more easily. One of the most important skills for any child to learn is mastery. In essence, mastery means that they can change things. Instead of feeling that they are essentially powerless, children can change their behaviors to change their feelings, which improves the choices (and outcomes) they make, and their quality of life.

Exercise and physical play make a difference for all children, especially those with learning differences. Exercise increases neurochemicals that help the brain learn (such as brain-derived neurotropic factor or BDNF). Children with learning challenges learn new information at a different pace and may hit a level of "too much information" sooner than do children with neurotypical brains. Small breaks for jumping rope, wrestling with a parent, or any physically engaging activity, help a child's brain learn more rapidly, and reduce the feeling of frustration associated with learning new things.

Touch and Sensory Integration

Sensory integration is a buzzword in psychology these days. When we say that water feels wet, there are several sensations (cold, slick, soft, etc.) that combine to create the feeling of wetness. The next time you are in a large room with other people, look around, and then close your eyes. Listen to the sounds. Your mind will continue putting the sounds together with your memory of physical space of the room. Even without opening your eyes, you can tell where a voice is coming from or how far away footsteps are. This ability to integrate our senses can be disrupted by many factors (e.g., maternal stress during pregnancy, toxins, early childhood trauma and many others). Children face many mental health challenges—from anxiety to autism to bipolar disorder—which can disrupt their sensory integration. To imagine what this feels like, remember a time you had not slept well for several days, or were highly stressed. Then imagine your neighbor was playing a slightly annoying song very loudly while you were trying to study or read. Under these conditions, most people would find it hard to filter the noise, and the loudness of the music would be very difficult to tolerate. This is what it is like almost all the time for both children and adults with sensory integration challenges. Sensory gating is the ability to reduce the amount of sensation that comes in from the outside environment. If you want to experience this, put your full attention on the sensation of your shirt on your shoulders. When you focus on this sensation, you notice it; before focusing, you were probably oblivious to it. This is what happens when the brain, through habituation, reduces the impact of certain sensations. Contained, supportive touch is a powerful tool that helps children and adults with sensory integration challenges rewire their sensory world.

Touch interventions can affect sensory integration in several ways. High stress response levels can lead to more challenges for children with sensory integration difficulties, and touch interventions reduce stress response. Touch interventions provide physical grounding and help "anchor" their systems as their minds work to weave together their sensory world. Touch can also help children with proprioception—an often ignored or misunderstood process. Specifically, proprioception is the body's ability to understand, or sense, its relationship to itself in space; for example, knowing whether an arm is situated above the head or hanging beside the body. However, there are myriad internal stimuli that lead the body to determining where it is in relationship to objects, the ground, or others, For the sake of simplicity going forward I will subsume the copious number of internal sensory processes under the sense of proprioception. (This is not scientifically accurate but it helps keep the discussion contained. It is important to note that these internal sensory experiences of self are often subsumed under touch, but really represent a *sixth type of sensory experience quite distinct from touch.*) When this sensation is disrupted, children are more accident-prone—they may even lean, or bump into things or people as they try to get some feedback from the world. Deep pressure touch can increase a child's ability to feel a relationship with the physical world. Some research indicates that elevated stress reactivity can alter the process of sensory integration and regulation, or proprioceptive feedback. By learning self-touch skills and having parents provide safe, containing touch, a child can begin to orient to the world and integrate proprioception with other sensations. The best treatment these days for sensory integration challenges is working with a well-trained occupational therapist that specializes in treating sensory processing disorders (SPD). The occupational therapist will: provide skills and home practices (including touch), develop a sensory diet (a personalized activity plan that provides appropriate sensory input to help a child remain focused) and a staged plan to help the child grow the neurocognitive ability to integrate their senses.

Cultural Differences in Touch and Their Impact on Mental Health Treatment

Rates and quality of touch vary across cultures. The amount of physical contact considered normal in France might be viewed as extreme in Russia or the United States. The type and rate of expected touch an individual uses is defined by their culture and is influenced by age and gender. In setting treatment goals for individuals from different cultural backgrounds, it is important for the clinician to understand that *health is often defined by culture.* Culture creates a balance of relationship that establishes the ecosystem of development. In one culture, lower levels of touch are balanced by more verbal instruction; in another culture, a child learns more by watching the behaviors of the adults in their life.

In Jamaican culture, many mothers perform deep massage on their infants and stretch their arms regularly; this practice (associated with advanced motor development in children) would probably shock an American parent. In yet another culture, children are held frequently and attended with intense focus, with the expectation that they will be highly autonomous upon reaching their adulthood. When trying to understand an individual or a culture, one needs to be open, willing to learn, and able to challenge one's basic assumptions about what health is. Clinicians who are able to do this will be more successful in helping their clients achieve their own best health, rather than attempting to make their clients conform to their own ideals.

Dr. Paul Ekman described a universal ability to read emotions through facial expression. Current research indicates that people can effectively decode emotions communicated through touch. Also, many forms of self-touch are used to communicate emotions. While flirting, a woman may stroke and flip her hair; an individual communicating sympathy may put a hand on his or her own cheek as they lean in towards another person. Culture defines display rules for appropriate touch.

Display rules tell us when and where touch is appropriate. For example, touch between a husband and wife in their home will be different than if they are in a coffee shop, and more different yet if they are visiting relatives. Along with display rules, there are physical symbols of emotional communication—the stylized patterns of behavior used to communicate an idea. Symbols commonly used in this country (such as the okay gesture and the peace gesture) can have very different meanings in other cultural contexts. The high-five and the fist-bump are symbols of acceptance and celebration between individuals in the United States, but could be interpreted as aggressive in another culture. Since touch is used even more often once an individual has achieved a certain level of acceptance and safety within a group, understanding cultural norms around the communication of emotion and display rules for touch is vital for development of effective touch-based interventions.

It is reasonable to assume that since touch patterns are non-verbal, many clinicians have not given sufficient attention to how display rules for touch influence their work. One could easily imagine American or British clinicians—blinded by their own cultural assessment—viewing an individual from a culture with high amounts of displayed affection as exhibiting pathological behavior. Such an assumption may even occur beneath the clinicians' awareness, since the impact of display rules tends to occur through non-verbal communication. To date, no research that this author is aware of has been conducted about cultural display rules and how they influence therapists' assumptions; such research could shed light on this important and interesting aspect of treatment. While research has been conducted on display norms and touch, another series of studies on how misunderstood cultural touch display rules impact clinical assumptions, thus leading to a cultural disconnect between therapists and their clients, would be very useful.

Optimal Mental Health and Touch

Flow is the state of being in optimal engagement, fully engaged in a task and solving a problem just as quickly as it comes up. In sports, this is called being "in the zone". It is possible for people to increase the periods of time they spend in flow. Some of the best ways to increase your time in flow are: choose to do things that you love; make sure your tasks are challenging, but not too challenging; build a quiet time into each day; practice focusing on one thing at a time; and, notice any small successes towards flow! Attention is like water for a plant. That which we pay attention to, grows. Researchers argue that flow occurs when our innate resources and skills are challenged just enough. If we are bored, we need more challenge. If we are overwhelmed, we need more skill.

It is possible to continue to develop mental health far beyond the point of having no symptoms of mental health problems. Touch plays an important role in optimal mental health. Individuals who regularly get massage have decreased stress and increased dopamine. This could translate into better problem solving and being more effective on the job and in school. Touch interventions can increase happiness for couples who are struggling, because touch is a vital part of a healthy, intimate relationship. Learning how to touch in different ways, from listening touch to supportive, containing touch, could help relationships shift from being merely enjoyable to being vibrant and thriving. The same can be true for the family system as well. Healthy touch within a family can increase the experience of happiness for family members as well as serve as a buffer against stressful times.

All individuals have areas where they are more developed than are other individuals. Optimal mental health may begin with recognizing strengths and enhancing them, and working on improving areas that need more development. For a doctor in a high-stress job, increasing the amount of supportive touch could reduce stress levels and generally make all aspects of his or her life more enjoyable. The same medical provider might also increase effectiveness in the work place by learning to touch patients with more subtle sensitivity, increasing job satisfaction while simultaneously reducing his or her own stress levels. At least one study has shown that patients whose doctors touch their shoulder, shake their hand, or offer another form of safe touch, are more likely to comply with their doctors' recommendations.

Some domains of optimal mental health could include increased joy in the moment, continued learning and skill development over a lifetime, increased ability to understand and accurately communicate one's emotions, and development of good relationship habits. Effective communication of emotions can include learning to read and express emotions through touch. Relationships, particularly close relationships, include some aspect of physical contact. The ability to be in relationship and feel loving connection with a spouse, child or friend, is enhanced by safe, supportive touch. Along with learning about the world, we are always learning about and adjusting to our bodies. As we age and develop, our bodies change. Safe touch interventions are major factors in developing a healthy relationship with our bodies.

Understanding how to help people reach optimal mental health is still in its infancy. Because touch is such a vital aspect of a healthy life, astute clinicians and theorists can help many people by developing effective touch-based interventions that individuals can use to continue improving their physical and mental health across their lifespan.

Chapter 8

Changing the Code:
The Genetics of Contact

It looks like a blueprint for a spiraling staircase, but it is not. When Watson and Crick first revealed the little packages of chemicals we call DNA to be a blueprint for life on this planet, their discovery resulted in an explosion of research. Initially, the research seemed to indicate that the genes we carry determine everything about who we are. Even today, more than fifty years later, news stories continue to appear about genetics—how this gene or that gene determines nearly every aspect of human physiology and behavior. Most of these stories neglect to mention that the picture is far more complex. Many of these genes are responsible for just a part of the development of a trait or disease. Only in extremely rare situations will one gene, or even a handful of genes, predict with complete certainty that a disease will develop. If one gene predicts a sixty percent likelihood of a condition developing, and that likelihood exists for only seventy percent of people carrying the gene, there must be other factors.

In the 1960s, researchers studied the development of psychosis. As we have discussed, people with this mental health challenge can experience hallucinations, difficulty socializing, and challenges with problem solving. Professor Wayne Drevets was one of the proponents of a term that is now used to explain how under certain conditions our genetic predisposition can lead to the development of a physical or mental health condition. Termed "diathesis-stress model," this concept proposes that while some individuals are born with a biologically increased risk for the development of psychosis, that risk is not one-hundred percent. A significant stressful event (or series of events), or a specific environmental factor (or factors) needs to occur, thus providing a catalyst for the development of a psychological or physiological challenge. Within the mental health community, a trove of research discusses the transition from genotype (the genetic disposition for a trait or disease) to phenotype (the actual development of a measurable trait or disease).

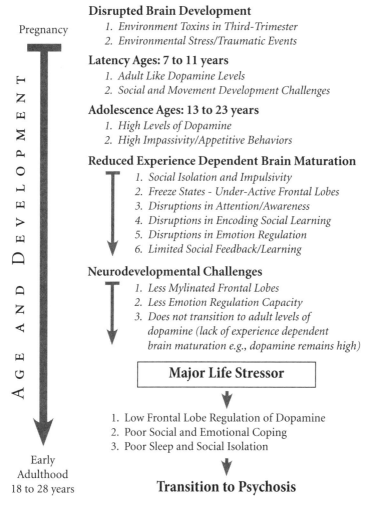

Disrupted Brain Development
Pregnancy
1. *Environment Toxins in Third-Trimester*
2. *Environmental Stress/Traumatic Events*

Latency Ages: 7 to 11 years
1. *Adult Like Dopamine Levels*
2. *Social and Movement Development Challenges*

Adolescence Ages: 13 to 23 years
1. *High Levels of Dopamine*
2. *High Impassivity/Appetitive Behaviors*

Reduced Experience Dependent Brain Maturation
1. *Social Isolation and Impulsivity*
2. *Freeze States - Under-Active Frontal Lobes*
3. *Disruptions in Attention/Awareness*
4. *Disruptions in Encoding Social Learning*
5. *Disruptions in Emotion Regulation*
6. *Limited Social Feedback/Learning*

Neurodevelopmental Challenges
1. *Less Mylinated Frontal Lobes*
2. *Less Emotion Regulation Capacity*
3. *Does not transition to adult levels of dopamine (lack of experience dependent brain maturation e.g., dopamine remains high)*

Major Life Stressor

1. Low Frontal Lobe Regulation of Dopamine
2. Poor Social and Emotional Coping
3. Poor Sleep and Social Isolation

Transition to Psychosis

Early Adulthood 18 to 28 years

AGE AND DEVELOPMENT

Figure 8.1 **Diathesis-Stress Model Transition to Psychosis**

In any diathesis-stress model, there are factors that increase risk for the development of a disease, as well as protective factors. The number of stressors and traumas a person encounters can affect the likelihood of them developing a disease. However, the quality and quantity of resiliency factors, the relationships in a person's life, and a feeling of empowerment—being able to change difficulties in life by one's own effort—can buffer the impact of even the most difficult life events.

Some have argued that the differences between the human genome and the ape genome are too small to account for all the differences between the species. Perhaps more relevant to humans, some individuals carry genes for terrible diseases, yet they do not develop disease. Is it possible that for these individuals, the genes are not "expressed" (switched on)? Current research has found that along with our genetic code, or DNA, there is another code, namely the "epigenetic code" which conducts our individual genes like notes in a symphony. Epigenetics is the study of heritable changes in gene activity that are *not* caused by changes in the DNA sequence; an epigenome consists of a record of the chemical changes to the processes that regulate the expression of DNA. Some of these processes can be passed through successive generations; however research has yet to demonstrate whether this also holds true for other processes.

Epigenome: Coding Life Events in our Genetics

Biologist Conrad Waddington first envisioned the epigenetic code, and the many factors that direct it, as a landscape that determines how the genetics can develop: in the same way that available foods, available sunlight, and types of predators in their environment determine how different species of birds develop. The epigenome is now thought of as one of the bridges linking nature (the genes we are born with) to nurture (the environment we are born into). One molecular basis of epigenetics is histone modification of DNA. If you think of our genes as an expandable file (like an accordion), you can imagine that when the file is fully expanded, information is easier to extract. This is exactly what happens with histone modification of DNA. Under certain circumstances, DNA is compressed, or so tightly wrapped it is inaccessible to the cell, and cannot be expressed. Because it is not expressed, it cannot lead to development of a disease.

While the body has its own code for expression of DNA (epigenome), life events can change the histone modification of DNA and other epigenetic factors. Life events are not just psychological memories or experiences; they are biological processes. When we narrowly avoid being hit by another car while we are driving our own vehicle, a biological cascade of stress hormones increases our breathing rate, and those of us who have a little road rage may yell at the other driver and pound the horn. When we smile at our spouse, that action also creates a biological cascade; this may be why some studies indicate that something as simple as the type of smile on a person's face as their photo is taken, can predict their lifespan. (A genuine smile for a photo—at least in some research—predicts a longer life.) The biological cascade brought about by smiling changes the chemical composition in the body and the mind. A smile, repeated often enough, could change the chemicals that trigger histone modification.

When we get a massage, hold a child, or pet an animal, it changes our inner chemistry. While typically no single event taken in isolation (this may not be true for extremely severe traumatic events) can change our DNA expression, a host of events together that occurs regularly can begin changing this process.

As an example of this, Professor Maleszka of Australian National University points out that researchers looking at colony collapse disorder (CCD: honey bees abandon their hives over winter and eventually die) are finding that it is not a single gene that regulates the death of the bees, but a complex interaction between a number of genes and the environment. Because so many of our planet's plant food sources need bees for pollination, the increasing incidence of CCD is of extreme concern. Bees play such a crucial part in the planet's entire ecosystem that many have posited that colony collapse disorder could be an early signal of increasing fragility developing in Earth's ecosystem.

Histone modification is mostly changed within a single lifespan. The jury is still out as to whether patterns of histone modification can transfer from parent to child. However, we do know that another

epigenetic factor, DNA methylation, can be passed to the next generation. It may be that some of the processes that interact between nature
and nurture and lead to colony collapse disorder are due to histone
modification.

DNA methylation is different from histone modification. DNA methylation is highly active during the first few years of life and may have
an effect on the expression of a child's genes over a lifetime, as well as
the gene expression of that child's eventual offspring. Methyl groups,
some of the most common structural units of organic compounds, are
chemicals that bind to the DNA strands and switch them off. In essence,
they tell the cell that certain strands of DNA are irrelevant. Genes can be
present, but if they are not switched on, they do not affect us.

There is a fascinating gene called the Agouti gene that is responsible
for the patterns and colors of some mammals' fur. The Agouti gene is
primarily responsible for regulating a chemical called agouti signaling peptide (ASP). It is associated with large-scale differences in coat
coloration and in mice, aspects of metabolism. Certain mice—agouti
mice, have more of the Agouti gene, and they give us a striking example of the power of gene regulation. When the Agouti gene is perma-
nently switched on, the mouse has yellow fur and a propensity to over-
eat until it perishes from obesity-related factors. One lab developed a
pair of genetically identical twin mice. What we expect from identical
twins is that they be identical. However, these genetically identical
mice could not have been more different from each other. One mouse
was of normal weight with a grayish coat. The other mouse was fat
with a yellow coat. Both mice had a copy of the Agouti gene, because
they had identical DNA. In one mouse, the Agouti gene was perma-
nently on; in the other it was not; thus the *genes* were the same, but the
epigenetics were different. The yellow mouse with the actuated Agouti
gene ate constantly and eventually died of heart complications. The
gray mouse maintained a normal weight and enjoyed a natural life
span. Both mice had the same genome, but different epigenomes, and
profoundly different phenotypes.

Current data indicate that there are periods in a child's life when
certain aspects of DNA methylation are established—particularly in

the early years. As we saw in chapter one, removing an infant from their parent for even a short time during early infancy can change the way that infant/child/adult responds to stress for the rest of its life. This has been observed in multiple species including, but not limited to, non-human primates, humans, and rodents. (Interestingly, at least one study of horses did not find this pattern.)

There are many processes that change epigenetics. Four of the most studied processes are: DNA methylation, which turns off strands of DNA; histone modification, which makes the DNA unavailable by compressing it so it cannot be expressed (part of the acetylating process and triggered through a binding to histone strands); phosphorylation, which also turns expression of genes on and off; and sumoylation, which regulates the way the cell manages its lifespan, stress, and the stability of proteins, and affects the way DNA is expressed.

Adverse Childhood Experiences and Adult Health

An ambitious and talented doctor at Kaiser Permanente in Santa Barbara set out to create a highly effective weight loss program. Dr. Vincent J. Felitti worked on the project for some time and had significant successes—patients who were losing one-hundred or more pounds! This was exciting. He knew all too well how the current American diet induces some, even many, people to become significantly overweight, and that obese individuals are at severe risk for many health problems—even early death. Sometimes, along the way to scientific discovery, there is a moment of insight that changes everything. Or, as John Lennon said so well, "Life is what happens while you are busy making other plans." Dr. Felitti's program was highly successful, except that the very people experiencing the most success were dropping out. The people who were reaching their goals were leaving the program early; moreover, typically they were quickly regaining the weight, which made very little sense. As a doctor who cared about his patients and as a scientist who needed to find a solution, Dr. Felitti started doing something quite radical: he began *listening* to his patients.

Doctors want to be involved in the healing relationship. Many doctors are aware that how they relate to their patients impacts how well those patients heal. However, more and more, doctors are pushed to treat their patients within fifteen-minute appointments, and they have very full daily schedules. This has made an environment for medical practitioners wherein, as one doctor said to me recently, "I do not have time to be a doctor." In this context, studies of medical providers show that they often interrupt a patient within the first *fifteen seconds* of a conversation about health. Most patients trying to communicate their health issues quite understandably do not use medical nomenclature, thus expressing their health issue(s) takes time—time that a doctor in our current culture simply does not have. When Dr. Felitti and his colleges stopped, listened, and then began asking questions, it was a radical departure from the norm.

When he talked with his patients, Dr. Felitti found they had one thing in common: childhood adversity. The patients who had gained the most weight, lost the most weight, and dropped out of the program the soonest, had all experienced significant childhood adversity. In his "John Lennon moment," Dr. Felitti had an insight: an individual's childhood adversity might be a root cause for excessive weight gain and its associated health problems. His first challenge was to identify types of childhood adversity and find a way to ask his patients about their childhood. After copious research and extensive discussion with patients, Dr. Felitti developed the Adverse Childhood Experiences Study (ACE). In this survey, people are asked about multiple adverse childhood events: for example; did they have a parent who was diagnosed with a mental illness, or a parent who had been in jail; had they experienced physical abuse; had they experienced the death of a family member? In collaboration with Dr. Robert F. Anda of the Centers for Disease Control and Prevention, and Kaiser Permanente's Health Appraisal clinic in San Diego, Dr. Felitti instigated the largest study of this type to date; over seventeen-thousand people participated in the research. He talked to the majority of the Kaiser Permanente members in the San Diego area. The title of one of his first research papers says it all, "Reverse Alchemy in Childhood: Turning Gold into Lead." Findings from the study show that the number of adverse childhood experiences (ACEs) correlates directly not just with an individual's weight, but with many forms of negative health behaviors, such as smoking, not exercising, or drug abuse. *Dr. Felitti considers this deplorable situation to be a public health crisis.*

One dramatic finding of his study: if an individual experienced six types of childhood adversity, they were *forty-six-hundred percent* (4,600.0%) more likely to use intravenous drugs than an individual who had experienced none. Results concerning smoking were similar and also quite dramatic: an individual who had experienced five adverse childhood events was *five-hundred and forty percent* (540.0%) more likely to take up smoking than one who scored a zero on the survey-scale. Dr. Felitti's ground-breaking research has changed and continues changing the practice of medicine in this country.

The public health impact of adverse childhood events does not stop there. Individuals with a high number of ACEs have increased risk for autoimmune diseases such as multiple sclerosis, Crohn's disease, and lupus. This finding, that childhood adversity can negatively impact an individual's health even fifty years later, is simply staggering. Other findings link ACEs to type II diabetes and other public health problems. Dr. Felitti and his colleagues established a pathway to health problems through ACEs, summarized in figure 8.2 below:

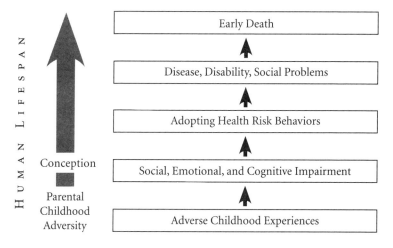

Figure 8.2 **Adverse Childhood Events and Health and Longevity**

ACEs do relate to a shortened lifespan. Other research on the effect of poverty on lifespan shows that simply not having enough money can reduce life expectancy by nearly four and one-half years (not to mention the impact on quality of life). Since the ACEs study was conducted with individuals in the middle class or middle socioeconomic group, the impact of poverty was not assessed; however one could anticipate that poverty would make most, or even all, of the ACEs findings worse.

Childhood Adversity and Health Behaviors

Childhood adversity impacts three factors that influence human health and development throughout a life; the first is challenges with building relationships and friendships. Isolation has a powerful impact on our health. The lack of social connections expressed through hugs, smiles, conversations, and feeling understood, creates terrible strain on human physiology. This may be due to in part to oxytocin, the hormone of safe emotional connection, affecting the stress hormone cortisol. Social relationships also help us solve problems, which nobody can accomplish alone within their own mind. (Because we all make perfect sense to ourselves all of the time; we need others to point out if and when we are not making sense.) We talk to friends, reason things out, consider the opinions of others; those of us who do such things can expect to be more successful in life.

A second factor impacted by childhood adversity is emotion regulation. As demonstrated in studies of mice that were not regularly licked and groomed by their mothers (resulting in a tendency to act more aggressively in social settings), people who experience childhood adversity can find it more challenging to regulate their emotions. They are therefore more vulnerable to the impacts of difficult emotional situations, and may choose behaviors that are ineffective and possibly health adverse. The popular term "self-medicating" describes this concept very well. Many individuals engage in what is called "emotional eating." Individuals with poor emotion regulation may choose over-eating as a way to manage their feelings. This even makes biological sense: When we are in the grip of terrible emotions, our fight-flight system activates, making us feel anxious, angry, and sometimes powerful enough to accomplish difficult tasks. (Where would the American Revolution, the civil rights movement, or the women's movement be, if people had not channeled their justifiable anger effectively?) For some individuals, eating stimulates the opposite system, the "rest and digest" system. Food becomes a way to physiologically soothe a difficult emotion. A possible pathway from childhood adversity to health challenges is via high levels of fight-flight stimulation, leading to overeating and unhealthy weight gain. Smoking, drug use, and other aspects of challenges to emotion regulation may have a similar pathway. In laypersons' terminology, these self-destructive behaviors may be self-medicating a common problem—childhood adversity.

However, this is not the time to despair and reach for fries and a cheeseburger—there is hope. Jon Kabat-Zinn, the founder of mindfulness-based stress reduction (MBSR), taught programmers working at one firm to meditate. These individuals experienced dramatic changes in how they regulated their emotions. While MBSR does not explicitly offer touch work, mindfulness often requires bringing attention to the body's connection with the world. There are also myriad direct touch-based ways to increase emotion regulation. As many of Dr. Tiffany Field's studies indicate, massage can change the fight-flight system, and many other neurochemicals associated with challenges to emotion regulation.

A third factor leading to adopting risky health behaviors is cognitive impairment. We saw earlier that childhood adversity can lead to adverse changes in brain development: Who can forget the extreme cases of neglected children in Romanian orphanages, some of whose brains were as much as thirty-eight percent smaller than the brains of children who did not experience such adversity? However, less extreme events can also affect brain development; consistently high stress levels make it more challenging for a person to form memories and learn.

Dr. Felitti proposes that these factors (challenges with social relationships, emotion regulation, and cognitive impairment) lead to what he calls "adoption of health-risk behaviors" that can result in disease, disability, and long-term social problems. In his keynote addresses, Dr.

Felitti discusses the ACE Study and its relevance to everyday medicine, mental health, and healthcare costs. Defying conventional belief, he explains that time does not heal all wounds, as humans convert traumatic emotional experiences in their childhood into organic disease later in life. One does not "just get over" some things, not even fifty years later. Dr. Felitti also points out that there are still many gaps in our scientific understanding of all of the negative impacts of early childhood adversity.

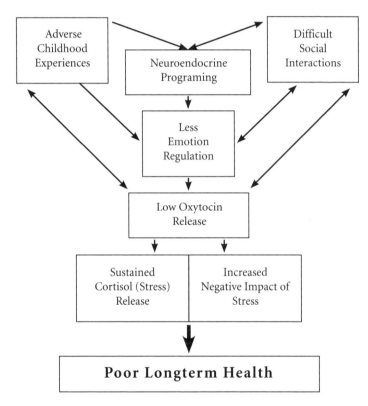

Figure 8.3 **Oxytocin and Poor Long-term Health**

Getting Beneath the Skin:
Long-Term Health and Childhood Adversity

Consider figure 8.3 below (this model has not been tested), which proposes at least one way that childhood adversity and lack of social support can lead to poor health, including cardiovascular disease. Adverse early childhood experiences can lead to challenges with emotion regulation. Childhood adversity can include a lack of sufficient supportive and loving touch, leading to less oxytocin release overall.

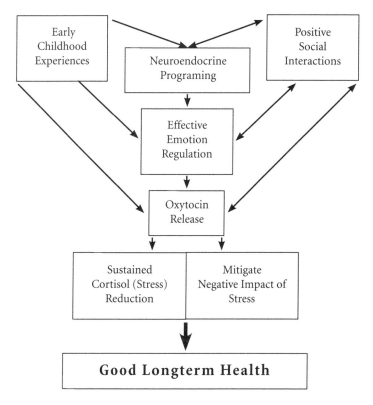

Figure 8.4 **Oxytocin and Good Long-term Health**

Current challenges with social relationships—stress with a spouse, conflicts at work, or social isolation—lead to less oxytocin release. Lower oxytocin increases the impact of existing cortisol and stress on the brain and body, and causes higher cortisol levels. Elevated stress leads to the development of health-risk behaviors, hence to the likelihood of poor health, and also many conditions such as arthritis, type II diabetes, and autoimmune diseases.

One critique of the ACEs study is that it is correlational work and, as any good scientist will say, "correlation is not causation." The problem of correlation is that some things can occur close together in time or in relationship, but not have any real relationship. For instance the number of murders goes up in a direct relationship to the number of ice cream cones purchased. This is a well-documented correlation that was discussed in a previous chapter. However, before starting an anti-ice cream coalition, it is important to remember that correlation is not causation. In this case there is third variable that affects both ice cream cone purchases and violence. That third variable is heat. It turns out that moderate to mildly hot temperatures make people uncomfortable and more likely to lash out with violence. This may be an example of a bottom up process of emotion regulation, as previously discussed. It is interesting to note that this relationship does not stay the same at very hot temperatures. When temperatures are extremely hot, people don't want to do anything; they just don't go anywhere or interact very much. Thus people at very hot temperatures may be even testier than they are at moderately hot temperatures, but the world will not be affected because people are just too hot to move. As it turns out this third variable (temperature) probably accounts for both increased rates of violence, and ice cream cone sales.

Now take that idea and apply it to genetics and childhood adversity. It is possible that childhood adversity causes a change in genetics, or that it changes epigenetics. It may also be that there is a third factor affecting them both. For instance, it could be that there are several genes controlling the likelihood that someone who experiences childhood adversity will develop health-adverse behaviors. This is the problem of correlation: The truth is that correlation is not causation.

Nonetheless, there is a wealth of data indicating early childhood adversity has major negative impacts on adult health. There are also many other sources of data on how adversity impacts health; these studies were conducted in a manner such that we can infer causation. These are experimental studies in which key variables are changed by the researcher. Considering the big picture, and the entirety of the body of literature on adversity, it looks to be even more probable that there *is* a causal relationship between adverse childhood events, adverse health behaviors, and subsequent poor health in adulthood.

Violence and Genetics

We are all hoping to find the cure for human violence. Researchers hoped they had found it with the discovery of the MOA-A gene (Monoamine oxidase-A, often referred to in the popular press as the "warrior" gene"). This gene relates to people whose ancestors lived in cultures that farm livestock, rather than grains or vegetables. These cultures displayed more violence because it was easier and more profitable to steal a cow than to steal unharvested grain. (Stealing grain requires hours of intensive labor and does not have quite the payoff that "rustling" a herd of cattle does.) Some researchers hypothesized that the MOA-A gene might be the missing link connecting violence to genetic predisposition. Initial research was exciting. Some carriers of this gene *are* more likely to be imprisoned for a violent offense. However, there is one catch: Dr. David Fergusson, in his longitudinal study (study measuring a group of people over a length of time) in New Zealand, found something more amazing: *if children with this gene had a loving, supportive home, they were no more likely than anyone else to lead a life of crime.* Let me say that again: if a child, even a child carrying the MAO-A gene, was well loved, they were no more likely to commit a violent crime than was anyone else. However, if these "warrior gene" children *were* treated with violence, aggression, or abuse, the risk factor for criminal behaviors shot back up!

Consider the impacts of this finding. Imagine a young boy with the MAO-A gene. He is part of a good family. They read to him at night. He sits on his mother's lap as she sings to him. His father loves to throw him up in the air and play airplane. He has good friends at his pre-school. These interactions, through some yet-to-be identified mechanism, tell the MOA-A gene to express itself in a way that makes this child relaxed, calm, and no more at risk than anyone else for violent behavior. So this child, who had the luck of being born into a kind family, has the continued luck to have an easier journey through life because the MOA-A gene is not expressed.

If this boy had another life situation, things could be quite different. What would happen if this young boy had a father, a kind and gentle man, who fought in a war and then returned with symptoms of post-traumatic stress disorder? The traumatized father would frequently lose his temper. The child would get angry in response. This aggression puts the child at risk for increased violent behavior and probable imprisonment.

However, what if the father seeks help? What if the father receives the right support and healing, and the house calms? What happens to this child as his genes are being expressed? What would it take to reverse the impact on his gene expression? Would good therapy for the father change the course of this child's life?

This is a profound question. More research is needed but there are indications that even for kids in violent homes, increased emotion regulation is possible. Thus there is reason to hope. Another even more profound question regarding this child and how their life develops is, "Who is at fault for the gene expression?" Should the child be punished for being in a difficult situation and having a genetic predisposition? If so, do the genetics direct what form and severity the punishment should take? These are profoundly important questions that we, as a society, should discuss.

Dr. Field's studies on the impact of massage on youth violence point in an interesting direction. There are reduced rates of depression in youths who receive massage. In a correlational study, she found indications that the rate and quality of touch between teens may influence rates of aggression. Further studies are certainly needed, but one factor that may be missing in the lives of children who commit violent acts is appropriate, safe, supportive touch. The research on licking and grooming behavior in mice seems to indicate that touch, at least during a critical period of development, is vital for optimal health and social skills for that animal; and remember—genetically, humans are very similar to mice.

Building a Resilient Lifestyle

Resilience is the ability to bounce back after a stressful event. Like anyone else, resilient individuals will often feel stressed and overwhelmed, but they are able to shift quickly out of that state of overwhelm back to a state of equilibrium. Results from the ACEs study point to a powerful implication: Even when all the risk factors are present, some people do not display challenges with health behavior. What makes the difference? Is there a list of factors that make people resilient to the stressors? Can an inverse list, perhaps the "positive childhood experiences" scale be created? Would such a scale shed light on the processes by which people bounce back from difficulty?

What helps resilient people survive? Is it a gene, epigenetics, or another as yet undiscovered factor? A large amount of research in the area of resilience has been conducted. Resulting data seem to point to many protective factors. Just as with violence and the MAO-A gene, when a person has many protective factors, they tend to be resilient against stress. It should be possible to conduct the ACE study in reverse and look at how positive childhood experiences reduce the risk of disease and health-adverse behavior. Such research would provide us with vital information about what we can do to create a happy, healthy, and resilient culture. Certainly, touch is a part of this mix.

Touch and Metabolic Syndrome

He walked into his doctor's office and received some tough news. He was at risk of heart disease, diabetes, and stroke. His doctor told him he had metabolic syndrome.

Metabolic syndrome has affected increasing numbers (some studies indicate up to 34%) of Americans over the last decade. This condition is a collection of three (or more) out of five major risk factors (abdominal (central) obesity, elevated blood pressure, elevated fasting plasma glucose, high serum triglycerides, and low levels of high-density cholesterol) that together indicate a substantially greater risk of many health conditions. One of the hallmarks of metabolic syndrome is an apple-shaped belly that sticks out in front of the body, more commonly referred to as beer belly. This is an indication that the body is overloaded, and the metabolism is not functioning well. Our modern life style—eating processed foods, stress from our jobs, insufficient exercise, demands of family life without community support, and for some individuals, profound social isolation—is leading to an epidemic of metabolic syndrome.

Let us take a moment and look at metabolism. Metabolism is the balance among multiple functions all regulating energy production in the body. I was out at dinner the other night and ate a piece of cake. I was laughing and talking as the sugar processed in my belly, entered my blood, and started a series of events. First, it gave me a bit of an energy boost, as sugar is a highly available energy source. However, sugar needs to be balanced in the body. Thus second, the large amount of sugar in the cake caused my body to produce insulin to reduce the excess sugar in my body. Excessive sugar ingested too often taxes the body's ability to excrete, or produce, insulin. Interestingly, insulin appears to be implicated in longevity. While there is still some controversy about this, better regulated insulin function is related to increased longevity.

Metabolism and Life Stress—The Picture of Complexity

If metabolism were as simple as it seems in the paragraph you just read, the problem of metabolic syndrome would be much easier to solve. But consider what happens when a person is highly stressed—metabolism increases so that a person facing danger can either fight or get away. Stress helps the body initially increase metabolism. However, chronic stress can do quite the opposite. Think of chronic stress as being analogous to always making less money than you owe. At first, you might balance the difference with savings, then credit cards, help from friends, or even taking a second job. Nonetheless, unless income is more than expenses, you will always be draining your reserves, and when those reserves are gone, your challenges really begin. This is similar to how the body works. Stress changes how our body produces insulin, and if the stress goes on for too long it puts the body into a more vulnerable state. Sleep also effects metabolism. If we do not get enough sleep, levels of ghrelin and leptin (hormones that regulate insulin, metabolism and hunger) are altered. Poor sleep also adversely affects our body's stress response.

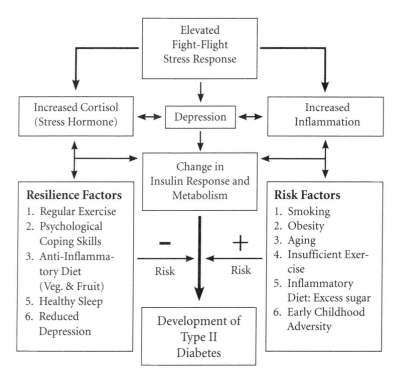

Figure 8.5 **Development of Type II Diabetes**

An Attack of Heart—Stress and Cardiac Function

In one very interesting study, a group of men with high levels of anger was found to have an increased risk of heart attack. Remember that the stress system is the *fight*-flight system. Anger is just as stressful as fear. Perhaps this is why philosophers such as Marcus Aurelius and the

Buddha pointed out that anger hurts the person who is angry more than it hurts the person who angered them. Another study determined that stress increased platelet reactivity, resulting in increased clotting, which is a risk factor for myocardial infarction (heart attack). Now, imagine blood coursing through your arteries. As long as there are no blockages, it can flow smoothly. If there is an injury to the blood vessel, the platelets, small disk-like cells in your blood, react by making a clot. If the platelets are too reactive, they may adhere to the walls of the arteries. Over time and in some places in the body, the accumulation of platelets can block the arteries. When the blood supply to the heart is blocked, the heart tissue dies, leading to myocardial infarction.

What does touch have to do with metabolism? In our nearest relatives, the non-human primates, we see something quite profound. The primates most stressed by aggression from other primates have the same hardening and blockage of the arteries that we find in humans. As discussed earlier, primates who received more supportive touch through grooming had less risk of heart disease. It is possible that regular, connected touch reduced their stress response, making the primates less vulnerable to developing heart disease.

Loneliness and Health

Another body of research shows that loneliness is a profound stressor with a powerfully adverse influence on health. Humans are highly social beings. The ecosystem of human development was one of connection, collaboration, and working towards common goals. A person from a hunter-gatherer group would rarely be completely isolated. Our bodies' genetic and epigenetic codes evolved in a high-touch, highly social environment. It is no surprise then that our body would sound an alarm if we were out of contact with our support. Research has found that supportive touch can reduce loneliness and increase a sense of connection.

Let us look at touch as a way to increase biological resilience and the impact of metabolic syndrome. It is well-documented that losing weight, reducing overall stress, and increasing social support can reduce the chance of developing diabetes, heart disease, and stroke.

Touch is one tool that crosses many borders of mind, body, and health. Healthy contact can reduce the stress response in general, and even reduce stress reactivity, or the intensity with which a person reacts to a stressor.

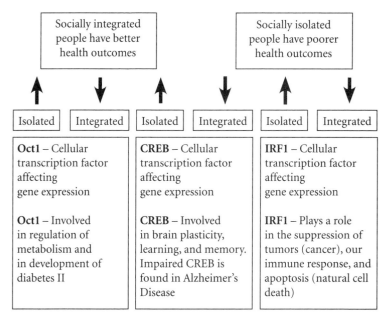

Figure 8.6 **Loneliness and Health**

One of the many challenges that infants born prematurely contend with, is gaining sufficient weight. Massage and skin-to-skin contact have been found to increase healthy metabolism in an infant. The risk factors for developing metabolic syndrome can occur throughout a lifetime, even in early infancy. The set point (set point is akin to the thermostat in a house: it can be set to 65° or 90°, telling the heater when to function) of the stress response can be changed by early-life exposure to events, chemicals, and other factors. In a very real sense, early-life contexts train, or prime, key aspects of metabolism, including insulin production and other vital factors. Factors like maternal-fetal nutrition can influence body events, such as how the body processes sugar, makes and stores fat, and produces mitochondria (the part of the cell involved in energy production). Later life events can also alter this programming. It may be that metabolic syndrome, and even type II diabetes, are results of a complex change in the set point of the body's metabolic regulatory complex. In addition to physical health problems (heart disease, diabetes, stroke), metabolic syndrome has been associated with mental health challenges such as depression. Current thinking is that there is a bi-directional interaction between depression and these health conditions (e.g., arthritis, hypertension, eczema, etc.). In other words, depression can contribute to the development of these illnesses, and conversely, these illnesses can contribute to increased risk for depression. Any good social scientist knows that just being with other people who care reduces the stress response and can help to lift depression. In controlled studies, massage reduces symptoms of depression. Since our modern environment is vastly different from the biological cultural contexts in which humans developed, it is truly imperative that we find ways to develop a healthy human context in our current culture. Touch is a vital part of this context.

One afternoon, awaiting my turn at a massage studio, I observed a woman going in just before me. Her face was tight. Her shoulders were practically glued to her ears. She was rushed. I watched as the therapist kindly led her to the room. After my massage (and feeling the post-massage glow myself), I saw the woman emerge. Her cheeks were rosier (more blood flow), her shoulders relaxed—far from the rushed, stressed, and tense person she had been—she was open, smiling, and expressing her gratitude. I recognized the shift she had gone through. I could feel it in how I felt in my own skin. I just liked life more than before I went in for my massage. This shift is more than just feeling good; it represents a shift in many biological structures—from how the blood flows to how the body regulates sugar.

An important study of stress and couples points to the importance of touch to the physical health of each individual in the couple, and the emotional health of a couple. In this study, sixty-seven women who had been in relationship for at least twelve months were subjected to a stressful event: after doing all of the preparation work and filling out consent forms, the women were shown a room with two examiners, a video camera, and bright lights. They were told that they were taking a verbal math test, aloud, in front of the examiners, and on-camera. Not surprisingly, this is qualifies as stressful. At times like these, the body produces tremendous amounts of stress hormones. One group of these women was left alone on a couch to stew and think about having to do this onerous task for ten minutes. Members of the second group of women were given verbal social support by their significant others. Members of the third group of women were given physical support by their romantic partners. It may be slightly shocking to learn that verbal support alone did not help reduce cortisol levels or heart rates. Many might be laughing as they think about their significant other's pitiful attempts to make them feel better, saying things like, "It will be okay" or, "You've got this." The more powerful finding was that the group of women receiving physical support through touch showed significant drops in cortisol level and heart rate. In other words, in this well-conducted study (randomized, controlled), physical contact reduced stress, while verbal support did not. This may point to the fundamental human need for contact. While a picture can communicate a thousand words, touch expresses the inexpressible.

Psychotherapy is called the talking cure. There is extensive research showing how talking can help. Nevertheless, all of the research discussed herein very clearly indicates that touch is a vital part of human health and healing. Most mental health challenges people suffer elicit increased stress response. There are times when expressed verbal empathy does not support an individual enough to shift from stress to rest, and increase their ability to regulate emotions. Our current cultural inability to support people through healthy touch may be leading to poor treatment and poor outcomes.

Chapter 9

Touched by Spirit:
Touch and Connection to It All

Her entire body ached from the chemotherapy treatment and occasionally she convulsed with a sob. She lay on a table with six of her friends around her, each with a hand on her body. Cancer causes intense feelings. For many it can be deeply traumatic, even producing symptoms of post-traumatic stress disorder. The experience of going through cancer treatment can be very isolating. It can feel like no one understands what you are going through. The women standing in the circle with their hands on their friend were often sobbing themselves. They loved their friend and it was deeply painful to see her so sick. At these incomprehensible moments, people look for meaning, depth, and purpose. Connecting with others is a way to connect to meaning. Getting up from the table some time later, the sick woman wept, saying she felt more at peace within herself. As she stood up, her face was softer and her body more relaxed.

Viktor Frankl, an Austrian neurologist of Jewish descent began working on his theory of meaning and purpose before the beginning of the Second World War. As he was taken to a concentration camp by the Austrian Nazi police, he still clutched his manuscript to his chest. Eventually the manuscript was taken. His wife was taken as well, and later killed by the Nazis. He explored his loss and his own journey to find meaning in his now classic book, "Man's Search for Meaning," originally titled (in the first English language translation), "From Death-Camp to Existentialism." Frankl made a powerful statement in this book: "Those who have a 'why' to live, can bear with almost any 'how.'" He pointed out that the people who were able to survive the meaningless horror of Auschwitz were those who believed their lives had meaning and purpose. He described what he called the "universal will towards meaning." As an individual who survived the worst that humanity had to offer (the Holocaust), Frankl's statement carries weight. Many, if not most, individuals view themselves as spiritual people, people who look for meaning in their lives, and throughout the world, touch is a way of connecting to spirituality.

Spirituality has been a taboo subject in psychology for some time. However, research is clear that connecting with a sense of meaning and purpose, or a higher power, has an impact psychologically. Learning to listen to clients' beliefs and supporting their efforts to connect with community and heal through their spiritual tradition is important, even for therapists who are atheists. Therapists need to listen past their own beliefs, and find ways to hear their clients' beliefs about spirituality. Meaning and purpose are powerful and necessary, no matter whether a person believes in the existence of a deity or not.

Laying on of Hands

When a new bishop is ordained in the Catholic Church, there is a ceremony called the Sacrament of Holy Orders. In this ceremony, the initiate kneels before another bishop (designated by the Pope) and bows his head as the other bishop places his hands on him, thus bestowing the direct continuation of the priesthood of Christ. The Eastern Orthodox Church has a similar practice. Jewish tradition has a ceremony for a new rabbi called *semikhah*. Many in the Jewish faith believe that there is an unbroken chain of authority from the ordained rabbi back to Moses. The word semikhah has three meanings, one of which is "the leaning of hands," although there is no formal laying on of hands in rabbinical ordination. While some people who have reviewed historical records believe that this formal ordination had a break in the chain between the 4th and 5th century, the ceremony is a powerful and ancient tradition with roots in early Jewish faith. The symbolism of this ceremony is one of communicating a spiritual transmission of the authority to lead the congregation through physical contact. Touch is a means of connection to the Divine in cultures throughout our world.

Laying on of hands has a predictable biological effect, and the physical connection between persons has emotional meaning. Feeling connected through this wordless expression of heart impacts us—it connects us to a greater sense of self and a larger sense of meaning and purpose.

I accompanied a friend who is a minister to visit another friend who was ill. The minister laid hands over our friend's body and prayed for his healing. I observed, remaining detached from the process. Over the course of the prayer, the sick man's face softened. He relaxed. The prayer had touched him. The results of research on the power of prayer to heal are mixed and unclear. Currently, the clarity is … that there is no clarity. However, it is apparent that prayer has an impact on people who believe in it. Many people argue that any impact of prayer is merely placebo effect. People of faith dispute this, and the intellectual battle continues today—as it probably will for all the days to come.

The placebo effect is an interesting phenomenon that typically changes the physiology of a disease in a disease-specific manner. For instance, if an individual receives a placebo to reduce pain, a real biological mechanism leads to the reduction of pain. *The Lancet*, a leading journal of medical research, stated in one of their articles, "Recent research shows that placebo effects are genuine psychobiological events attributable to the overall therapeutic context, and that these effects can be robust in both laboratory and clinical settings." In other words, there are aspects of a placebo that lead directly to a biological change.

Parkinson's disease is very difficult to live with. I sat in a nursing home cafeteria with a client who suffered from Parkinson's disease, as he ate. His hand shook so badly he could barely get food to his mouth. He talked about how difficult and embarrassing it was to have his hands shake like this in public. I listened to him and supported him as he grieved about the changes his body was going through. While some people live for many years with only minor parkinsonism—shaking, rigidity, slowness of movement and difficulty with walking and gait, other people's minds shut down (depression and dementia) more and more as the disease progresses, and their bodies become rigid and waxy. One of the biological hallmarks of Parkinson's is reduction in dopamine production; this is due to the death of dopamine-generating cells in an area of the motor system called the substantia nigra (a part of the brain that modulates key aspects of movement, regulates mood and is the main center for the production of dopamine), so named because it is black to the naked eye. The brain cells are black because they are filled with dopamine, which in addition to being involved with pleasure and addiction, is a vital part of the movement system. Too little dopamine causes the body to display symptoms of Parkinsonism. Too much dopamine produces symptoms of Huntington's disease. Sufferers of Huntington's disease cannot control their movements—their bodies writhe uncontrollably in involuntary, jerky movements called chorea. As of yet, there is no cure for Huntington's; the implacable progression of this disease makes it, like Parkinson's, a very difficult disease to cope with.

Placebos can have effects even in challenging diseases such as Parkinson's; hence, researchers devised a study to determine what mechanism causes the changes a person with Parkinson's exhibits when given a placebo. In a now famous 2001 study, Raul de la Fuente-Fernandez and colleagues at the University of British Columbia in Vancouver, Canada, gave people afflicted with Parkinson's disease a placebo and measured changes in their brains as the placebo took effect. What their research uncovered is shocking in its implications: Not only did the placebo diminish the symptoms of Parkinson's; there was a substantial increase in secretion of dopamine. In other words, *the placebo affected the core difficulty of Parkinson's disease.* A patient's faith in the treatment they are receiving clearly influences their healing. Belief matters in the healing process.

As too many people know, the diagnosis of cancer can shake a person to their core, undermining their sense of connection and safety. Spiritual traditions attempt to help people connect to something larger, so they can find meaning and purpose in their suffering.

Research about the types of care people receive makes it clear that connected touch helps people feel at ease and safe. When I visit individuals in nursing facilities, it is common for a client or a family member to hold my hand as they pray. The simple, warm connection of touching hands brings about a deepening connection of hearts.

In a study conducted in Korea, thirty-nine people were interviewed in depth about the impact of touch on their healthcare. Some people were medical professionals; others were suffering from illness. Five major themes emerged from the interviews about how touch affected people's care. Touch is complex, but meaningful to people on multiple levels. The answers people gave indicated that touch promoted physical, emotional, and mind-body comfort, influenced social relationships, and provided a means of sharing spirituality. In their conclusions about their research, the authors make a significant statement: these five areas are all important treatment goals; therefore, all five areas should be targets of treatment.

Indigenous Knowledge

Meta-analysis is what researchers use as a systematic way of deriving a coherent understanding of a large body of research. A meta-analysis of the role of complementary and alternative medicine used by refugees given asylum in America, examined the findings of two-hundred-thirty-seven studies; the meta-analysis then focused on forty-seven studies that met selection criteria and found that these refugees used alternative treatments at what our culture considers a high rate. Many individuals used mind-body therapies. In thirty-six percent of the trials assessed in the meta-analysis, people were using touch treatments to address symptoms of trauma.

An acquaintance recently sent me photos of a healer he met in Bali. The healer had experienced a difficult childhood and in reaction to this, he journeyed into the forest attempting to find healing. The healer described his sojourn as learning how to heal from his *connection* with trees, plants, and animals. In his healing work, he rubs and massages herbs and poultices on those individuals willing to make the trek to his home. In no small part because of his connection to nature, this healer also enjoys a powerful connection to the people he treats.

In literature about healers, the term "indigenous knowledge" is often used. We who live in post-industrial cultures do not connect to the world in the same way. People in a more indigenous context know everyone in their community. A person's grandparent, parent, or other elder teaches them much of what they need to know, passing down the ability to carve a tool for hunting, or create a bowl for grinding grain, from generation to generation. A deep knowledge of plants, animals, and the healing arts is woven into indigenous cultures. A child learns the medicinal plants by exploring and observing with an elder, and by listening to talk around the evening fire. In many cultures, touch plays a role in these healing arts. Such a relationship with the natural world is hard for most of us to fathom from within our post-industrial mindset. Any group of humans has good and bad knowledge woven together, and it is not helpful to romanticize indigenous cultures; nonetheless, there are differences in how people learn what they know. Learning about rituals and touch that help connect and heal people is one type of indigenous knowledge. The knowledge obtained through observation and relationship with the natural world is a valid and vital form of empirical learning in indigenous *and* post-industrial cultures.

A similar type of learning happens for any healer. A doctor learns as much from her preceptors (the 'elder' doctor who mentors her during residency) as she does from medical texts. Human learning passed from one healer to another is a powerful part of the training process in any culture.

A 1979 study explored treatments offered by an indigenous healer, a shaman in Taiwan. The study's title is provocative: "Why Do Indigenous Practioners Successfully Heal?" The researchers followed the courses of treatment for twelve of the shaman's patients. Ten people reported improvement of their symptoms, stating that they were at least partially improved—despite the fact that several of these individuals had no noticeable improvement in symptoms. In fact one individual who reported improvement had become worse. The authors believe that many of the physical symptoms being treated were masking psychological symptoms. They argue that the indigenous healers were probably effecting psychological changes and improving social functioning for the individuals that showed no noticeable improvement despite reporting it. It is likely that for the individuals who reported and displayed actual improvement, there is an impact of placebo effect. It is possible that a complex interaction between placebo effect and psychological symptoms that are present may account for the impact of indigenous healers.

Healing rituals bring together symbolism, meaning, and connection with spirituality. It is important for psychologists working with cultures different from their own to find ways to adapt to their customs and patterns of healing. In many cultures, healing takes place within ritual settings. Many therapists work with non-governmental organizations to support individuals who have experienced terrible, traumatic atrocities. Our experience of trauma is influenced by meaning, or context. As Dr. Peter Levine, the founder of Somatic Experiencing™ says, "Trauma is not in the event, but in a person's reaction to the event." This means that trauma occurs within a person's cultural context. It is important for clinicians who work in varied settings to understand their patients' culture, their common beliefs about trauma, and how their culture would choose to heal trauma.

In Angola, a boy returning home from war—numb, disconnected, feeling dead inside—is taken to the House of Spirits. This structure, built by the residents on the outskirts of their village, is their site for rituals of healing and transformation. In this ritual, his grandfather presents the traumatized boy to the family's ancestral spirits, thanking them for this child's safe return. A few days later, an indigenous healer performs a cleansing. The healer leads the boy into the bush and dresses him in the filthy clothes he wore during his time at war. The healer builds a small house out of dry grass, which the boy enters to remove his dirty clothing. When the naked boy emerges to rejoin his family and community, the hut and everything he has left within, is burned. A chicken is sacrificed; the boy inhales the smoke from herbs the healer burns. Finally, the boy is bathed in clean water.

Often, individuals who have experienced trauma feel estranged from their community and culture. This boy has been through extreme traumas. Traditional western psychological healing techniques such as talking, skills development, and exposure are powerful in the treatment of trauma, and may be important for this boy. However, the symbolism in this ritual successfully mended his frayed connection with his family and his village. For this boy, the physicality of letting his clothes burn and his body be washed is steeped in meaning. There is a letting go of the past and a preparing for the renewal of entering into community life again.

The intensity of the process a ritual contains within it has many curative properties of meaning and biology. Documented reports show that symptoms of post-traumatic stress are reduced or relieved by participation in ritual ceremonies. Going through the ceremony washes away the horrors of war; now this boy sees himself, and is seen by his family and his village, as clean, forgiven and whole. For this boy from Angola, there is a reestablishment of harmony with the spirits of his ancestors. The boy is returned as a member of his family and community—able to sit with the elders and leaders in his tribe without stigma or shame.

A therapist in an indigenous community may support healing through dance, movement, art, and other expressive forms, as well as supporting the changing of experiential meaning that occurs when a person undergoes a cleansing and healing ritual. It is possible that ritual has a place in healing the wounds of trauma in industrial cultures as well. This often-ignored aspect of psychological transformation can be harnessed for victims of trauma, and even for those who suffer from illness or depression. One veteran (American) of the Iraq war transformed his uniform into art by grinding it into pulp and using the pulp to make paper. He now leads other returned soldiers through a similar process, and discusses the powerful meaning in the expression, or forcing out, of trauma through the visceral transformation of a uniform from a symbol of war, to paper, and finally to a work of art.

The Ultimate Hug

Her followers call her the hugging saint. She has hugged more than thirty-two million people in her lifetime. She has a practice of connecting, through her heart and maternal hugs, to the depth of what it means to be human. This is a difficult and real practice of looking past all the difficulties and brambles of the human heart, and opening to the willingness to love. She describes connecting to the truth through love, and she expresses this love through contact. When she visits towns and cities, thousands of people attend her gatherings. She calls the charity she founded "Embracing the World." Amṛtānandamayī Devī, fondly called Amma (mother), one of India's foremost spiritual leaders, greets the entire world with open arms.

Touched

Many people report feeling "touched" after spiritual experiences and those who follow monotheistic religions often report feeling "touched by God." This touch can be a quiet movement of inner feelings, or a palpable contact on the skin. As one client on the bodywork table reported, "I feel like I am loved again." She said this as she explored her spiritual experience of connection with something greater than herself. Her therapist gently held her shoulders to support her exploration of these feelings, as she developed and deepened this sense of meaning and connection.

There is one koan in the Zen tradition that uses touch as a doorway to the awakening experience. Koans are teaching stories intended to guide a person past their usual "reasoned" experience of the world, to an experience of connection with all beings. This koan contains an image of ten individuals jumping into a pool of cold water. As one, they jump into the pool and through the direct connection of the cold water on their skins, awaken to their true natures, seeing beyond what and who they are, and immediately connecting to all life.

This koan is an illustration of one way touch affects people. It pushes them past what they "know" to a direct, intuitive connection. In cases of hands-on healing, physical connection between healer and patient may in fact, be a catalyst for a biological change leading to healing. For some spiritual practitioners, physical touch is part of how they connect, both to each other and to their view of the Divine. Psychologists play the role of midwife in aiding psychological transformation for their clients. Psychologists with a deep understanding of the importance of touch and meaning in the process of reconnecting with life, effectively support healing for individuals feeling a disconnection between themselves and their community. Working in conjunction with a community's values and beliefs about healing, a motivated psychologist can develop truly powerful tools and techniques.

Irvin D. Yalom, Professor Emeritus of Psychiatry at Stanford University, and the preeminent researcher on group therapy, found that the fundamental curative factor in a group setting is what he calls "the universality principle." This is the connected feeling people get from discovering that others share their experience. The group context allows people to express deeply hidden feelings and find ways to see the validity of their own humanity through the experience of being a member in a community.

This same experience exists in an old folk story that crosses borders and continents. One version of this story features Solomon, the wisest of Jewish kings, and another version features the Buddha. A woman came to the healer in her community and said, "I have had a terrible loss. It is breaking my heart. I find it unbearable." The healer said to her, "I know how to heal your wound. But you must follow my instruction without fail." The suffering woman agreed. The healer then said, "Go out into the village and bring me back a single grain of rice from a house that has seen no suffering." Upon leaving, the woman immediately knocked on the door of the most prosperous person in town saying, "Please help me. Can you tell me if you have had any suffering in this house?" The woman who opened the door sobbed as she talked about the loss of her child. The woman sent by the healer sat with this devastated woman, listening and consoling. This happened over and again as she knocked on door after door. Eventually, the woman came to understand the healer's intent. She saw that all people have suffering; her suffering was part of the human suffering everyone faces. While this did not make her loss retreat, hearing the stories of others enabled her to find her own meaning and purpose in the loss she had experienced. She discovered for herself the universality principle and her shared humanity. She was 'touched' by her connection with others.

Chapter 10

Heal Thyself:
Touch Tools to Connect to Life

What role does touch play in our lives? In a simple and yet profound way, touch connects us to the world, to other people, and even to ourselves. When we arise in the morning, we feel the rough brush of a cotton shirt pulling across our shoulders, and the sensation of our feet touching the fibers of a carpet or the crispness of a hardwood floor. Touch is our contact with the world. It lets us know where we are. Even our emotions contain an element of physical sensation. When we are angry or embarrassed: our face flushing as heat rises in our body, the sensation of our jaws clenching—these are physical markers of how and what we are feeling. Extremely intense emotions can feel unbearable; it is not surprising that people turn to opiates like nicotine and heroin, or other substances like alcohol, attempting to numb the pain they feel.

We even refer to being "touched" when something affects our emotions—perhaps one of those Society for the Prevention of Cruelty to Animals or Christmas Hallmark commercials. When we pet an animal, play with a child, or make love with our spouse, touch is our medium of connection. For many of us, an accumulation of difficulties in life makes it challenging to feel connected. For some, touch feels profoundly unsafe and frightening. Others find it hard to be sure whether the touch they are experiencing is safe; they may override their inner feeling of wanting a particular type of touch to stop—thinking something like, "I *should* like it." Or a person may not be able to ask for the type of contact they most need, because they believe they *should not* need or want it."

When we refer to people who are at peace with themselves and act with confidence, we say they are "comfortable in their skin." However, some people have intellectual or emotional challenges in how they regard physical contact and the body; moreover we live in a culture where many, perhaps even most, people are chronically touch-deprived. Our culture has normalized this deprivation: We routinely move across the country for our careers, uprooting our children, leaving our extended families and our long-term friendships. These upheavals leave us bereft of those relationships in which we receive nurturing contact from others.

Thich Nhat Hanh, a Buddhist monk and peace activist, talks about learning to walk with enjoyment. He describes how walking and noticing the way our feet contact the ground, the brush of air on our face, and even the sensation of the clothes on our backs, are all doorways to happiness. *We live inside our bodies and yet we spend much of our time attempting to escape them.* Learning to connect to ourselves, each other, and our world through touch, offers the possibility of living a richer, more fulfilling life.

Jon Kabat-Zinn, a graduate of Massachusetts Institute of Technology (MIT), teaches at Harvard Medical School. He often jokes that in his mindfulness-based stress reduction classes, he teaches his students … nothing. He says people just walk around, paying attention, or just sit still … paying attention. What he has learned is powerful: Through connecting to their bodies by slowing down in this manner, learning to observe their minds instead of control them—people begin healing. Kabat-Zinn's work on "coming to the senses" is used to treat ailments from chronic pain to depression, and has changed many lives for the better. We live in our body—we cannot escape it except by dying. Learning how to connect with our body and with each other is a vital part of psychological and physiological healing.

Touch can be a critical part of healing physiological and psychological wounds, but it is equally a part of a healthy lifestyle for all individuals. Touch plays a vital role in knitting family into a unit. Touch is crucial in parenting relationships, and plays a large role in friendships. Children and adults need to learn how to have healthy, supportive contact with others, just as they must learn what unhealthy contact is and how to avoid it. Touch builds resiliency. It helps us "keep calm and carry on" through the inevitable challenges we encounter in life. Touch is part of how we engage with our world at every stage of our life.

Healthy Contact: Families, Couples and Touch

Hugs are powerful therapy, but only when they are received from, or exchanged with, people we trust. Hugs reduce stress and increase expression of the social bonding hormone, oxytocin. However, if we do not like, let alone trust a person, that hug increases our stress response rather than reducing it. Whom we feel safe with is constantly changing. In any family or couple, there are times when a hug feels unsafe or unwelcome, while at other times a hug creates safety, because our boundaries with each other are constantly shifting. We may not feel much trust after a particularly vehement argument, but when sufficient time has passed, a hug or a soft pat on the shoulder can initiate forgiveness. One key relational skill is noticing when contact feels supportive in couple or family relationship. In other words, it is important to recognize signals showing there is enough safety and trust in a moment such that contact will reduce, rather than increase, stress.

One great first step in learning to recognize how others react to touch is understanding how *you* react—what you enjoy, and how you already connect with people using touch. *The ability to pay attention and learn from life is one of the most powerful tools we have.* Most of the time, we can start by just paying attention to ourselves. The next time you get a hug, shake someone's hand, or slap the back of a friend, notice how it feels for you. Observe how the other person responds. Observe how you respond. What do you like? What don't you like? Such investigation builds good intuitions about improving your connections with beings outside yourself, human and otherwise.

The jury is in: Touch is a healthy part of family life. It is a powerful buffer against stress and emotional challenges and creates a bonded family unit. Families that go through stressful times often stop using supportive touch, which can make the stressful times even worse. One problem I often encounter in my practice with families is a lack of safe hugs. Teenagers come into my office feeling unloved, undervalued, and angry—stressed by believing they are a disappointment to their parents. Parents often feel hurt and pushed away, or even hated by the child whom they love, but who now seems like a stranger. Often, neither the teenagers nor their parents feel much inclination to offer the olive branch of forgiveness, preferring to wait until the other gives in first.

I often tell parents in this unenviable situation that four factors aid in keeping children from having major life difficulties: discipline, supervision, friendships, and regular displays of love and affection. I ask parents which factor they think is the most important. What has rigorous research shown to be the most important factor that predicts a child will avoid difficult life paths? Most parents say discipline. They are correct that discipline is vital; however, the most important factor is expressed love and affection. Without expressed love and affection, no amount of discipline will suffice.

As one of the excellent clinicians who trained me said, "There are three ways a child can hear you when you tell them "I love you." The first is saying it to them directly using spoken words. The second is saying it directly in writing and small notes. The third is saying it with hugs, kisses, and kind, caring touch. It is important to bring loving, supportive touch into a family if it is insufficient or absent. Children easily forget that they are loved: daily love and affection is crucial.

We adults forget easily too. John Gottman, a researcher who has looked extensively at what factors help couples' relationships last, discusses creating a "culture of appreciation" in relationships. This involves making moments in each day to appreciate the people around us by offering small, loving touches. The kiss on the neck of your partner when he is cleaning dishes, or the hug when your child comes home from school, these touches are as important as the food your family eats for creating a happy, healthy life together.

Touch and Learning—Early Childhood

Touch plays an important part in learning. Multiple studies show that parents who take active roles in their children's learning increase their children's ability to pay attention and learn independently. In educational literature this process is called scaffolding. Scaffolding is a parent using their own skills to extend the skills of their child. One crucial skill every child needs is paying *and sustaining* attention. Touch and human connection are vital for this process. Three factors support expansion of a child's ability to pay attention through touch and relationship—stress reduction, positive emotions, and redirecting attention. Young children can pay attention for only so long before they run off to something else. After a time, attention fatigues. Holding a child in one's lap, or just providing body contact as they read, helps redirect the child's attention when it wanders, and helps their body feel less stress reaction to new learning (which is inherently stressful), thus reducing attention fatigue. There is currently a movement in education to allow service animals to sit with young children as they read in school for just this purpose. Contact with their parent makes a child feel loved. Lots of holding, sitting closely together, and working together is vital. It actually hones the child's ability to pay attention and handle emotions. William James, known as the father of modern psychology said, "The training of attention is an education, par excellence." Through supportive touch and contact, the parent becomes scaffolding for the child's ability to pay attention and tolerate feelings. For our children, receiving good parenting is an "education par excellence."

Middle Childhood and Touch

In middle childhood, touch can be a hug when the child is upset, sitting together playing a game, wrestling or physical play, sports, high-fives, tickling matches, or playing pretend games. Proximity of parent to child still has a calming, supportive effect. I often encourage parents whose child is struggling with schoolwork to sit down at a table next to their child and do their own work. As they work together, the parent can see when the child is stuck, determine what kind of support is needed, and offer positive reinforcement to keep the child on task. Far from coddling their child into dependency, parents are thus modeling how to work, and allowing the child to learn at their own pace. It may be quite revealing for you to observe the touch occurring in your family. Some families do a lot of hugging, but not enough playful physical tussling. Some do plenty of playful tussling, but not much congratulatory touching—high-fives, fist bumps, handshakes and "atta-boys" or "atta-girls." If you notice that one or more type of healthy touch are lacking, see if you can change the culture of your family, one high-five at a time.

Change happens slowly, often encountering vehement resistance at its initiation. I have seen families become so angry that there are no hugs occurring at all. When parents start trying to change the family culture by offering daily hugs and kisses, children may protest at first, rolling their eyes, and even cursing at their parents. However, two or three weeks into the culture shift, a child who had been so angry might, as they are on their way out the door for school, ask, "Can I have my hug now?" Should she forget the good-night kiss, the child asks, "Mom, aren't you going to give me a kiss?" This is a powerful shift for a family that was previously more prone to yelling at each other than saying, "I love you."

Family Contact During Teen Years

The teen years are fraught with challenges: Teens are often awkward in their own skin, trying to find their own identity as individuals, which can make them prickly and standoffish. Adding to the awkwardness are the physical changes teens go through in puberty, which can make many fathers feel uncomfortable offering their daughters touch, and make mothers feel awkward in how they care for their teenage boys. Nevertheless, this hurdle is scalable by using safe, supportive contact. Teens need safe, loving, supportive touch—often even more than younger children, because of how awkward they feel. Teens may not need contact as often as a toddler, but they do need it regularly. Loving touch helps teens believe they are part of the family that cares for them, and is a vital factor (as is the knowledge that there will be clear, predictable consequences for their actions) in stopping a teen from making some terrible decisions.

Touch and Stages of Relationship

Healthy touch looks different at different stages of a relationship. For a new couple, touch will be frequent, a primary part of forming the relationship. For a couple that has been together for a few years, this often changes as the relationship has more business to handle, and people start taking on more defined roles. Touch can tend to fall by the wayside. Making a real effort to play together—wrestling and goofing around—as well as going on "dates" is important to keep a relationship strong through this period. Sexual intimacy is also vital in bonding. As the fire of early passion gives way to a steady connection, making sex a time of safety, exploration, and play will enable a couple in relationship to keep sex vibrant and exciting.

Tools for Creating Family Connection through Contact

Parenting is a difficult job. Even parents who agree with each other on most subjects, who enjoy great jobs and support from family, still experience stress. Most families do not have all of those circumstances in place. In truth, many families would feel lucky to have even one of them.

Stress Reduction Tools

Three types of touch-based tools help reduce a couple's stress. The first reduces long-term stress through regular practice. The second helps a couple recover from a deeply stressful event, and rebuild feelings of connection and love. The third helps a couple to discover, perhaps for the first time, how to connect with each other through touch.

Supporting Each Other to Sleep

Good sleep is often hard to come by when one or both members of a couple are under stress. It is ironic that when we are stressed and need rest the most is usually when it is most difficult to fall (and remain) asleep. Lack of sleep makes life so much more difficult. It creates a loop: we become more vulnerable, more easily overwhelmed, and more irritable, which increases our stress, thus making it even harder to sleep. Fortunately, touch can improve sleep patterns.

Foot Massage: As Simple as It Sounds

Materials: lotion, a towel and a willing partner

In the evening after a stressful day, ask your partner if they have enough energy to help you fall asleep. Describe this tool for your partner, telling them how it will help you. About an hour before going to sleep, turn down the lights in the house so the lighting is dim. If possible, turn off the television, or at least reduce the volume. About thirty minutes before sleep, as you get ready for bed, gently remind your partner that you are overly stressed and a foot massage will help you sleep well. Ready the materials for your partner, put the towel under your feet, and remember to thank your partner in advance—as well as after the fact—an appreciated partner will be more likely to do this for you again! Do not forget to show your partner when something they are doing feels good, whether with words, or simply a sigh. This will help your partner learn what your body likes. Remember to tell your partner that you will return the favor, and follow through on that promise.

For the Willing Partner: Offering Massage

Most people tend to enjoy firm, broad pressure that moves at a moderate pace over the skin. The best way to begin is by asking your partner what feels good to them. Sometimes it is good to just hold solid, broad pressure for a few seconds before using lotion and starting massage. (Remember to warm your hands by rubbing them briskly, or dipping them in warm water before offering foot massage. Our feet have numerous temperature sensors and therefore are quite sensitive to cold.) One guide for giving a good massage or making good contact is noticing the breath. If your partner takes a deep breath, sighs, or relaxes their upper body tension, you know you are moving in the right direction. Remember the moves or techniques that make your partner feel good and use them again another time. Another important clue for giving good, connected touch is noticing how you feel inside, that is, keep part of your attention within yourself as you massage your partner.

Increasing Connection through Touch

Life is full of things that make it difficult for couples to feel connection with each other. One way to increase connection is to offer more regular affection such as hugs, kisses on the shoulder, pats on the back, flirtatious touches, or sitting close to each other while watching television together. However, couples often do not really know how to give or receive supportive touch. This tool of regular, affectionate touch supports couples in learning how to feel increased connection with each other, and how to offer or receive touch in ways that feel supportive.

Creating Connection: Offering and Receiving Touch

Materials: two people and twenty minutes

It may sound obvious; nonetheless, it is important to note that paying attention to good feelings engenders more good feelings. Our minds are primed to look for problems. This can mean that we often ignore good feelings when they occur, making us more vulnerable to stress, and our relationship more vulnerable to conflict. Recognizing and acknowledging good feelings helps a couple pay more attention to their connection. This feeling of connection reduces the intensity of arguments, and makes people more invested in supporting each other. Good touching increases expression of the bonding hormone oxytocin, creating feelings of trust and closeness.

Offering and Receiving Touch: How to Practice the Skill

This technique develops the skill of connected touch. Remember to check in with your *feelings*, not with your thoughts—your body will be a stronger guide than your mind in this exercise.

BUILDING CONNECTION EXERCISE

- Decide who will offer supportive touch first and who will receive touch first.
- The person receiving touch guides the touch.
- The guide identifies an area to receive touch by examining the feelings in their body (the body will be a more effective place to look for signals in this exercise than the mind).

- The guide then asks for contact on the part of their body that feels it would enjoy it the most. Remember to tell your partner what type of contact you would like.
- The member of the couple giving touch offers contact to the specified area.
- The guide then asks the partner to shift the pressure, type of contact, and/or area of contact until the contact is "just right."
- The person offering touch complies, moving and changing the contact until it is "just right."
- When the contact feels right, the guide pays attention to the connection—how it feels to have contact that is right for them, and asks for small adjustments as their feelings change.
- The person offering touch notices the feeling of connection. Even if the sense of connection is minimal, or other feelings like fear or desire arise, just let those feelings be there, and continue paying close attention to the feeling of connection.
- The partners then make eye contact for thirty seconds to one minute, paying attention to any feeling of contact and closeness, even if it is small and fleeting.
- After a few minutes, the guide checks in with their body and finds another place that would feel supported by contact from their partner. The process repeats.
- The partners switch roles.

Reconnection After Stress: Forgiveness and Contact

Relationships are often wonderful, but just as frequently, living with other people is slightly annoying or even entirely irritating. It is just part of the human condition. Each of us is both quite wonderful and a bit of a nincompoop. Some fortunate people are masters at relationship; they experience less conflict, more fun and longer relationships. Until recently, it was unclear what they were doing to make them so successful in relationship.

Enough research has now been done for us to identify many of the good habits practiced by people with good relationship skills. One of the most important habits is relationship repair. Repair occurs after a conflict. When a conflict is *overtly* over, some people *covertly* stew in their unresolved anger. Others look at their own mistakes, accept responsibility for those mistakes, and begin repairing the relationship. However, there is no tool for convincing another person to allow repair to occur. For repair to happen, both people have to be willing. Physical contact can be a powerful way to repair after arguing, once people are willing to let repair happen. If a child acts out, effective parents elicit a verbal apology, then ask the child for a hug and reaffirm their love. The same is true in adult relationships.

Usually, during and after an argument, every person involved feels he or she is in the right. Therefore, making a move towards peace is difficult, albeit a worthy choice. The best and most effective way out of an argument is for both people to take responsibility, apologize for their part in the argument, and then take time to reconnect physically, even if only with a sincere hug. Relationships that repair after a conflict are much healthier and stronger than relationships that try to avoid conflict altogether. After conflict, it is important to let your partner know that you still love him or her. Additionally, it is crucial not to behave like a doormat (letting your partner walk all over you), or allow yourself to fall into the trap of anger and retaliation. Both of these behaviors will significantly corrode any relationship over time. Instead, let your partner know what you believe would help avoid the conflict in the future, and apologize for any overly aggressive statements you made in support of your point of view; however, unless it has changed, do not apologize for your point of view: it shares equal validity with that of your partner.

After the verbal expression is accomplished, there are two possible routes back to connected relationship. Some people find they need time before they feel ready to work on repair. If that is true for you, take time away from the relationship (go for a walk, read: whatever activity will feel better than what you are currently doing); when enough time has passed, make a moment to reconnect to your partner with a hug, by holding a hand, or verbally expressing your love. This allows both people to begin feeling their connection again. We often have mixed feelings after conflict; it is important to acknowledge them, and during the process of repair, to focus attention on feelings of safety and connection through touch.

Destructive Touch

It is important to note here that some relationships, despite the qualities of the people in them, are not healthy. If your spouse, partner, or lover hits or otherwise intimidates you physically or verbally, it is a clear indication that this relationship is not safe. The first action to take is connecting with a nearby support system for people who are experiencing partner abuse and making a safety plan. There are support systems in your area: look on the internet or in a phonebook.

When experiencing an abusive relationship, it is normal to feel confusion and believe that increasing your love and affection will stop your partner's violent behaviors. What really happens is the rupture-repair cycle becomes destructive. Instead of repair and change in behaviors, the couple falls into a repetitive cycle of violence. The abuser hurts their partner, thus relieving their own stress; that relief allows them to calm, becoming loving and nurturing. The abuser may beg for forgiveness and promise that their abusive behavior will never happen again. A honeymoon period follows, only to inevitably crumble under rebuilding tension. During this phase, conflict increases until again erupting into violence. Then the cycle starts again—except it often worsens—because the couple "normalizes" or habituates to the abuse.

If any of the above situations describe your relationship, please contact a local abuse hotline and seek help from a licensed therapist.

Touch: Habits for Long-Term Relationships

If you remember all the way back to the early chapters about touch and its vital role in human development, you may remember the studies of families that measured how frequently family members gave small, affectionate touches. It is clear that these touches make the family or couple healthier; people who touch often report liking their partner more than do people in couples who do not practice frequent touch. Obviously a resilient relationship can weather storms more easily than can a stressed relationship. When you work on strengthening your relationship, you are investing in your future happiness, just as you save part of your paycheck for your retirement. You are making your life and your family's life easier and far more enjoyable over the long-term.

FOUR TOUCH HABITS
TO STRENGTHEN RELATIONSHIPS

One—Practice regular, safe, affectionate touch: If you make the culture of your relationship a culture of appreciation, your relationship will be stronger. We humans often say, "I love you" and those words are very important, but touch communicates love directly—heart-to-heart. Building affectionate touch into your relationship is not complicated; for the closest relationships in your life, give a pat on the shoulder, a hug, a kiss, and so forth, several times every day. At first, it may be hard to remember to do this, and it may even feel a little awkward. One of the best ways to build a new habit is to make a time for reflection about your successes each day. For the first couple of weeks, at the end of each day ask yourself how often you gave your partner affectionate touch. If it was more than five times, give yourself a pat on the back! If it was less, make an agreement with yourself to increase it the next day. Habit One is very much like putting money in the bank and may well enable your relationship to survive, even thrive and grow, after a "live" stress test.

Two—After a stressful period, reconnect: All people experience stress, but when it is over, make time to reconnect with loved ones. Spend time with your partner. Give a massage. Ask for a massage. Stress pushes us out of our social bonding system. It can also deplete a relationship's emotional reserve. After a relationship experiences and survives stress is always a good time to go back to basics! Get good rest, good food, good sleep, good play, and make time to connect with each other at a body-to-body level.

Three—Do not forget about playful touch: Flirting is enjoyable and touch is a wonderful way to flirt and play with your partner.

Four—Build a touch love map: John Gottman talks about "touch love maps" as being an important tool. We all like people who know us deeply. It helps us feel cherished and appreciated. The way we like being touched, or the way our partners like being touched in relationships, is often unknown territory to everybody involved. Some couples forget to touch each other unless they are having sex. Some partners have not learned to recognize what their partner likes and doesn't like when they touch them. If you pay attention to what your partner likes, you can begin offering touch, love, and support that helps make your partner feel understood and truly cherished. *Paying attention is one of the best, perhaps even the very best habit for making your relationship last.*

A good way to begin building a touch love map is to simply start paying close attention to what touch makes your partner feel good. As we learned before, deep breaths, increased eye contact, relaxing, soft sighs, or moving into your touch are all good indications (although not foolproof!) of what feels good to your partner. After paying this close attention, make a small list of the types of touch your partner likes at different times: when you are having sex, when you are in public, when joking around, when driving, when stressed, or when working together on a project. I know it sounds simplistic, but offer your partner more of the touch they like and less of what they do not! This will have a powerful effect on love and connection in your relationship.

Touch in Family:
Parents and Children Building Attachment for a Lifetime

Our early relationships are where we learn how to be in relationship. The feelings of safety, connection, and support that begin in infancy play out over a lifetime. During the early 20th century, the assumption was that children needed food and water, but not love and affection. In fact, doctors of the time went so far as to suggest that parents not touch their children except with a handshake or a pat on the head. This extended to how children were treated in hospital. Children in hospital were kept away from their families due to the belief that if parents visited, it made the child more upset after they left. Children could spend many months alone in hospital cared for only by strangers. What researchers of attachment discovered was that children left alone in hospital did not form healthy social bonds. Like children growing up in orphanages, they never learned feelings of safety and support in their relationships or, more simply described—they never learned to feel love. Fortunately, today a hospitalized child would never be left alone for even days, let alone for months.

Many individuals face traumatic events during their early childhood, which can affect their ability to feel safe, and to support nurturing interaction with their own children. Other individuals did grow up in supportive homes, but still never learned how to connect with their children. We can help children build strong, healthy attachments by modeling supportive interaction.

Some touch-based tools parents can utilize to aid them in connecting to their children are used for soothing their child and reducing stress, reconnection after discipline, and supporting resilience. These tools are not rocket science. In truth, many families use some or all of them (albeit not necessarily systematically or enough). Understanding and practicing the principles behind touch-based tools will guide and support parents in building safe bonds in their family that will last not only for their lifetime, but for generations to come.

First and foremost, it is crucial to have safe touch between children and their parents. Safety is an interesting concept. It is feeling that things are going to be okay. Many children report feeling safe even when things are stressful, because of their confidence in their parents and the resultant trust that things will work out. Establishing safety does not mean everything in life must be perfect, but it does require some key factors. The first is that a child is *seen*—that his or her reactions and opinions are considered. All children have different experiences of the world. Part of the job of being a parent is helping your child grow in new ways; an equally important job is discovering your child's likes and dislikes. Children whose parents pay attention and help them discover who they are, feel stronger and more confident, and face challenges with more ease. As a parent, you can learn along with your child. This is true for touch and physical support as well.

In my early twenties, I worked with children in an afterschool program. In the afternoon, I would collect the children from kindergarten and take them to a small playground. The kids loved the playground. They made up fortresses, fought dragons, and loved playing tag. Every so often, during a rough and tumble day of fun, a child would fall and scrape a knee. Some children really needed support; they would want a hug, or to hold my hand as we went to the office to get a Band-Aid. Some children hated that type of support. They wanted to be left alone until they got their Band-Aid. As an instructor in this program, it was important that I *saw* each child and understood his or her needs. Over time, this helped the children feel safe. I taught this skill to the children I worked with. Many of them would want to run to a friend and help after a fall. I taught them to ask if their friend wanted their support, or to be given space. It was profound when I first heard a five-year-old boy ask his friend, "Do you want me to just sit here, give you space, or do you want a hand up?"

Touch and physical contact can feel intrusive. One of the most difficult aspects of working with children is that their boundaries change all the time. One day a hug feels like it saved the child's world. In another moment on another day, a hug is rejected as "baby" stuff. Parents have to stay alert and find ways to adapt their interventions to the changing needs of their children. A child's reactions will indicate if touch is feeling intrusive. If a child's body becomes tense, it may indicate that the contact feels invasive. If a child's body becomes tense and then goes limp, it often means that they felt scared, but were too overwhelmed to tell you; their fear overrode their needs. When contact feels safe, the child will often move closer or relax into the contact, as opposed to going limp, which is quite different. Often when a child feels supported through touch, their breathing slows and deepens. It is not uncommon for children (and adults) who are very stressed or hurt to begin crying when contact feels safe, and they can finally let go.

Making the Emotional Sound Track of Life

I remind parents that *the words they say to their children become the words their children will say to themselves* when they become adults.

Parents' voices become part of the fabric of thoughts—the inner voice in a child's mind. Children, along with internalizing the words their parents utter, internalize feelings. Some researchers consider feelings—emotions—a vital part of thinking. Feelings or emotions set the tone, thus they help a child determine what response would be the most appropriate.

Where do we learn which actions go with which emotions? We learn through our interactions with friends, family, and other adults. Many people have difficult emotions playing in their minds, and in the same manner as a reel-to-reel tape; people can loop, or ruminate over negative and unrealistic thoughts. While it is entirely possible to change our emotion and thought tapes in adulthood, as parents, we have the opportunity to support good emotional tapes in a child's mind from day one!

Building good emotion tapes is simple: The first step is to spend time in positive emotions. Again, this is simple. If we spend more time in positive actions and emotions such as play and joy, we have more play and joy on our tape! This is true for adults as well as children, but children are more open to learning new tapes than are most adults. Spending more time in positive emotions is akin to the way frequent demonstrations of love and affection between two people will strengthen their relationship. Parents can offer hugs, kisses, and loving contact to their child many times throughout each day. Here is the good news: When parents provide this type of love and support to their children, they feel better too. Offering love makes us feel good— what a great deal!

Building good emotional loops for children through touch can begin very early with infant massage (this also helps babies with challenges in sleeping or eating). The supportive massage builds feelings of being loved, supported, and cared for in relationship. It programs positive emotion tapes. Parents can learn infant massage from a video or class, and it is a lot of fun! In the medical office where I work, whenever there is a newborn, doctors bring the infant around to all the staff. The doctors joke that we are getting a "baby" contact-high. In truth, we are. Simply seeing, smelling (you know which end smells best!), and smiling at a brand-new baby increases our expression of oxytocin.

Teaching Siblings About Touch

I was talking with the parents of two young children. One of their children is four-years old and the other is six. The four-year-old girl dotes on her older brother. She follows him wherever he goes. When the parents try to teach their girl something, it takes time. But! When her brother does it in front of her, she learns it in seconds. That is the power of the sibling relationship. While many siblings experience conflict with each other (often competing for their parents' attention), siblings play a powerful role each other's development. At a holiday celebration this year, I saw four sisters, now all over forty, laughing and talking together, draped over each other on the couch. Contact and closeness are important parts of sibling relationships, but some children are not given much guidance about how to connect with each other through touch.

Parents can teach children from a young age to observe how their touch and contact affects other people and animals. What children learn from their brothers and sisters lasts a lifetime, and will have much more immediate impact than anything their parents say. An older sibling can be more effective than parents at showing a younger sibling how to pet a dog or a cat. Like "mini-parents," siblings can teach each other about the impact of touch, as well as how to give "good" touch.

Touch is often about attunement. Think of turning a radio dial until it lands on a clear signal. In a relationship, people send signals all the time. They indicate what they like, what they don't like, what makes them angry, and what makes them happy. Attunement is learning to recognize the signals coming from other people. Children can learn to recognize these signals in their siblings.

Parents of young children can be good models of safe contact. They can ask a child how certain contact feels. They can demonstrate the signals that show when touch and contact feel good to others; for example, "Look! Your sister liked it when you gave her a hug. She smiled and took a deep breath." Parents can also build a young child's ability to assess their effect on an animal when they pet it by asking them, "Can your eyes see if (animal's name) likes it?" I talk to older children about how sometimes hugs feel good and other times they don't. I ask them to figure out how they know when they like being hugged and when they do not. It is also important to ask them how they know what their brother or sister likes.

Educating the Next Generation: Teaching Healthy Touch

While the majority of human touch is healthy, touch can be violent, and damaging. There are people whose bodies and psyches have been profoundly hurt by touch. There are many who live with internal wounds from not having their body's basic needs respected by the very people who should have been protecting and caring for them. Such tragic situations have led to a taboo: People do not talk about touch or what healthy touch is. We as a culture have thrown out the baby with the bathwater. It is quite possible that by not being taught about healthy touch and contact, our children are more at risk of being inappropriately touched.

What is healthy touch? It is contact that respects the integrity of another person's boundaries. Touch builds social connection. It also helps people learn to respect themselves and have compassion for their own needs. As we teach our children how to touch, we can also teach them how to respect other people's boundaries. It is crucial to teach children about "red and green flags" regarding touch and contact with peers and adults. If they experience "red flag" touch, children must know and feel safe to tell their parents or another adult immediately.

Teaching Children Red Flag Touch

- Being forced or coerced in any way to hug or touch someone (peer or adult) is a red flag. Acceptable contact only occurs when there is safety. Safety requires respect for the boundaries of both parties.
- Children need to learn about types of touch that are off limits (contact with private parts, or removing clothes). *Parents protect their children by making it safe for children to talk to them.* Parents should

teach their children that if anyone attempts to touch them under their clothes or near their private parts, the child must tell their parent or another safe adult immediately.

- Threats are a huge red flag. Children need to know to tell their parents or another safe adult immediately if another child or an adult threatens them.

Teaching children how to recognize unhealthy touch will help parents keep children safe. Many children do not know which types of touch are acceptable and which are not, and this can make the child feel confused if an adult or peer crosses a boundary. If children are taught to distinguish good touch from bad and have trusted adult confidants, they are much more likely to stay safe than if this topic is ignored.

Emotion Regulation and Touch

Children can also learn to help themselves manage their emotions. Finding safe, supportive contact can help them reach this goal. In order to attend school, children need to be able to sit in a chair, receive criticism from teachers, and manage conflict with peers. Children can learn to recognize when they are overwhelmed by emotion. We have all witnessed a two-year-old having a meltdown. Face flushed with anger, they stomp and cry and yell about something that they won't even care about in another hour. Parents can help children recognize signs that they are feeling bad (anger makes the face feel hot) and help them think of ways to get support. Parents can ask their child a series of questions that help the child find a better way to calm down: "When you get mad, what do you feel inside?" The parent can sit with the child and make a drawing of the feeling together. Parents can tell their child what they themselves feel like inside when they are angry. The next important question to ask is, "Does it feel good or bad to be (angry/upset/sad/hurt)?" Most children will say "bad" quite promptly. Parents can then help children think of things they could do to help themselves feel better or worse. Things that help children feel better might include getting a hug from mommy or daddy, spending quiet time with a toy, reading a book with their parent, hugging a stuffed animal, or throwing a ball in the back yard. Things that might make the feeling get worse might include yelling, breaking things, fighting with a sibling, sulking, and so forth. Parents can help children figure out their best choices for managing intense feelings.

Developing Self-Regulation

Many parents mistakenly believe that if they help their child to feel better, their child will become weak. It is quite the opposite. Every time children experience the cycle of intense feeling and returning to rest, they are increasing their ability to be self-regulating. Self-regulation is the ability to manage a wide range of emotional experiences and stressful events through inner resources, support from family and friends, and implementing behaviors that help a person feel better after a difficult event. Parents can help children learn to be self-regulating through five processes:

- Validate a child's experience (not the same as agreeing with the child). Validating is recognizing the child's experience and their emotional reactions while understanding the connection between events and the emotions. A statement like, "I see you are upset that I did not buy a toy. I know you are disappointed." is a validating statement, but it does not give in to the child's demand for a new toy.
- Help a child recognize the signs of feeling good versus feeling bad.
- Help a child learn to make choices that make him or herself feel better.
- Help a child recognize that all feelings change, and that even the worst feelings will change to good or neutral feelings eventually. Parents can point out this shift as it happens: "You were so mad twenty minutes ago! Isn't it nice that you are feeling better now? Isn't it good to know that bad feelings change?"
- Help a child recognize their successes in handling their emotions effectively.

Touch plays an important role in this process. It is one of the most effective tools for helping a child shift from a difficult emotion to feeling safe again. Being held is vital for young children. For older children, an adult willing to sit with a hand on their back or shoulder and bear witness to their feelings—without trying to change them—can be truly profound. It communicates to the child that the adult trusts them to make it through the difficult emotion, while giving the child support for the process. Over time, these interactions train the child's innate ability to regulate their emotions. The child's body will naturally express more oxytocin, reducing cortisol levels as the front brain engages to regulate emotion.

Touched by Knowledge

Touch is not just a part of learning in the home; *it is a part of learning!* The quality of touch younger children receive directly impacts their educational outcomes. Recall the study wherein a teacher began offering more supportive touch to her students, and the children with the worst behavioral problems shifted and exhibited fewer problem behaviors. This is profound and has important implications for education and parenting.

Experts argue that the frontal lobes of the brain are highly involved in learning and attention. While the brain is highly complex and there may be many other systems involved in attention, the mainstream biological explanation of attention deficit hyperactivity disorder (ADHD) is that children with ADHD lack dopamine, leading to under-activation of the frontal lobes. If dopamine is increased with medication, the frontal lobes become more active. While no one would suggest that touch cures ADHD, safe, physical contact is associated with increased activation in the frontal lobes. It may be that increasing ability to regulate emotion by using touch helps increase attention and learning abilities. It is well-documented that reducing stress response can increase cognitive ability, such as the rate of solving math problems or the ability to sustain focus. It is probable that a teacher who walks by a struggling student and offers a brief, supportive pat on the back will help the child maintain attention for a little longer.

Self-Help through Touch: Tools for a Happy Life

Touch is a powerful tool for increasing happiness and a vital aspect of good quality of life. Our current culture often leaves us isolated and touch-deprived. We tend to have more physical contact with people that we feel safe with, but frequently life journeys involve moving away from family and childhood friends. Changes in when people marry, how long they stay married, and how often they remarry, profoundly impact family relationships. The current trend of changing jobs more frequently over our working-lives makes it likely we will be working with, attending school with, and living in community with people we have known for less time. All these factors can reduce the amount of touch people enjoy in their lives. So what can we do?

We can find ways to increase our contact with others. Massage and bodywork increase the amount of healthy touch one experiences and have a powerful impact on physical and mental health. We can participate in sports and activities, thus meeting people with whom we can socialize. As these relationships mature, they will probably include more contact. We can increase the contact we get through giving, and thus receiving more hugs. No one wants a hug forced upon him or her, but more people than you probably realize are open to hugging. We can use touch as a part of our self-care. We need enough good food, enough good sleep, enough exercise, enough play, and enough love. By making contact and physical support part of our daily self-care, we can build up resources in our "resiliency bank."

Getting the Most Out of Affection

Most of us have some affection in our lives, although given our current culture, many of us experience far less touch and affection than we really need. It is possible to increase the amount of affection we get in our day-to-day life, and meanwhile we can get the most out of the affection we do receive. Even if we already enjoy a lot of affection and caring touch, we can help ourselves "take in" more of the nurturing we receive.

The key to this skill is learning to *manage our attention*. Depending on how we use our attention, we can get more or less benefit from our connection with others. At any moment in time, we are paying attention to something. Often, when we give or receive casual affection, our concern about the appropriateness of the hug or pat on the shoulder can engage our entire mental field. In other words, we pay attention to only the negative feelings. At other times, the affection just happens, but our attention is skipping off to another thing and missing the moment that we are in. Learning to shift our attention and learning to stay present in the moment will help us get the most benefit from the affection we receive.

We can move our attention around in the same way we move our eyes. I can focus on sounds in the room. I can focus on the words on this page. I can focus on my own thoughts. I can focus on how my body feels as I sit in this chair. Most of us, most of the time, let our attention be dragged about hither and yon out of habit. However, we can begin consciously shifting our attention to help ourselves. When feeling stressed, we tend to focus all our attention on the stressful thoughts or feelings. Learning to shift our attention away from these feelings and thoughts to a more pleasant feeling or helpful thought will help us shift our mood. Being conscious of our attention can have a similar effect on how we receive and give affection.

When you give a hug, a high-five, or even a handshake, you can move your attention to any aspect of the event. You could for instance, focus solely on the nose of the person you are talking with, ignoring everything else, although I would not suggest it. You can focus on some discomfort you are feeling; this will have a predictable effect. However, you can just as easily focus on the connection you feel with another being. Let yourself be a detective; find out what is it like to feel connection and safety when contacting another person. Next time you are with a friend and give them a hug, notice the sensations in your body that let you know you are in contact with them. Let yourself pay full attention to the positive feelings of contact and get the most out of the touch you are receiving!

Getting Your Mind Out of Stress and Your Body Relaxed

Touch and physical contact can be a very good distraction for us. Sometimes it is necessary to shift our minds away from a difficulty. There are many ways we can use touch to accomplish this. We can pay attention to how our feet contact the ground, or touch a cold table and notice the sensations. Often the sensations of contact can override, however briefly, the difficult sensations of an emotion. A warm shower is a great self-soothing tool. Feeling one's contact with a chair can help, as can massage of one's feet or hands. I often recommend a foot massage for difficulty falling asleep: get a lotion you enjoy, sit on the edge of your bed or a couch, and rub your feet one at time. Notice any tight or sore spots and use the massage to help them relax a bit. Alternatively (if there are no witnesses), lie on your back on the bed with your feet in the air and massage them. Then just shake and kick your legs wildly in the air as though you were an infant again. Trust me, you will feel entirely different (in a good way) if you try this.

The skill of distraction requires two parts to make it as effective as humanly possible. These are both ways of using your attention wisely: being one-hundred percent mindful of what you are currently doing (staying entirely present in the moment), and being one-hundred percent unmindful of the difficult feelings. This is a wonderful skill to shift our minds out of a "rumination loop" whenever we feel stuck.

Touch During Pregnancy—Growing a Family

When one of my dear friends was pregnant, she talked about how her body just hurt and how uncomfortable she was. As a massage therapist, I supported many women through their pregnancies. All too often, a mother-to-be would arrive at the office stressed and overwhelmed. I would sit and listen to her for a moment to understand what she needed. As the massage helped relax tight tissues in her body, I could see and *feel* the layers of stress drain away. A couple can easily learn pregnancy massage; however, it is important to learn the correct techniques: what to watch out for, and which areas of the body to avoid. Loving contact like pregnancy massage can buttress a relationship against the exhausting and stressful period that follows the arrival of a newborn human being.

Touch can play a vital part in the birthing process. One man I spoke with recently told me that while she was in labor, his wife nearly broke a bone in his hand during her contractions. Touch can help the body soothe through this stressful event. Many childbirth classes teach these techniques. Support and pressure in the right areas can help a woman in labor tolerate difficult sensations.

After their birth, it is important that the newborn be placed on the mother's chest or body for skin-to-skin contact. This will increase bonding between mother and child and even help the infant's development. Infant massage can help "grow" a baby—increasing weight and length at a faster pace. What's more, parents report that massaging their baby just feels good.

Romantic Bonding

She had just started the relationship and she wasn't yet sure if he was "the one" for her. She liked him and felt good with him, but still, she had doubts. At the same time, he felt close to her and enjoyed her company, but wondered whether she was right for him. He experienced her as smart and kind, but he still wasn't sure about the long-term. During this critical time in relationship, touch plays an important role. We make contact with people when we feel safe. The level of safety we feel helps us discern whether a relationship is right. Touch increases oxytocin and that neurochemical, along with vasopressin, is integral to connection. However, it is not just any touch that enhances social bonding—it is *attuned* touch.

When a couple holds hands, either there is a feeling of connection, or there isn't. Attunement is the ability to recognize and understand the emotional state of another and to enter into that state to some degree. This can happen through the simple act of holding hands. Touch can be wildly disconnected, or highly attuned, and most people feel the difference very quickly. To a large extent (besides breaking social norms of touch), the primary difference between a touch that feels creepy and a touch that feels enjoyable, is the quality of attunement. Most people can feel this in a handshake. Many of us have experienced shaking hands with, or hugging someone who is not connected or attuned—it just feels … off. Happily, the reverse occurs when we are in contact with attuned romantic partners.

One of the most challenging aspects of early bonding in relationships is that stress makes it harder to attune. Imagine that you are in college; you are approaching someone to whom you are deeply attracted, with the intention of asking for a date. Your heart pounds, your breathing is rapid, and your palms are sweaty. This is a normal stress response, making it harder to find the right words, and, worse yet, making it difficult for our bodies to attune. This can make even the most interesting conversation feel awkward. However, if we master those intense feelings and remain engaged, we enter the zone or "flow" state, which can be an intoxicating way to begin a romantic relationship. In early social bonding, touch plays two major roles. It helps us soothe ourselves and stay in an emotional state that enables us to reach attunement, and it helps create a sense of connection and love. This is important—even for two people who have been together for years. Building connection through attuned touch can rekindle a spark dimmed by the business of life.

Play in Adulthood

Play is one of the most important and sadly, most ignored aspects of adult life. Touch is a part of all play. Even if we are just playing a video game, *our body* is playing the game. There are many ways to increase touch-based play, but most important is recognizing when you are not getting enough touch and play and finding ways to increase both!

Touch for Eldership

With the exception of Dorian Gray, we all age, and for many of us, our connections with others change. We lose close friends and family more often. While many people reach their elder years with all of their physical and cognitive abilities intact, many do not. As family or friends of an elder, we can create opportunities to connect through safe, supportive contact.

I sat with a woman who had mid-stage Alzheimer's disease. She was weeping because she was so scared about the changes her mind was going through. I just sat with her and held her hand as she cried and talked about her fears, her losses, and what she wished she were doing instead of suffering this disease. At one point, she was able to find a bright spot of meaning in her losses, and look for ways to connect with what she cared about most—her family. We did a life review and looked at everything she had accomplished and the things in which she took the most pride. There were quite a lot. As her disease progressed and she lost more and more of her words, I showed her children other ways to feel their connection with her. I taught them to feel the contact of holding her hand and walking with her. I explained that there is more to a relationship than remembering a name. I have cared for many patients with Alzheimer's who never remembered my name, but they remembered our relationship.

I taught a husband whose wife was experiencing cognitive changes to give her hand and foot massages; this allowed them to feel their connection and closeness even as she lost more of her memories of their life together. There are always two parts of a relationship; one is facts and memories and the other is the experience of the relationship in the moment. Despite her cognitive decline, this woman was *present* for that relationship. It is very important to understand that the brain circuit responsible for verbal memory is not the same circuit responsible for emotional memory. Even if verbal memory becomes damaged or is lost altogether, often the memories for emotional connection remain.

Touch is Vital—Even at the End

Touch is an important part of the process of dying. I sat with a dying woman. Her breath hitched in her chest. As I held her hand, her breathing became steadier. I thought of the work we had done together and the connection we had formed, and spoke about that to her. As I held her hand, she seemed to fluctuate in and out of awareness, at times surfacing enough for eye contact, then drifting again into the vast sea of her inner world. Holding the hand of a loved one during this passage can be a powerful gift for everyone. Touch can help a dying person face their ending with equanimity. Touch can be an anchor of safety, love, and connection as consciousness fluctuates. Touch can assure people that even as they leave this world, they are loved.

Concluding Contact

Touch is woven into the fabric of what it is to be alive. At a biological level, it provides protection against stress, and builds resiliency in the face of many difficulties. Even casual contact sparks a neurobiological cascade. Psychology, despite its successes in reducing suffering from mental illness or overwhelming challenges, has ignored this deep and powerful part of human life for far too long. Despite its importance in human development, it has been only within recent years that psychology has dared put forth suggestions about what type of touch benefits the health of infants, children, adults, couples, and families. Psychology has too often ignored the importance of touch, focusing only on verbal communication, leaving some people with unresolved trauma, and others feeling disconnected from their body—unable to recognize and experience safe touch in relationship. Research on touch is still in its infancy, but even so, its role in human health and happiness is clear and indisputable.

Touch matters. Touch is a vital part of experiencing meaning, purpose, and joy in our life. Touch is the first sensation we experience when we arrive into this world, and the last sensation we experience when we depart this life. Touch keeps us present, mindful of our common human bond—enabling us to experience our connection with ourselves, with each other, and with our world—directly, authentically, and profoundly.

References

Chapter 1

46 Smith, E. (1870). *On the wasting diseases of infants and children.* Henry C. Lea.

46 Field, T. (2001). Violence and touch deprivation in adolescents. *Adolescence, 37*(148), 735-749.

46 Barber, B. K., & Thomas, D. L. (1986). Dimensions of fathers' and mothers' supportive behavior: The case for physical affection. *Journal of Marriage and the Family*, 783-794.

46 Dainton, M., Stafford, L., & Canary, D. J. (1994). Maintenance strategies and physical affection as predictors of love, liking, and satisfaction in marriage. *Communication Reports, 7*(2), 88-98.

46 Durana, C. (1998). The use of touch in psychotherapy: Ethical and clinical guidelines. *Psychotherapy: Theory, Research, Practice, Training, 35*(2), 269.

46 Wilson, J. M. (1982). The value of touch in psychotherapy. *American Journal of Orthopsychiatry, 52*(1), 65-72.

47 Geib, P. G. (1982). *The experience of nonerotic physical contact in traditional psychotherapy: A critical investigation of the taboo against touch* (Doctoral dissertation, ProQuest Information & Learning).

47 Gleeson, M., & Timmins, F. (2005). A review of the use and clinical effectiveness of touch as a nursing intervention. *Clinical Effectiveness in Nursing, 9*(1), 69-77.

47 DeCasper, A. J., & Fifer, W. P. (1980). Of human bonding: Newborns prefer their mothers' voices. *Science, 208*(4448), 1174-1176.

48 Pereira, P. K., Lovisi, G. M., Lima, L. A., Legay, L. F., de Cintra Santos, J. F., Santos, S. A., ... & Valencia, E. (2011). Depression During Pregnancy: Review of Epidemiological and Clinical Aspects in Developed and Developing Countries. *PSYCHIATRIC DISORDERS–TRENDS AND DEVELOPMENTS, 267.*

49 Lundy, B. L., Jones, N. A., Field, T., Nearing, G., Davalos, M., Pietro, P. A., ... & Kuhn, C. (1999). Prenatal depression effects on neonates. *Infant Behavior and Development, 22*(1), 119-129.

49 Field, T., Diego, M., Dieter, J., Hernandez-Reif, M., Schanberg, S., Kuhn, C., ... & Bendell, D. (2004). Prenatal depression effects on the fetus and the newborn. *Infant Behavior and Development, 27*(2), 216-229.

49 O'Connor, T. G., Heron, J., Golding, J., Beveridge, M., & Glover, V. (2002). Maternal antenatal anxiety and children's behavioural/emotional problems at 4 years Report from the Avon Longitudinal Study of Parents and Children. *The British Journal of Psychiatry, 180*(6), 502-508.

49　O'Connor, T. G., Heron, J., Golding, J., & Glover, V. (2003). Maternal ante-natal anxiety and behavioral/emotional problems in children: a test of a programming hypothesis. *Journal of Child Psychology and Psychiatry, 44*(7), 1025-1036.

49　Field, T., Diego, M., Hernandez-Reif, M., Salman, F., Schanberg, S., Kuhn, C., ... & Bendell, D. (2002). Prenatal anger effects on the fetus and neonate. *Journal of Obstetrics & Gynecology, 22*(3), 260-266.

51　Goleman, D. (2003). Finding happiness: Cajole your brain to lean to the left. *New York Times, 4*(3).

51　Field, T., & Diego, M. (2008). Maternal depression effects on infant frontal EEG asymmetry. *International Journal of Neuroscience, 118*(8), 1081-1108.

51　Field, T., Diego, M. A., Hernandez-Reif, M., Schanberg, S., & Kuhn, C. (2004). Massage therapy effects on depressed pregnant women. *Journal of Psychosomatic Obstetrics & Gynecology, 25*(2), 115-122.

52　Lobel, M., Dunkel-Schetter, C., & Scrimshaw, S. C. (1992). Prenatal mater-nal stress and prematurity: a prospective study of socioeconomically disad-vantaged women. *Health Psychology, 11*(1), 32.

52　Feldman, P. J., Dunkel-Schetter, C., Sandman, C. A., & Wadhwa, P. D. (2000). Maternal social support predicts birth weight and fetal growth in human pregnancy. *Psychosomatic Medicine, 62*(5), 715-725.

52　Graven, S. N., & Browne, J. V. (2008). Sensory development in the fetus, neonate, and infant: introduction and overview. *Newborn and Infant Nurs-ing Reviews, 8*(4), 169-172.

52　Blackburn, S. T. (2012). *Maternal, fetal, and neonatal physiology.* WB Saun-ders Company.

52　Buss, C., Davis, E. P., Class, Q. A., Gierczak, M., Pattillo, C., Glynn, L. M., & Sandman, C. A. (2009). Maturation of the human fetal startle response: evi-dence for sex-specific maturation of the human fetus. *Early human develop-ment, 85*(10), 633-638.

53　Mikic, B., Johnson, T. L., Chhabra, A. B., Schalet, B. J., Wong, M., & Hun-ziker, E. B. (2000). Differential effects of embryonic immobilization on the development of fibrocartilaginous skeletal elements. *Journal of rehabilita-tion research and development, 37*(2), 127-134.

54　Jain, S., Sharma, R., & Wadhwa, S. (2004). Effect of prenatal species-specific and music stimulation on the postnatal auditory preference of the domestic chick. *Indian journal of physiology and pharmacology, 48*(2), 174.

54　Gottlieb, G., Tomlinson, W. T., & Radell, P. L. (1989). Developmental inter-sensory interference: Premature visual experience suppresses auditory learning in ducklings. *Infant Behavior and Development, 12*(1), 1-12.

55　Leader, L. R., Baillie, P., Martin, B., & Vermeulen, E. (1982). The assessment and significance of habituation to a repeated stimulus by the human fetus. *Early Human Development, 7*(3), 211-219.

55 Khazipov, R., Sirota, A., Leinekugel, X., Holmes, G. L., Ben-Ari, Y., & Buzsáki, G. (2004). Early motor activity drives spindle bursts in the developing somatosensory cortex. *Nature*, *432*(7018), 758-761.

56 Birnholz, J. C., Stephens, J. C., & Faria, M. (1978). Fetal movement patterns: a possible means of defining neurologic developmental milestones in utero. *American journal of Roentgenology*, *130*(3), 537-540.

56 Mirmiran, M., Maas, Y. G., & Ariagno, R. L. (2003). Development of fetal and neonatal sleep and circadian rhythms. *Sleep medicine reviews*, *7*(4), 321-334.

56 Faure, J., Uys, J. D., Marais, L., Stein, D. J., & Daniels, W. M. (2006). Early maternal separation followed by later stressors leads to dysregulation of the HPA-axis and increases in hippocampal NGF and NT-3 levels in a rat model. *Metabolic brain disease*, *21*(2-3), 172-179.

58 Gilmer, W. S., & McKinney, W. T. (2003). Early experience and depressive disorders: human and non-human primate studies. *Journal of affective disorders*, *75*(2), 97-113.

58 Greisen, M. H., Altar, C. A., Bolwig, T. G., Whitehead, R., & Wörtwein, G. (2005). Increased adult hippocampal brain-derived neurotrophic factor and normal levels of neurogenesis in maternal separation rats. *Journal of neuroscience research*, *79*(6), 772-778.

59 Meaney, M. J. (2001). Maternal care, gene expression, and the transmission of individual differences in stress reactivity across generations. *Annual review of neuroscience*, *24*(1), 1161-1192.

59 Champagne, F., & Meaney, M. J. (2001). Like mother, like daughter: evidence for non-genomic transmission of parental behavior and stress responsivity. *Progress in brain research*, *133*, 287-302.

60 Anderson, G. C. (1991). Current knowledge about skin-to-skin (kangaroo) care for preterm infants. *Journal of perinatology: official journal of the California Perinatal Association*, *11*(3), 216-226.

60 Charpak, N., Ruiz-Peláez, J. G., Zita Figueroa de C, M. D., & Charpak, Y. (1997). Kangaroo mother versus traditional care for newborn infants≤ 2000 grams: a randomized, controlled trial. *Pediatrics*, *100*(4), 682-688.

60 Johnston, C. C., Stevens, B., Pinelli, J., Gibbins, S., Filion, F., Jack, A., ... & Veilleux, A. (2003). Kangaroo care is effective in diminishing pain response in preterm neonates. *Archives of pediatrics & adolescent medicine*, *157*(11), 1084.

61 Feldman, R., & Eidelman, A. I. (2003). Skin-to-skin contact (Kangaroo Care) accelerates autonomic and neurobehavioral maturation in preterm infants. *Developmental Medicine & Child Neurology*, *45*(4), 274-281.

61 Messmer, P. R., Rodriguez, S., Adams, J., Wells-Gentry, J., Washburn, K., Zabaleta, I., & Abreu, S. (1996). Effect of kangaroo care on sleep time for neonates. *Pediatric nursing*, *23*(4), 408-414.

62 Feldman, R., Weller, A., Sirota, L., & Eidelman, A. I. (2002). Skin-to-skin contact (kangaroo care) promotes self-regulation in premature infants: sleep-wake cyclicity, arousal modulation, and sustained exploration. *Developmental Psychology, 38*(2), 194.

62 Ludington-Hoe, S. M., Lewis, T., Morgan, K., Cong, X., Anderson, L., & Reese, S. (2006). Breast and infant temperatures with twins during shared kangaroo care. *Journal of Obstetric, Gynecologic, & Neonatal Nursing, 35*(2), 223-231.

62 Ludington-Hoe, S. M., Anderson, G. C., Swinth, J. Y., Thompson, C., & Hadeed, A. J. (2004). Randomized controlled trial of kangaroo care: Cardiorespiratory and thermal effects on healthy preterm infants. *Neonatal Network: The Journal of Neonatal Nursing, 23*(3), 39-48.

63 Chen, F. S., Kumsta, R., von Dawans, B., Monakhov, M., Ebstein, R. P., & Heinrichs, M. (2011). Common oxytocin receptor gene (OXTR) polymorphism and social support interact to reduce stress in humans. *Proceedings of the National Academy of Sciences, 108*(50), 19937-19942.

63 Detillion, C. E., Craft, T. K., Glasper, E. R., Prendergast, B. J., & DeVries, A. C. (2004). Social facilitation of wound healing. *Psychoneuroendocrinology, 29*(8), 1004-1011.

63 Feldman, R., & Eidelman, A. I. (2003). Skin *Journal of Family Psychology*, Vol 17(1), Mar 2003, 94-107.-to-skin contact (Kangaroo Care) accelerates autonomic and neurobehavioral maturation in preterm infants. *Developmental Medicine & Child Neurology, 45*(4), 274-281.

64 Feldman, R., Eidelman, A. I., Sirota, L., & Weller, A. (2002). Comparison of skin-to-skin (kangaroo) and traditional care: parenting outcomes and preterm infant development. *Pediatrics, 110*(1), 16-26.

69 Doyon, J., Song, A. W., Karni, A., Lalonde, F., Adams, M. M., & Ungerleider, L. G. (2002). Experience-dependent changes in cerebellar contributions to motor sequence learning. *Proceedings of the National Academy of Sciences, 99*(2), 1017-1022.

69 Greenough, W. T., Black, J. E., & Wallace, C. S. (1987). Experience and brain development. *Child development, 58*(3)539-559.

70 Eliot, L. (2010). *What's going on in there? How the brain and mind develop in the first five years of life.* Random House Digital, Inc.

71 Walker, C. D. (2010). Maternal touch and feed as critical regulators of behavioral and stress responses in the offspring. *Developmental Psychobiology, 52*(7), 638-650.

71 Feldman, R., Weller, A., Sirota, L., & Eidelman, A. I. (2003). Testing a family intervention hypothesis: the contribution of mother-infant skin-to-skin contact (kangaroo care) to family interaction, proximity, and touch. *Journal of Family Psychology, 17*(1), 94.

72 Dainton, M., Stafford, L., & Canary, D. J. (1994). Maintenance strategies

and physical affection as predictors of love, liking, and satisfaction in marriage. *Communication Reports, 7*(2), 88-98.

72 Feldman, R., & Eidelman, A. I. (2007). Maternal postpartum behavior and the emergence of infant–mother and infant–father synchrony in preterm and full-term infants: The role of neonatal vagal tone. *Developmental Psychobiology, 49*(3), 290-302.

Chapter 2

76 Gordon, I., Zagoory-Sharon, O., Leckman, J. F., & Feldman, R. (2010). Oxytocin, cortisol, and triadic family interactions. *Physiology & Behavior, 101*(5), 679-684.

77 Takeuchi, M. S., Miyaoka, H., Tomoda, A., Suzuki, M., Liu, Q., & Kitamura, T. (2010). The effect of interpersonal touch during childhood on adult attachment and depression: a neglected area of family and developmental psychology? *Journal of Child and Family Studies, 19*(1), 109-117.

77 Gallace, A., & Spence, C. (2010). The science of interpersonal touch: an overview. *Neuroscience & Biobehavioral Reviews, 34*(2), 246-259.

77 Field, T. (2010). Touch for socioemotional and physical well-being: A review. *Developmental Review, 30*(4), 367-383.

77 Feldman, R., Keren, M., Gross-Rozval, O., & Tyano, S. (2004). Mother–child touch patterns in infant feeding disorders: relation to maternal, child, and environmental factors. *Journal of the American Academy of Child & Adolescent Psychiatry, 43*(9), 1089-1097.

78 Fredrickson, B. L., Mancuso, R. A., Branigan, C., & Tugade, M. M. (2000). The undoing effect of positive emotions. *Motivation and Emotion, 24*(4), 237-258.

78 Ditzen, B., Nater, U. M., Schaer, M., La Marca, R., Bodenmann, G., Ehlert, U., & Heinrichs, M. (2012). Sex-specific effects of intranasal oxytocin on autonomic nervous system and emotional responses to couple conflict. *Social Cognitive and Affective Neuroscience.*

78 Quirin, M., Kuhl, J., & Düsing, R. (2011). Oxytocin buffers cortisol responses to stress in individuals with impaired emotion regulation abilities. *Psychoneuroendocrinology, 36*(6), 898-904. Narvaez, D. (2012). Moral neuroeducation from early life through the lifespan. *Neuroethics, 5*(2), 145-157.

79 Narvaez, D., & Gleason, T. (2013). Developmental optimization. *Evolution, early experience and human development: From research to practice and policy*, 307-325.

79 Oddy, W. H. (2002). The impact of breastmilk on infant and child health. *Breastfeeding review: professional publication of the Nursing Mothers' Association of Australia, 10*(3), 5.

80 Jackson, K. M., & Nazar, A. M. (2006). Breastfeeding, the immune response, and long-term health. *JAOA: Journal of the American Osteopathic Association, 106*(4), 203-207.

80 Jung, M. J., & Fouts, H. N. (2011). Multiple caregivers' touch interactions with young children among the Bofi foragers in Central Africa. *International Journal of Psychology, 46*(1), 24-32.

81 Hess, E. H. (1958). Imprinting in animals. *Scientific American, 198*(3), 81-90.

81 Harlow, H. F. (1958). The nature of love.

82 Cho, M. M., DeVries, A. C., Williams, J. R., & Carter, C. S. (1999). The effects of oxytocin and vasopressin on partner preferences in male and female prairie voles (< em> Microtus ochrogaster). *Behavioral neuroscience, 113*(5), 1071.

83 Tannock, Michelle T. "Rough and tumble play: An investigation of the perceptions of educators and young children." *Early Childhood Education Journal* 35.4 (2008): 357-361.

83 Ardiel, E. L., & Rankin, C. H. (2010). The importance of touch in development. *Paediatrics & child health, 15*(3), 153.

83 Andrzejewski, C. E., & Davis, H. A. (2008). Human contact in the classroom: Exploring how teachers talk about and negotiate touching students. *Teaching and Teacher Education, 24*(3), 779-794.

83 Owen, P. M., & Gillentine, J. (2011). Please touch the children: appropriate touch in the primary classroom. *Early Child Development and Care, 181*(6), 857-868.

85 Brown, S. L. (2009). *Play: How it shapes the brain, opens the imagination, and invigorates the soul.* Penguin. com.

85 Xu, Y. (2010). Children's social play sequence: Parten's classic theory revisited. *Early Child Development and Care, 180*(4), 489-498.

86 Burgdorf, J., Kroes, R. A., Beinfeld, M. C., Panksepp, J., & Moskal, J. R. (2010). Uncovering the molecular basis of positive affect using rough-and-tumble play in rats: a role for insulin-like growth factor I. *Neuroscience, 168*(3), 769-777.

86 Himmler, B. T., Pellis, S. M., & Kolb, B. (2013). Juvenile play experience primes neurons in the medial prefrontal cortex to be more responsive to later experiences. *Neuroscience letters, 556*, 42-45.

87 Trezza, V., Baarendse, P. J., & Vanderschuren, L. J. (2010). The pleasures of play: pharmacological insights into social reward mechanisms. *Trends in pharmacological sciences, 31*(10), 463-469.

87 Kirschner, S., & Tomasello, M. (2009). Joint drumming: Social context facilitates synchronization in preschool children. *Journal of experimental child psychology, 102*(3), 299-314.

88 Perry, B. D. (2002). Childhood experience and the expression of genetic potential: What childhood neglect tells us about nature and nurture. *Brain and mind, 3*(1), 79-100.

88 Field, T. (2010). Touch for socioemotional and physical well-being: A review. *Developmental Review, 30*(4), 367-383.

90 Siviy, S. M. (1998). Neurobiological substrates of play behavior: Glimpses into the structure and function of mammalian playfulness. *Animal play: Evolutionary, comparative, and ecological perspectives*, 221-42.

92 Silver, M.E., Field, T., Sanders, C., Diego, M. (2000). Angry adolescents who worry about becoming violent. *Adolescence, 35*, 663-669.

92 Toledo-Rodriguez, M., & Sandi, C. (2011). Stress during adolescence increases novelty seeking and risk-taking behavior in male and female rats. *Frontiers in behavioral neuroscience, 5*.

92 Sterlemann, V., Rammes, G., Wolf, M., Liebl, C., Ganea, K., Müller, M. B., & Schmidt, M. V. (2010). Chronic social stress during adolescence induces cognitive impairment in aged mice. *Hippocampus, 20*(4), 540-549.

94 Steward, A. L., & Lupfer, M. (1987). Touching as teaching: The effect of touch on students' perceptions and performance. *Journal of Applied Social Psychology, 17*(9), 800-809.

94 Jankord, R., Solomon, M. B., Albertz, J., Flak, J. N., Zhang, R., & Herman, J. P. (2011). Stress vulnerability during adolescent development in rats. *Endocrinology, 152*(2), 629-638.

96 Ruttle, P. L., Shirtcliff, E. A., Serbin, L. A., Ben-Dat Fisher, D., Stack, D. M., & Schwartzman, A. E. (2011). Disentangling psychobiological mechanisms underlying internalizing and externalizing behaviors in youth: Longitudinal and concurrent associations with cortisol. *Hormones and behavior, 59*(1), 123-132.

99 Prescott, J. W. (1975). Body pleasure and the origins of violence. *The Bulletin of The Atomic Scientists*, 10-20.

Chapter 3

101 Franz, C. E., & White, K. M. (1985). Individuation and attachment in personality development: Extending Erikson's theory. *Journal of personality, 53*(2), 224-256.

101 Turp, M. (2000). Touch, enjoyment and health: in adult life. *European Journal of Psychotherapy, Counselling & Health, 3*(1), 61-76.

103 Field, T., Hernandez-Reif, M., LaGreca, A., Shaw, K., Schanberg, S., & Kuhn, C. (1997). Massage therapy lowers blood glucose levels in children with Diabetes Mellitus. *Diabetes Spectrum, 10*, 237-239.

103 Andersson, K., Wändell, P., & Törnkvist, L. (2004). Tactile massage improves glycaemic control in women with type 2 diabetes: a pilot study. *Practical diabetes international, 21*(3), 105-109.

103 Field, T. (2010). Touch for socioemotional and physical well-being: A review. *Developmental Review, 30*(4), 367-383.

103 Oliveira, D. S., Hachul, H., Goto, V., Tufik, S., & Bittencourt, L. R. A. (2012). Effect of therapeutic massage on insomnia and climacteric symptoms in postmenopausal women. *Climacteric, 15*(1), 21-29.

105 Major, B. (1981). Gender patterns in touching behavior. In *Gender and nonverbal behavior* (pp. 15-37). Springer New York.

105 Major, B., Schmidlin, A. M., & Williams, L. (1990). Gender patterns in social touch: The impact of setting and age. *Journal of Personality and Social Psychology, 58*(4), 634.

105 Remland, M. S., Jones, T. S., & Brinkman, H. (1995). Interpersonal distance, body orientation, and touch: Effects of culture, gender, and age. *The Journal of social psychology, 135*(3), 281-297.

105 Jourard, S. M. (1966). An Exploratory Study of Body Accessibility1. *British Journal of Social and Clinical Psychology, 5*(3), 221-231.

105 Jourard, S. M. (1966). Some psychological aspects of privacy. *Law and Contemporary Problems, 31*(2), 307-318.

105 Hall, J. A., & Veccia, E. M. (1990). More" touching" observations: New insights on men, women, and interpersonal touch. *Journal of Personality and Social Psychology, 59*(6), 1155.

105 Guéguen, N., & Jacob, C. (2005). The effect of touch on tipping: an evaluation in a French bar. *International Journal of Hospitality Management, 24*(2), 295-299.

105 Smith, D. E., Willis, F. N., & Gier, J. A. (1980). Success and interpersonal touch in a competitive setting. *Journal of Nonverbal Behavior, 5*(1), 26-34.

105 Kosfeld, M., Heinrichs, M., Zak, P. J., Fischbacher, U., & Fehr, E. (2005). Oxytocin increases trust in humans. *Nature, 435*(7042), 673-676.

106 Guerrero, L. K., & Andersen, P. A. (1994). Patterns of matching and initiation: Touch behavior and touch avoidance across romantic relationship stages. *Journal of Nonverbal Behavior, 18*(2), 137-153.

106 Schneiderman, I., Zagoory-Sharon, O., Leckman, J. F., & Feldman, R. (2012). Oxytocin during the initial stages of romantic attachment: relations to couples' interactive reciprocity. *Psychoneuroendocrinology, 37*(8), 1277-1285.

107 Aron, A., Fisher, H., Mashek, D. J., Strong, G., Li, H., & Brown, L. L. (2005). Reward, motivation, and emotion systems associated with early-stage intense romantic love. *Journal of neurophysiology, 94*(1), 327-337.

107 Floyd, K., Boren, J. P., Hannawa, A. F., Hesse, C., McEwan, B., & Veksler, A. E. (2009). Kissing in marital and cohabiting relationships: Effects on blood lipids, stress, and relationship satisfaction. *Western Journal of Communication, 73*(2), 113-133.

107 Bauer, B. A., Cutshall, S. M., Wentworth, L. J., Engen, D., Messner, P. K., Wood, C. M., ... & Sundt III, T. M. (2010). Effect of massage therapy on pain, anxiety, and tension after cardiac surgery: a randomized study. *Complementary therapies in clinical practice, 16*(2), 70-75.

108 Harrist, A. W., Pettit, G. S., Dodge, K. A., & Bates, J. E. (1994). Dyadic synchrony in mother-child interaction: Relation with children's subsequent kindergarten adjustment. *Family Relations*, 417-424.

108 Stier, D. S., & Hall, J. A. (1984). Gender differences in touch: An empirical and theoretical review. *Journal of Personality and Social Psychology, 47*(2), 440.

108 Thompson, E. H., & Hampton, J. A. (2011). The effect of relationship status on communicating emotions through touch. *Cognition and emotion, 25*(2), 295-306.

108 Tucker, J. S., & Anders, S. L. (1998). Adult attachment style and nonverbal closeness in dating couples. *Journal of Nonverbal Behavior, 22*(2), 109-124.

108 Naber, F., van IJzendoorn, M. H., Deschamps, P., van Engeland, H., & Bakermans-Kranenburg, M. J. (2010). Intranasal oxytocin increases fathers' observed responsiveness during play with their children: a double-blind within-subject experiment. *Psychoneuroendocrinology, 35*(10), 1583-1586.

108 Guerrero, L. K., & Andersen, P. A. (1991). The waxing and waning of relational intimacy: Touch as a function of relational stage, gender and touch avoidance. *Journal of Social and Personal Relationships, 8*(2), 147-165.

108 Schneiderman, I., Zagoory-Sharon, O., Leckman, J. F., & Feldman, R. (2012). Oxytocin during the initial stages of romantic attachment: relations to couples' interactive reciprocity. *108 Psychoneuroendocrinology, 37*(8), 1277-1285. Smith, J. C. S., Vogel, D. L., Madon, S., & Edwards, S. R. (2011). The power of touch: Nonverbal communication within married dyads. *The Counseling Psychologist, 39*(5), 764-787.

108 Fredrickson, B. L. (2001). The role of positive emotions in positive psychology: The broaden-and-build theory of positive emotions. *American psychologist, 56*(3), 218.

108 Bush, E. (2001). The Use of Human Touch to Improve the Well-Being of Older Adults A Holistic Nursing Intervention. *Journal of holistic nursing, 19*(3), 256-270.

108 Hollinger, L. M., & Buschmann, M. B. T. (1993). Factors influencing the perception of touch by elderly nursing home residents and their health caregivers. *International Journal of Nursing Studies, 30*(5), 445-461.

108 Adomat, R., & Killingworth, A. (1994). Care of the critically ill patient: The impact of stress on the use of touch in intensive therapy units. *Journal of Advanced Nursing, 19*(5), 912-922.

108 Langer, E. J. (1989). *Mindfulness.* Addison-Wesley/Addison Wesley Longman.

108 Rodin, J., & Langer, E. J. (1977). Long-term effects of a control-relevant intervention with the institutionalized aged. *Journal of personality and social psychology, 35*(12), 897.

109 Campbell, F. A. K. (2008). Exploring internalized ableism using critical race theory. *Disability & Society, 23*(2), 151-162.

109 Downing, J. E., & Chen, D. (2003). Using tactile strategies with students who are blind and have severe disabilities. *Teaching Exceptional Children, 36*(2), 56-60.

109 Tarr, J. (2011). Educating with the hands: working on the body/self in Alexander Technique. *Sociology of health & illness, 33*(2), 252-265.

109 Mason, H., & McCall, S. (Eds.). (2013). *Visual impairment: access to education for children and young people*. Routledge.

110 Thai-Van, H., Veuillet, E., Norena, A., Guiraud, J., & Collet, L. (2010). Plasticity of tonotopic maps in humans: influence of hearing loss, hearing aids and cochlear implants. *Acta oto-laryngologica, 130*(3), 333-337.

110 Wilson, B. S. (2013). Toward better representations of sound with cochlear implants. *Nature medicine, 19*(10), 1245-1248.

110 Sampaio, E., S. Maris., and P. Bach-y-Rita. 2001. Brain plasticity: 'Visual' acuity of blind persons via the tongue. Brain Research 908(July 13):204.

110 Heller, M. A. (1989). Picture and pattern perception in the sighted and the blind: the advantage of the late blind. *Perception, 18*(3), 379-389.

110 A. Bhattacharjee, A. J. Ye, J. A. Lisak, M. G. Vargas, D. Goldreich. Vibrotactile Masking Experiments Reveal Accelerated Somatosensory Processing in Congenitally Blind Braille Readers. Journal of Neuroscience, 2010; 30 (43): 14288 DOI: 10.1523/JNEUROSCI.1447-10.2010

110 Cramer, S. C., Sur, M., Dobkin, B. H., O'Brien, C., Sanger, T. D., Trojanowski, J. Q., ... & Vinogradov, S. (2011). Harnessing neuroplasticity for clinical applications. *Brain, 134*(6), 1591-1609.

113 Buschmann, M. T., Hollinger-Smith, L. M., & Peterson-Kokkas, S. E. (1999). Implementation of expressive physical touch in depressed older adults. *Journal of Clinical Geropsychology, 5*(4), 291-300.

113 Bush, E. (2001). The Use of Human Touch to Improve the Well-Being of Older Adults A Holistic Nursing Intervention. *Journal of holistic nursing, 19*(3), 256-270.

113 Allison, L. K., Kiemel, T., & Jeka, J. J. (2006). Multisensory reweighting of vision and touch is intact in healthy and fall-prone older adults. *Experimental brain research, 175*(2), 342-352.

113 Skinner, H. B., Barrack, R. L., & COOK, S. D. (1984). Age-related decline in proprioception. *Clinical orthopedics and related research, 184*, 208-211.

113 Kraaij, V., & De Wilde, E. J. (2001). Negative life events and depressive symptoms in the elderly: a life span perspective. *Aging & Mental Health, 5*(1), 84-91.

115 Kraaij, V., Arensman, E., & Spinhoven, P. (2002). Negative Life Events and Depression in Elderly Persons A Meta-Analysis. *The Journals of Gerontology Series B: Psychological Sciences and Social Sciences, 57*(1), P87-P94.

115 Alexander, C. N., Langer, E. J., Newman, R. I., Chandler, H. M., & Davies, J. L. (1989). Transcendental meditation, mindfulness, and longevity: an experimental study with the elderly. *Journal of personality and social psychology, 57*(6), 950.

116 Allan, L. M., Ballard, C. G., Allen, J., Murray, A., Davidson, A. W., McKeith,

I. G., & Kenny, R. A. (2007). Autonomic dysfunction in dementia. *Journal of Neurology, Neurosurgery & Psychiatry, 78*(7), 671-677.

116 Zulli, R., Nicosia, F., Borroni, B., Agosti, C., Prometti, P., Donati, P., ... & Padovani, A. (2005). QT dispersion and heart rate variability abnormalities in Alzheimer's disease and in mild cognitive impairment. *Journal of the American Geriatrics Society, 53*(12), 2135-2139.

116 Albinet, C. T., Boucard, G., Bouquet, C. A., & Audiffren, M. (2010). Increased heart rate variability and executive performance after aerobic training in the elderly. *European journal of applied physiology, 109*(4), 617-624.

116 Delaney, J., Leong, K. S., Watkins, A., & Brodie, D. (2002). The short-term effects of myofascial trigger point massage therapy on cardiac autonomic tone in healthy subjects. *Journal of advanced nursing, 37*(4), 364-371.

117 Crane, J. D., Ogborn, D. I., Cupido, C., Melov, S., Hubbard, A., Bourgeois, J. M., & Tarnopolsky, M. A. (2012). Massage therapy attenuates inflammatory signaling after exercise-induced muscle damage. *Science translational medicine, 4*(119), 119ra13-119ra13.

117 Gordon, I., Zagoory-Sharon, O., Leckman, J. F., & Feldman, R. (2010). Oxytocin, cortisol, and triadic family interactions. *Physiology & behavior, 101*(5), 679-684.

117 Pettit, G. S., & Harrist, A. W. (1993). Children's aggressive and socially unskilled playground behavior with peers: Origins in early family relations. *Children on playgrounds: Research perspectives and applications*, 240-270.

117 Carlson, M. C., Saczynski, J. S., Rebok, G. W., Seeman, T., Glass, T. A., McGill, S., ... & Fried, L. P. (2008). Exploring the effects of an "everyday" activity program on executive function and dementia: Introduction to the Special Issue. *Dementia, 11*(3), 281-285.

118 Ward, R., Howorth, M., Wilkinson, H., Campbell, S., & Keady, J. (2012). Supporting the friendships of people with dementia. *Dementia, 11*(3), 287-303.

119 Rinck, C. M., Willis, F. N., & Dean, L. M. (1980). Interpersonal touch among residents of homes for the elderly. *Journal of Communication, 30*(2), 44-47.

119 Edvardsson, J., Sandman, P. O., & Rasmussen, B. H. (2003). Meanings of giving touch in the care of older patients: becoming a valuable person and professional. *Journal of Clinical Nursing, 12*(4), 601-609.

119 Gescheider, G. A., Edwards, R. R., Lackner, E. A., Bolanowski, S. J., & Verrillo, R. T. (1996). The effects of aging on information-processing channels in the sense of touch: III. Differential sensitivity to changes in stimulus intensity. *Somatosensory & motor research, 13*(1), 73-80.

119 Gleeson, M., & Timmins, F. (2005). A review of the use and clinical effectiveness of touch as a nursing intervention. *Clinical Effectiveness in Nursing, 9*(1), 69-77

120 Golberg, B. (1998). Connection: an exploration of spirituality in nursing care. *Journal of Advanced Nursing, 27*(4), 836-842.

121 Patterson, A. C., & Veenstra, G. (2010). Loneliness and risk of mortality: A longitudinal investigation in Alameda County, California. *Social science & medicine, 71*(1), 181-186.

121 Kozak, L. E., Kayes, L., McCarty, R., Walkinshaw, C., Congdon, S., Kleinberger, J., ... & Standish, L. J. (2009). Use of complementary and alternative medicine (CAM) by Washington state hospices. *American Journal of Hospice and Palliative Medicine, 25*(6), 463-468.

121 Snyder, M., & Olson, J. (1996). Music and hand massage interventions to produce relaxation and reduce aggressive behaviors in cognitively impaired elders: a pilot study. *Clinical gerontologist, 17*(1), 64-69.

122 Snyder, J. R. (1997). Therapeutic touch and the terminally ill: healing power through the hands. *The American journal of hospice & palliative care, 14*(2), 83.

122 Kutner, J. S., Smith, M. C., Corbin, L., Hemphill, L., Benton, K., Mellis, B. K., ... & Fairclough, D. L. (2008). Massage Therapy versus Simple Touch to Improve Pain and Mood in Patients with Advanced Cancer A Randomized Trial. *Annals of internal medicine, 149*(6), 369-379.

122 Post-White, J., Kinney, M. E., Savik, K., Gau, J. B., Wilcox, C., & Lerner, I. (2003). Therapeutic massage and healing touch improve symptoms in cancer. *Integrative cancer therapies, 2*(4), 332-344.

122 Sharpe, P. A., Williams, H. G., Granner, M. L., & Hussey, J. R. (2007). A randomised study of the effects of massage therapy compared to guided relaxation on well-being and stress perception among older adults. *Complementary Therapies in medicine, 15*(3), 157-163.

123 Edvardsson, J., Sandman, P. O., & Rasmussen, B. H. (2003). Meanings of giving touch in the care of older patients: becoming a valuable person and professional. *Journal of Clinical Nursing, 12*(4), 601-609.

123 Adomat, R., & Killingworth, A. (1994). Care of the critically ill patient: The impact of stress on the use of touch in intensive therapy units. *Journal of Advanced Nursing, 19*(5), 912-922.

123 Bush, E. (2001). The Use of Human Touch to Improve the Well-Being of Older Adults: A Holistic Nursing Intervention. *Journal of holistic nursing, 19*(3), 256-270.

123 Chang, S. O. (2001). The conceptual structure of physical touch in caring. *Journal of Advanced Nursing, 33*(6), 820-827.

123 Holt-Lunstad, J., Smith, T. B., & Layton, J. B. (2010). Social relationships and mortality risk: a meta-analytic review. *PLoS medicine, 7*(7), e1000316.

124 Sorkin, D., Rook, K. S., & Lu, J. L. (2002). Loneliness, lack of emotional support, lack of companionship, and the likelihood of having a heart condition in an elderly sample. *Annals of Behavioral Medicine, 24*(4), 290-298.

Chapter 4

4 Benjamin Jr, L. T. (2007). *A brief history of modern psychology.* Blackwell Publ.

5 Ishikawa, T., & Mogi, K. Creativity and Visual One-shot Learning.

5 Beck, A. T. (1997). The past and future of cognitive therapy. *The Journal of psychotherapy practice and research, 6*(4), 276.

5 Kandel, E. (2013). The New Science of Mind and the Future of Knowledge. *Neuron, 80*(3), 546-560.

6 Van der Kolk, B. A., McFarlane, A. C., & Weisaeth, L. (Eds.). (1996). *Traumatic stress: The effects of overwhelming experience on mind, body, and society.* Guilford Press.

6 Damasio, A. (2005). *Descartes' error: Emotion, reason, and the human brain.* Penguin.com.

7 Damasio, A. R., Everitt, B. J., & Bishop, D. (1996). The somatic marker hypothesis and the possible functions of the prefrontal cortex [and discussion]. *Philosophical Transactions of the Royal Society of London. Series B: Biological Sciences, 351*(1346), 1413-1420.

7 Bechara, A., Damasio, H., Tranel, D., & Damasio, A. R. (2005). The Iowa Gambling Task and the somatic marker hypothesis: some questions and answers. *Trends in cognitive sciences, 9*(4), 159-162.

8 Field, T., Seligman, S., Scafidi, F., & Schanberg, S. (1996). Alleviating post-traumatic stress in children following Hurricane Andrew. *Journal of Applied Developmental Psychology, 17*(1), 37-50.

8 Field, T., Hernandez-Reif, M., Diego, M., Schanberg, S., & Kuhn, C. (2005). Cortisol decreases and serotonin and dopamine increase following massage therapy. *International Journal of Neuroscience, 115*(10), 1397-1413.

8 Jain, S., McMahon, G. F., Hasen, P., Kozub, M. P., Porter, V., King, R., & Guarneri, E. M. (2012). Healing Touch with Guided Imagery for PTSD in returning active duty military: a randomized controlled trial. *Military medicine, 177*(9), 1015-1021.

8 Field, T., Hernandez-Reif, M., Quintino, O., Drose, L. A., Field, T., Kuhn, C., & Schanberg, S. (1997). Effects of sexual abuse are lessened by massage therapy. *Journal of bodywork and movement therapies, 1*(2), 65-69.

9 Penfield, W., & Erickson, T. C. (1941). Epilepsy and cerebral localization.

10 Merzenich, M. M., Nelson, R. J., Stryker, M. P., Cynader, M. S., Schoppmann, A., & Zook, J. M. (1984). Somatosensory cortical map changes following digit amputation in adult monkeys. *Journal of comparative neurology, 224*(4), 591-605.

10 Altenmüller, E. (2008). Neurology of musical performance. *Clinical medicine, 8*(4), 410-413.

10 Meaney, M. J. (2001). Maternal care, gene expression, and the transmission of individual differences in stress reactivity across generations. *Annual review of neuroscience, 24*(1), 1161-1192.

10 Ekman, P., & Rosenberg, E. L. (Eds.). (1997). *What the face reveals: Basic and applied studies of spontaneous expression using the Facial Action Coding System (FACS)*. Oxford University Press.

11 Hertenstein, M. J., Keltner, D., App, B., Bulleit, B. A., & Jaskolka, A. R. (2006). Touch communicates distinct emotions. *Emotion, 6*(3), 528.

11 Gross, J. J., & John, O. P. (2003). Individual differences in two emotion regulation processes: implications for affect, relationships, and well-being. *Journal of personality and social psychology, 85*(2), 348.

11 Gross, J. J. (1998). The emerging field of emotion regulation: An integrative review. *Review of general psychology, 2*(3), 271.

13 Sterling, P., & Eyer, J. (1988). Allostasis: a new paradigm to explain arousal pathology.

13 McEwen, B. S., & Wingfield, J. C. (2003). The concept of allostasis in biology and biomedicine. *Hormones and behavior, 43*(1), 2-15.

13 McEwen, B. S. (2002). *The end of stress as we know it*. The National Academies.

14 Goleman, D. (2006). *Emotional intelligence: Why it can matter more than IQ*. Random House Digital, Inc.

16 Linehan, M. (1993). *Skills training manual for treating borderline personality disorder* (pp. 107-177). New York: Guilford Press.

17 Bonanno, G. A. (2004). Loss, trauma, and human resilience: Have we underestimated the human capacity to thrive after extremely aversive events? *American psychologist, 59*(1), 20.

17 Fredrickson, B. L., Tugade, M. M., Waugh, C. E., & Larkin, G. (2003). What good are positive emotions in crises? A prospective study of resilience and emotions following the terrorist attacks on the United States on September 11th, 2001. Journal of Personality and Social Psychology, 84, 365-376.

18 Levine, P. A. (1997). *Waking the tiger: Healing trauma: The innate capacity to transform overwhelming experiences*. North Atlantic Books.

19 Schore, A. N. (1994). *Affect regulation and the origin of the self: The neurobiology of emotional development*. Psychology Press.

19 Schore, A. N. (2001). The effects of early relational trauma on right brain development, affect regulation, and infant mental health. *Infant mental health journal, 22*(1-2), 201-269.

22 Iacoboni, M. (2009). *Mirroring people: The new science of how we connect with others*. Macmillan.

23 Porges, S. W. (2004). Neuroception: A Subconscious System for Detecting Threats and Safety. *Zero to Three, 24*(5), 19-24.

28 Herman, J. L. (1997). *Trauma and recovery*. Basic Books.

28 Chodron, P. (2007). *The places that scare you: A guide to fearlessness in difficult times*. Shambhala Publications.

29 Merino, J. G., & Martin, A. (2002). Neuroanatomy through clinical cases. *The Journal of Neuropsychiatry and Clinical Neurosciences, 14*(3), 351-352.

30 Nimer, J., & Lundahl, B. (2007). Animal-assisted therapy: A meta-analysis. *Anthrozoos: A Multidisciplinary Journal of The Interactions of People & Animals*, *20*(3), 225-238.

30 Trotter, K. S., Chandler, C. K., Goodwin-Bond, D., & Casey, J. (2008). A comparative study of the efficacy of group equine assisted counseling with at-risk children and adolescents. *Journal of Creativity in Mental Health*, *3*(3), 254-284.

31 Nathans-Barel, I., Feldman, P., Berger, B., Modai, I., & Silver, H. (2004). Animal-assisted therapy ameliorates anhedonia in schizophrenia patients. *Psychotherapy and Psychosomatics*, *74*(1), 31-35.

32 Penninx, B. W., Van Tilburg, T., Kriegsman, D. M., Deeg, D. J., Boeke, A. J. P., & van Eijk, J. T. M. (1997). Effects of social support and personal coping resources on mortality in older age: The Longitudinal Aging Study Amsterdam. *American journal of epidemiology*, *146*(6), 510-519.

32 Cacioppo, J. T., Hawkley, L. C., Crawford, L. E., Ernst, J. M., Burleson, M. H., Kowalewski, R. B., ... & Berntson, G. G. (2002). Loneliness and health: Potential mechanisms. *Psychosomatic Medicine*, *64*(3), 407-417.

32 McAuley, E., Blissmer, B., Marquez, D. X., Jerome, G. J., Kramer, A. F., & Katula, J. (2000). Social relations, physical activity, and well-being in older adults. *Preventive medicine*, *31*(5), 608-617.

32 Richeson, N. E. (2003). Effects of animal-assisted therapy on agitated behaviors and social interactions of older adults with dementia. *American journal of Alzheimer's disease and other dementias*, *18*(6), 353-358.

32 Filan, S. L., & Llewellyn-Jones, R. H. (2006). Animal-assisted therapy for dementia: a review of the literature. *International Psychogeriatrics*, *18*(4), 597-612.

32 Antonioli, C., & Reveley, M. A. (2005). Randomised controlled trial of animal facilitated therapy with dolphins in the treatment of depression. *Bmj*, *331*(7527), 1231.

33 Marcus, D. A., Bernstein, C. D., Constantin, J. M., Kunkel, F. A., Breuer, P., & Hanlon, R. B. (2012). Animal-Assisted Therapy at an Outpatient Pain Management Clinic. *Pain Medicine*, *13*(1), 45-57.

34 Lindgren, L., Westling, G., Brulin, C., Lehtipalo, S., Andersson, M., & Nyberg, L. (2012). Pleasant human touch is represented in pregenual anterior cingulate cortex. *Neuroimage*, *59*(4), 3427-3432.

34 Olausson, H., Lamarre, Y., Backlund, H., Morin, C., Wallin, B. G., Starck, G., ... & Bushnell, M. C. (2002). Unmyelinated tactile afferents signal touch and project to insular cortex. *Nature neuroscience*, *5*(9), 900-904.

35 Rolls, E. T. (2010). The affective and cognitive processing of touch, oral texture, and temperature in the brain. *Neuroscience & Biobehavioral Reviews*, *34*(2), 237-245.

35 Rolls, E. T., O'Doherty, J., Kringelbach, M. L., Francis, S., Bowtell, R., & McGlone, F. (2003). Representations of pleasant and painful touch in the

human orbitofrontal and cingulate cortices. *Cerebral Cortex, 13*(3), 308-317.

35 Björnsdotter, M., Löken, L., Olausson, H., Vallbo, Å., & Wessberg, J. (2009). Somatotopic organization of gentle touch processing in the posterior insular cortex. *The Journal of Neuroscience, 29*(29), 9314-9320.

32 Lamm, C., & Singer, T. (2010). The role of anterior insular cortex in social emotions. *Brain Structure and Function, 214*(5-6), 579-591.

36 Thomas, K. M., Drevets, W. C., Whalen, P. J., Eccard, C. H., Dahl, R. E., Ryan, N. D., & Casey, B. J. (2001). Amygdala response to facial expressions in children and adults. *Biological psychiatry, 49*(4), 309-316.

36 MacLean, P. D. (1990). *The triune brain in evolution: Role in paleocerebral functions.* Springer.

37 De Kloet, C. S., Vermetten, E., Geuze, E., Kavelaars, A., Heijnen, C. J., & Westenberg, H. G. M. (2006). Assessment of HPA-axis function in posttraumatic stress disorder: pharmacological and non-pharmacological challenge tests, a review. *Journal of psychiatric research, 40*(6), 550-567.

40 Lanius, R. A., Williamson, P. C., Boksman, K., Densmore, M., Gupta, M., Neufeld, R. W., ... & Menon, R. S. (2002). Brain activation during script-driven imagery induced dissociative responses in PTSD: a functional magnetic resonance imaging investigation. *Biological psychiatry, 52*(4), 305-311.

40 Gordon, I., Voos, A. C., Bennett, R. H., Bolling, D. Z., Pelphrey, K. A., & Kaiser, M. D. (2011). Brain mechanisms for processing affective touch. *Human brain mapping.*

40 Uvnas-Moberg, K., & Petersson, M. (2005). Oxytocin, a mediator of anti-stress, well-being, social interaction, growth and healing. *Z Psychosom Med Psychother, 51*(1), 57-80.

40 Rolls, E. T., O'Doherty, J., Kringelbach, M. L., Francis, S., Bowtell, R., & McGlone, F. (2003). Representations of pleasant and painful touch in the human orbitofrontal and cingulate cortices. *Cerebral Cortex, 13*(3), 308-317.

42 Le Carret, N., Lafont, S., Letenneur, L., Dartigues, J. F., Mayo, W., & Fabrigoule, C. (2003). The effect of education on cognitive performances and its implication for the constitution of the cognitive reserve. *Developmental neuropsychology, 23*(3), 317-337.

42 Fredrickson, B. L. (2001). The role of positive emotions in positive psychology: The broaden-and-build theory of positive emotions. *American psychologist, 56*(3), 218.

Chapter 5

126 Bonitz, V. (2008). Use of physical touch in the" talking cure": A journey to the outskirts of psychotherapy. *Psychotherapy: Theory, Research, Practice, Training, 45*(3), 391.

126 Sapolsky, R. M., Krey, L. C., & McEwen, B. S. (2002). The neuroendocrinology of stress and aging: the glucocorticoid cascade hypothesis. *Science of Aging Knowledge Environment, 2002*(38), 21.

126 McEwen, B. S. (2000). Effects of adverse experiences for brain structure and function. *Biological psychiatry, 48*(8), 721-731.

126 McEwen, B. S. (2002). *The end of stress as we know it.* The National Academies.

127 Zur, O., & Nordmarken, N. (2004). To touch or not to touch: exploring the myth of prohibition on touch in psychotherapy and counseling. *Retrieved December, 23,* 2006.

128 Field, T. M., Sunshine, W., Hernandezreif, M., Quintino, O., Schanberg, S., Kuhn, C., & Burman, I. (1997). Massage therapy effects on depression and somatic symptoms in chronic fatigue syndrome. *Journal of Chronic Fatigue Syndrome, 3*(3), 43-51.

128 Field, T., Fox, N. A., Pickens, J., & Nawrocki, T. (1995). Relative right frontal EEG activation in 3-to 6-month-old infants of" depressed" mothers. *Developmental Psychology, 31*(3), 358.

128 Field, T. M. (1998). Massage therapy effects. *American Psychologist, 53*(12), 1270.

128 Cassileth, B. R., & Vickers, A. J. (2004). Massage therapy for symptom control: outcome study at a major cancer center. *Journal of pain and symptom management, 28*(3), 244-249.

130 Beck, A. T. (Ed.). (1979). *Cognitive therapy of depression.* Guilford Press.

132 Linehan, M. (1993). *Skills training manual for treating borderline personality disorder* (pp. 107-177). New York: Guilford Press.

132 Yorke, J., Nugent, W., Strand, E., Bolen, R., New, J., & Davis, C. (2012). Equine-assisted therapy and its impact on cortisol levels of children and horses: a pilot study and meta-analysis. *Early Child Development and Care,* (ahead-of-print), 1-21.

132 Yount, R. A., Olmert, M. D., & Lee, M. R. (2012). Service dog training program for treatment of posttraumatic stress in service members. *US Army Medical Department Journal,* 63-69.

132 Friedmann, E., & Son, H. (2009). The human–companion animal bond: how humans benefit. *Veterinary Clinics of North America: Small Animal Practice, 39*(2), 293-326.

135 Grossman, P., Niemann, L., Schmidt, S., & Walach, H. (2004). Mindfulness-based stress reduction and health benefits: A meta-analysis. *Journal of psychosomatic research, 57*(1), 35-43.

135 Bohlmeijer, E., Prenger, R., Taal, E., & Cuijpers, P. (2010). The effects of mindfulness-based stress reduction therapy on mental health of adults with a chronic medical disease: a meta-analysis. *Journal of psychosomatic research, 68*(6), 539-544.

135 Hofmann, S. G., Sawyer, A. T., Witt, A. A., & Oh, D. (2010). The effect of mindfulness-based therapy on anxiety and depression: A meta-analytic review. *Journal of consulting and clinical psychology, 78*(2), 169.

135 Powers, M. B., Zum Vörde Sive Vörding, M. B., & Emmelkamp, P. M. (2009). Acceptance and commitment therapy: A meta-analytic review. *Psychotherapy and psychosomatics, 78*(2), 73-80.

143 In Narvaez, D., Panksepp, J., Schore, A., & Gleason, T. (Eds.) (for 2012). *Human Nature, Early Experience and the Environment of Evolutionary Adaptedness.* New York: Oxford University Press.

143 Schore, A. N. (2003). *Affect regulation and the repair of the self* (Vol. 2). WW Norton & Company.

143 Stone, V. E., Baron-Cohen, S., & Knight, R. T. (1998). Frontal lobe contributions to theory of mind. *Journal of cognitive neuroscience, 10*(5), 640-656.

143 Fletcher, P. C., Happe, F., Frith, U., Baker, S. C., Dolan, R. J., Frackowiak, R. S., & Frith, C. D. (1995). Other minds in the brain: a functional imaging study of "theory of mind" in story comprehension. *Cognition, 57*(2), 109-128.

143 Beckett, C., Bredenkamp, D., Castle, J., Groothues, C., O'Connor, T.G., & Rutter, M. (2002). Behavior patterns associated with institutional deprivation: a study of children adopted from Romania. *Journal of Developmental & Behavioral Pediatrics, 23*(5), 297-303.

143 Felitti, V. J. (2002). The relationship of adverse childhood experiences to adult health: Turning gold into lead. *Zeitschrift fur Psychosomatische Medizin und Psychotherapie, 48*(4), 359-369.

144 Bowlby, J. (2005). *A Secure Base: Clinical Applications of Attachment Theory* (Vol. 393). Taylor & Francis US.

149 MacLean, P. D. (1990). *The triune brain in evolution: Role in paleocerebral functions.* Springer.

151 Porges, S. W. (1995). Orienting in a defensive world: Mammalian modifications of our evolutionary heritage. A polyvagal theory. *Psychophysiology, 32*(4), 301-318.

152 Porges, S. W., Doussard-Roosevelt, J. A., Portales, A. L., & Greenspan, S. I. (1996). Infant regulation of the vagal "brake" predicts child behavior problems: A psychobiological model of social behavior. *Developmental psychobiology, 29*(8), 697-712.

152 Porges, S. W. (2007). The polyvagal perspective. *Biological psychology, 74*(2), 116-143.

153 Schmidt, N. B., Richey, J. A., Zvolensky, M. J., & Maner, J. K. (2008). Exploring human freeze responses to a threat stressor. *Journal of behavior therapy and experimental psychiatry, 39*(3), 292-304.

156 Stern, D. N. (2000). *Interpersonal world of the infant: A view from psychoanalysis and development psychology.* Basic books.

158 Bugental, J. F. (1965). *The search for authenticity: An existential-analytic approach to psychotherapy.* New York: Holt, Rinehart and Winston.

159 Hoagland, H., (1928). On the mechanism of tonic immobility in vertebrates. JGP, 11, 6715-741.

161 Young, C. (2011). The history and development of Body Psychotherapy: European collaboration. *Body, Movement and Dance in Psychotherapy, 6*(1), 57-68.

Chapter 6

166 Corbett, B. A., Schupp, C. W., Levine, S., & Mendoza, S. (2009). Comparing cortisol, stress, and sensory sensitivity in children with autism. *Autism Research, 2*(1), 39-49.

166 Salomon, D. From Marginal Cases to Linked Oppressions: Reframing the Conflict between the Autistic Pride and Animal Rights Movements. *Journal for Critical Animal Studies,* 47.

166 Field, T., Lasko, D., Mundy, P., Henteleff, T., Kabat, S., Talpins, S., & Dowling, M. (1997). Brief report: autistic children's attentiveness and responsivity improve after touch therapy. *Journal of Autism and Developmental Disorders, 27*(3), 333-338.

167 Malone, A., Carroll, A., & Murphy, B. P. (2012). Facial affect recognition deficits: A potential contributor to aggression in psychotic illness. *Aggression and Violent Behavior, 17*(1), 27-35.

191 Mittal, V. A., & Walker, E. F. (2007). Movement abnormalities predict conversion to Axis I psychosis among prodromal adolescents. *Journal of abnormal psychology, 116*(4), 796.

191 Gur, R. C., Calkins, M. E., Satterthwaite, T. D., Ruparel, K., Bilker, W. B., Moore, T. M., ... & Gur, R. E. (2014). Neurocognitive growth charting in psychosis spectrum youths. *JAMA psychiatry, 71*(4), 366-374.

167 Nederlof, A. F., Muris, P., & Hovens, J. E. (2011). Threat/control-override symptoms and emotional reactions to positive symptoms as correlates of aggressive behavior in psychotic patients. *The Journal of nervous and mental disease, 199*(5), 342-347.

167 Pedersen, C. A., Gibson, C. M., Rau, S. W., Salimi, K., Smedley, K. L., Casey, R. L., ... & Penn, D. L. (2011). Intranasal oxytocin reduces psychotic symptoms and improves Theory of Mind and social perception in schizophrenia. *Schizophrenia research, 132*(1), 50-53.

167 Polanczyk, G., Moffitt, T. E., Arseneault, L., Cannon, M., Ambler, A., Keefe, R. S., ... & Caspi, A. (2010). Etiological and clinical features of childhood psychotic symptoms: results from a birth cohort. *Archives of general psychiatry, 67*(4), 328.

168 Mittal, V. A., & Walker, E. F. (2007). Movement abnormalities predict conversion to Axis I psychosis among prodromal adolescents. *Journal of abnormal psychology, 116*(4), 796.

168 Pedersen, C. A., Gibson, C. M., Rau, S. W., Salimi, K., Smedley, K. L., Casey, R. L., ... & Penn, D. L. (2011). Intranasal oxytocin reduces psychotic symptoms and improves Theory of Mind and social perception in schizophrenia. *Schizophrenia research, 132*(1), 50-53.

169 Uvnäs-Moberg, K. (1998). Oxytocin may mediate the benefits of positive social interaction and emotions. *Psychoneuroendocrinology, 23*(8), 819-835.

169 Lloyd, C., Sullivan, D., & Williams, P. L. (2005). Perceptions of social stigma and its effect on interpersonal relationships of young males who experience a psychotic disorder. *Australian Occupational Therapy Journal, 52*(3), 243-250.

169 Rotarska-Jagiela, A., van de Ven, V., Oertel-Knöchel, V., Uhlhaas, P. J., Vogeley, K., & Linden, D. E. (2010). Resting-state functional network correlates of psychotic

170 Helldin, L., Kane, J. M., Karilampi, U., Norlander, T., & Archer, T. (2007). Remission in prognosis of functional outcome: a new dimension in the treatment of patients with psychotic disorders. *Schizophrenia research, 93*(1), 160-168.

170 Nederlof, A. F., Muris, P., & Hovens, J. E. (2011). Threat/control-override symptoms and emotional reactions to positive symptoms as correlates of aggressive behavior in psychotic patients. *The Journal of nervous and mental disease, 199*(5), 342-347.

171 Field, T. (2010). Touch for socioemotional and physical well-being: A review. *Developmental Review, 30*(4), 367-383.

172 Umberson, D. (1987). Family status and health behaviors: Social control as a dimension of social integration. *Journal of health and social behavior*, 306-319.

172 Murphy, M., Glaser, K., & Grundy, E. (1997). Marital status and long-term illness in Great Britain. *Journal of Marriage and the Family*, 156-164.

172 Diedrick, P. (1991). Gender differences in divorce adjustment. *Journal of Divorce & Remarriage, 14*(3-4), 33-46.

172 Schotte, C. K., Van Den Bossche, B., De Doncker, D., Claes, S., & Cosyns, P. (2006). A biopsychosocial model as a guide for psychoeducation and treatment of depression. *Depression and anxiety, 23*(5), 312-324.

172 Blackburn, I. M., Bishop, S., Glen, A. I., Whalley, L. J., & Christie, J. E. (1981). The efficacy of cognitive therapy in depression: a treatment trial using cognitive therapy and pharmacotherapy, each alone and in combination. *The British Journal of Psychiatry, 139*(3), 181-189.

172 Ehnvall, A., Mitchell, P. B., Hadzi-Pavlovic, D., Loo, C., Breakspear, M., Wright, A., ... & Corry, J. (2011). Pain and rejection sensitivity in bipolar depression. *Bipolar disorders, 13*(1), 59-66.

173 Frank, E., Swartz, H. A., & Kupfer, D. J. (2000). Interpersonal and social rhythm therapy: managing the chaos of bipolar disorder. *Biological psychiatry, 48*(6), 593-604.

176 Goleman, D. (2006). *Emotional intelligence: Why it can matter more than IQ.* Random House Digital, Inc.

176 Bracha, H. S. (2004). Freeze, flight, fight, fright, faint: Adaptationist perspectives on the acute stress response spectrum. *CNS spectrums, 9*(9), 679-685.

177 Gagne, D., & Toye, R. C. (1994). The effects of therapeutic touch and relaxation therapy in reducing anxiety. *Archives of Psychiatric Nursing, 8*(3), 184-189.

177 Turner, J. G., Clark, A. J., Gauthier, D. K., & Williams, M. (1998). The effect of therapeutic touch on pain and anxiety in burn patients. *Journal of Advanced Nursing, 28*(1), 10-20.

177 Simington, J. A., & Laing, G. P. (1993). Effects of therapeutic touch on anxiety in the institutionalized elderly. *Clinical Nursing Research, 2*(4), 438-450.

177 Hart, S., Field, T., Hernandez-Reif, M., Nearing, G., Shaw, S., Schanberg, S., & Kuhn, C. (2001). Anorexia nervosa symptoms are reduced by massage therapy. *Eating Disorders, 9*(4), 289-299.

177 Gupta, M. A., Gupta, A. K., Schork, N. J., & Watteel, G. N. (1995). Perceived touch deprivation and body image: some observations among eating disordered and non-clinical subjects. *Journal of psychosomatic research, 39*(4), 459-464.

177 Gupta, M. A., & Schork, N. J. (1995). Touch deprivation has an adverse effect on body image: Some preliminary observations. *International Journal of Eating Disorders, 17*(2), 185-189.

178 Iwasaki, S., Inoue, K., Kiriike, N., & Hikiji, K. (2000). Effect of maternal separation on feeding behavior of rats in later life. *Physiology & behavior, 70*(5), 551-556.

179 Hernandez-Reif, M., Field, T., Krasnegor, J., & Theakston, H. (2001). Lower back pain is reduced and range of motion increased after massage therapy. *International Journal of Neuroscience, 106*, 131-145.

179 Field, T., Hernandez-Reif, M., Diego, M., & Fraser, M. (2007). Lower back pain and sleep disturbance are reduced following massage therapy. *Journal of Bodywork and Movement Therapy, 11*, 141-145

179 Field, T., Hernandez-Reif, M., Taylor , S., Quintino, O., & Burman, I. (1997). Labor pain is reduced by massage therapy. *Journal of Psychosomatic Obstetrics and Gynecology, 18*, 286-291.

179 Kutner, J. S., Smith, M. C., Corbin, L., Hemphill, L., Benton, K., Mellis, B. K., ... & Fairclough, D. L. (2008). Massage Therapy versus Simple Touch to Improve Pain and Mood in Patients with Advanced Cancer A Randomized Trial. *Annals of internal medicine, 149*(6), 369-379.

180 So, P. S., Jiang, Y., & Qin, Y. (2008). Touch therapies for pain relief in adults. *Cochrane Database Syst Rev, 4.*

180 Corbin, L. W., Mellis, B. K., Beaty, B. L., & Kutner, J. S. (2009). The use of complementary and alternative medicine therapies by patients with

advanced cancer and pain in a hospice setting: a multicentered, descriptive study. *Journal of palliative medicine, 12*(1), 7-8

180 Erb, W. H. (1883). *Handbook of electro-therapeutics* (Vol. 46). Wood.

181 Schenck, C. H., & Mahowald, M. W. (2002). REM sleep behavior disorder: clinical, developmental, and neuroscience perspectives 16 years after its formal identification in SLEEP. *Sleep, 25*(2), 120.

181 Houdenhove, B. (2000). Psychosocial stress and chronic pain. *European journal of pain, 4*(3), 225-228.

181 Price, D. D. (2000). Psychological and neural mechanisms of the affective dimension of pain. *Science, 288*(5472), 1769-1772.

182 Hernandez-Reif, M., Field, T., Krasnegor, J., & Theakston, H. (2001). Lower back pain is reduced and range of motion increased after massage therapy. *International Journal of Neuroscience, 106*, 131-145.

183 Field, T., Hernandez-Reif, M., Diego, M., & Fraser, M. (2007). Lower back pain and sleep disturbance are reduced following massage therapy. *Journal of Bodywork and Movement Therapy, 11*, 141-145

183 Field, T., Peck, M., Krugman, S., Tuchel, T., Schanberg, S., Kuhn, C. & Burman, I. (1998). Burn injuries benefit from massage therapy. *Journal of Burn Care and Rehabilitation, 19*, 241-244.

183 Field, T., Peck, M., Hernandez-Reif, M., Krugman, S., Burman, I. & Ozment-Schenck, L. (2000). Post burn itching, pain, and psychological symptoms are reduced with massage therapy. *Journal of Burn Care and Rehabilitation, 21*, 189-193.

183 Felitti, V. J. (2002). The relationship of adverse childhood experiences to adult health: Turning gold into lead. *Zeitschrift fur Psychosomatische Medizin und Psychotherapie, 48*(4), 359-369.

183 Naqvi, N. H., Rudrauf, D., Damasio, H., & Bechara, A. (2007). Damage to the insula disrupts addiction to cigarette smoking. *Science, 315*(5811), 531-534.

183 Naqvi, N. H., & Bechara, A. (2009). The hidden island of addiction: the insula. *Trends in neurosciences, 32*(1), 56-67.

184 Rolls, E. T., O'Doherty, J., Kringelbach, M. L., Francis, S., Bowtell, R., & McGlone, F. (2003). Representations of pleasant and painful touch in the human orbitofrontal and cingulate cortices. *Cerebral Cortex, 13*(3), 308-317.

186 Rosenblatt, P. C. (1974). Behavior in public places: Comparison of couples accompanied and unaccompanied by children. *Journal of Marriage and the Family*, 750-755.

186 Takeuchi, M. S., Miyaoka, H., Tomoda, A., Suzuki, M., Liu, Q., & Kitamura, T. (2010). The effect of interpersonal touch during childhood on adult attachment and depression: a neglected area of family and developmental psychology?. *Journal of Child and Family Studies, 19*(1), 109-117.

186 Gordon, I., Zagoory-Sharon, O., Leckman, J. F., & Feldman, R. (2010). Oxytocin, cortisol, and triadic family interactions. *Physiology & behavior, 101*(5), 679-684.

186 Gottman, J. M. (1994). *What Predicts Divorce?: The Relationship Between Marital Processes and Marital Outcomes: John Mordechai Gottman.* Routledge.

187 De Waal, F. B. (2000). Primates—a natural heritage of conflict resolution. *Science, 289*(5479), 586-590.

187 Reader, S. M., & Laland, K. N. (2002). Social intelligence, innovation, and enhanced brain size in primates. *Proceedings of the National Academy of Sciences, 99*(7), 4436-4441.

187 Dunbar, R. I. (2003). The social brain: mind, language, and society in evolutionary perspective. *Annual Review of Anthropology,* 163-181.

192 Field, T., Lasko, D., Mundy, P., Henteleff, T., Kabat, S., Talpins, S., & Dowling, M. (1997). Brief report: autistic children's attentiveness and responsivity improve after touch therapy. *Journal of Autism and Developmental Disorders, 27*(3), 333-338.

192 Cullen, L., & Barlow, J. (2002). 'Kiss, cuddle, squeeze': The experiences and meaning of touch among parents of children with autism attending a touch therapy programme. *Journal of Child Health Care, 6*(3), 171-181.

193 Cullen, L. A., Barlow, J. H., & Cushway, D. (2005). Positive touch, the implications for parents and their children with autism: an exploratory study. *Complementary therapies in clinical practice, 11*(3), 182-189.

193 Escalona, A., Field, T., Singer-Strunck, R., Cullen, C., & Hartshorn, K. (2001). Brief report: improvements in the behavior of children with autism following massage therapy. *Journal of autism and developmental disorders, 31*(5), 513-516.

193 Grandin, T., & Johnson, C. (2009). *Animals in translation: Using the mysteries of autism to decode animal behavior.* Simon and Schuster.

195 Gori, M., Mazzilli, G., Sandini, G., & Burr, D. (2011). Cross-sensory facilitation reveals neural interactions between visual and tactile motion in humans. *Frontiers in psychology, 2.*

196 Matsumoto, D. (1990). Cultural similarities and differences in display rules. *Motivation and emotion, 14*(3), 195-214.

196 Malatesta, C. Z., & Haviland, J. M. (1982). Learning display rules: The socialization of emotion expression in infancy. *Child development,* 991-1003.

197 Remland, M. S., Jones, T. S., & Brinkman, H. (1995). Interpersonal distance, body orientation, and touch: Effects of culture, gender, and age. *The Journal of social psychology, 135*(3), 281-297.

199 D. L. (2005). A randomized controlled trial of meditation and massage effects on quality of life in people with late-stage disease: a pilot study. *Journal of Palliative Medicine, 8*(5), 939-952.

199 Land, D. (2008). Study shows compassion meditation changes the brain. *University of Wisconsin News.*

199 Ong, L. M., De Haes, J. C., Hoos, A. M., & Lammes, F. B. (1995). Doctor-patient communication: a review of the literature. *Social science & medicine, 40*(7), 903-918.

Chapter 7

202 Watson, J. D. (2011). *The double helix: A personal account of the discovery of the structure of DNA.* Scribner.

203 Walker, E. F., & Diforio, D. (1997). Schizophrenia: a neural diathesis-stress model. *Psychological review, 104*(4), 667.

203 Rutherford, S. L. (2000). From genotype to phenotype: buffering mechanisms and the storage of genetic information. *Bioessays, 22*(12), 1095-1105.

203 Strohman, R. (2002). Maneuvering in the complex path from genotype to phenotype. *Science, 296*(5568), 701-703.

204 Goldberg, A. D., Allis, C. D., & Bernstein, E. (2007). Epigenetics: a landscape takes shape. *Cell, 128*(4), 635-638.

204 Holliday, R. (2006). Epigenetics: a historical overview. *Epigenetics, 1*(2), 76-80.

204 McCarthy, N. (2013). Epigenetics: Histone modification. *Nature Reviews Cancer, 13*(6), 379-379.

204 Vaissière, T., Sawan, C., & Herceg, Z. (2008). Epigenetic interplay between histone modifications and DNA methylation in gene silencing. *Mutation Research/Reviews in Mutation Research, 659*(1), 40-48.

204 Tsankova, N., Renthal, W., Kumar, A., & Nestler, E. J. (2007). Epigenetic regulation in psychiatric disorders. *Nature Reviews Neuroscience, 8*(5), 355-367.

204 Oberlander, T. F., Weinberg, J., Papsdorf, M., Grunau, R., Misri, S., & Devlin, A. M. (2008). Prenatal exposure to maternal depression, neonatal methylation of human glucocorticoid receptor gene (NR3C1) and infant cortisol stress responses. *Epigenetics, 3*(2), 97-106.

204 Morgan, H. D., Sutherland, H. G., Martin, D. I., & Whitelaw, E. (1999). Epigenetic inheritance at the agouti locus in the mouse. *Nature genetics, 23*(3), 314-318.

206 Dong, M., Giles, W. H., Felitti, V. J., Dube, S. R., Williams, J. E., Chapman, D. P., & Anda, R. F. (2004). Insights into causal pathways for ischemic heart disease adverse childhood experiences study. *Circulation, 110*(13), 1761-6.

206 Dube, S. R., Fairweather, D., Pearson, W. S., Felitti, V. J., Anda, R. F., & Croft, J. B. (2009). Cumulative childhood stress and autoimmune diseases in adults. *Psychosomatic Medicine, 71*(2), 243-250.

206 Dahlquist, G. (2006). Can we slow the rising incidence of childhood-onset autoimmune diabetes? The overload hypothesis. *Diabetologia, 49*(1), 20-24.

210 Bazarko, D. M. (2011, July). Mindfulness Meditation in a Corporate Setting.

In *Sigma Theta Tau International's 22nd International Nursing Research Congress*. STTI.

210 Field, T., Hernandez-Reif, M., Diego, M., Schanberg, S., & Kuhn, C. (2005). Cortisol decreases and serotonin and dopamine increase following massage therapy. *International Journal of Neuroscience, 115*(10), 1397-1413.

212 McEwen, B. S. (2012). Brain on stress: How the social environment gets under the skin. *Proceedings of the National Academy of Sciences, 109* (Supplement 2), 17180-17185.

213 Lea, R., & Chambers, G. (2007). Monoamine oxidase, addiction, and the "warrior" gene hypothesis. *Journal of the New Zealand Medical Association, 120*(1250), U2441.

247 Fergusson, D. M., Boden, J. M., Horwood, L. J., Miller, A. L., & Kennedy, M. A. (2011). MAOA, abuse exposure and antisocial behavior: 30-year longitudinal study. *The British Journal of Psychiatry, 198*(6), 457-463.

214 Field, T. (1999). American adolescents touch each other less and are more aggressive toward their peers as compared with French adolescents. *Adolescence, 34*(136), 753-758.

214 Jones, N.A., & Field, T. (1999). Massage and music therapies attenuate frontal EEG asymmetry in depressed adolescents. *Adolescence, 34*, 529-534.

215 Ford, E. S., Giles, W. H., & Dietz, W. H. (2002). Prevalence of the metabolic syndrome among US adults. *JAMA: the journal of the American Medical Association, 287*(3), 356-359.

215 Golden, S. H. (2007). A review of the evidence for a neuroendocrine link between stress, depression and diabetes mellitus. *Current diabetes reviews, 3*(4), 252-259.

216 Pouwer, F., Kupper, N., & Adriaanse, M. C. (2010). Does emotional stress cause type 2 diabetes mellitus? A review from the European Depression in Diabetes (EDID) Research Consortium. *Discovery medicine, 9*(45), 112.

217 Kamarck, T. W., Everson, S. A., Kaplan, G. A., Manuck, S. B., Jennings, J. R., Salonen, R., & Salonen, J. T. (1997). Exaggerated Blood Pressure Responses During Mental Stress Are Associated With Enhanced Carotid Atherosclerosis in Middle-Aged Finnish Men Findings From the Kuopio Ischemic Heart Disease Study. *Circulation, 96*(11), 3842-3848.

217 Hemingway, H., & Marmot, M. (1999). Evidence based cardiology: psychosocial factors in the aetiology and prognosis of coronary heart disease: systematic review of prospective cohort studies. *BMJ: British Medical Journal, 318*(7196), 1460.

218 Patterson, A. C., & Veenstra, G. (2010). Loneliness and risk of mortality: A longitudinal investigation in Alameda County, California. *Social science & medicine, 71*(1), 181-186.

218 Cole, S. W., Hawkley, L. C., Arevalo, J. M., & Cacioppo, J. T. (2011). Transcript origin analysis identifies antigen-presenting cells as primary tar-

gets of socially regulated gene expression in leukocytes. *Proceedings of the National Academy of Sciences, 108*(7), 3080-3085.

218 Wallace, D. L., Han, M. H., Graham, D. L., Green, T. A., Vialou, V., Iñiguez, S. D., ... & Nestler, E. J. (2009). CREB regulation of nucleus accumbens excitability mediates social isolation–induced behavioral deficits. *Nature neuroscience, 12*(2), 200-209.

220 Ditzen, B., Neumann, I. D., Bodenmann, G., von Dawans, B., Turner, R. A., Ehlert, U., & Heinrichs, M. (2007). Effects of different kinds of couple interaction on cortisol and heart rate responses to stress in women. *Psychoneuroendocrinology, 32*(5), 565-574.

Chapter 8

223 Frankl, V. E. (1985). *Man's search for meaning.* Simon and Schuster.

223 Choi, M. S., & Kim, G. J. (2011). Effects of Paters' Duola Touch during Labor on the Paternal Attachment and Role Confidence to Neonate and Couple Attachment. *Korean Journal of Women Health Nursing, 17*(4), 426-437.

223 Chang, S. O. (2001). The conceptual structure of physical touch in caring. *Journal of Advanced Nursing, 33*(6), 820-827.

224 MacDuff, S., Grodin, M. A., & Gardiner, P. (2011). The use of complementary and alternative medicine among refugees: A systematic review. *Journal of Immigrant and Minority Health, 13*(3), 585-599.

226 de la Fuente-Fernández, R., Ruth, T. J., Sossi, V., Schulzer, M., Calne, D. B., & Stoessl, A. J. (2001). Expectation and dopamine release: mechanism of the placebo effect in Parkinson's disease. *Science, 293*(5532), 1164-1166.

226 Finniss, D. G., Kaptchuk, T. J., Miller, F., & Benedetti, F. (2010). Biological, clinical, and ethical advances of placebo effects. *The Lancet, 375*(9715), 686-695.

224 Kleinman, A., & Sung, L. H. (1979). Why do indigenous practitioners successfully heal? *Social Science & Medicine. Part B: Medical Anthropology, 13*(1), 7-26.

228 Green, E. C., & Honwana, A. (1999). Indigenous healing of war-affected children in Africa. *IK Notes, 10,* 1-4.

233 Yalom, I. D. (1995). *The theory and practice of group psychotherapy.* Basic Book

Chapter 9

236 Gordon, I., Zagoory-Sharon, O., Leckman, J. F., & Feldman, R. (2010). Oxytocin, cortisol, and triadic family interactions. *Physiology & behavior, 101*(5), 679-684.

236 Field, T. (2010). Touch for socioemotional and physical well-being: A review. *Developmental Review, 30*(4), 367-383.

236 Grewen, K. M., Girdler, S. S., Amico, J., & Light, K. C. (2005). Effects of partner support on resting oxytocin, cortisol, norepinephrine, and blood pressure before and after warm partner contact. *Psychosomatic medicine, 67*(4), 531-538.

236 Holt-Lunstad, J., Birmingham, W. A., & Light, K. C. (2008). Influence of a "warm touch" support enhancement intervention among married couples on ambulatory blood pressure, oxytocin, alpha amylase, and cortisol. *Psychosomatic Medicine, 70*(9), 976-985.

237 Gottman, J. M., & Krokoff, L. J. (1989). Marital interaction and satisfaction: a longitudinal view. *Journal of consulting and clinical psychology, 57*(1), 47.

240 Quote by William James—Palmer, P. J., Zajonc, A., & Scribner, M. (2010). *The heart of higher education: A call to renewal.* John Wiley and Sons.

Acknowledgements

It is never one person who makes a piece of writing or any work for that mater. One of the deep messages of this book is that we are not alone and could never be. Their are countless people to thank who's work has make this work possible.

My heart felt gratitude for Deborah Freeman, Fred Hageneder and Siegmar Gerken all of whom worked diligently on this book to make it available to you. Their kindness strength and wisdom is reflected through out.

A deep debt of gratitude to Peter Levine for his insight and dedication, Allan Schore for teaching me how to see the relationship between neurobiology and our basic humanity and to the many researchers and thinkers who's work made this book possible. Some of these visionaries are Dacher Keltner, Steven Porges, Bessel Van Der Kolk, Bob Scare, Phyllis Stein, Mardi Crane, Tiffany Fields and many many others.

Also to my teacher and mentor in Zen practice Daniel Terragno, Roshi who's steady practice taught me how to sit in the unknown for long enough for truth to emerge. I have been blessed by some of the most amazing teachers who know how to help information turn into knowledge and challenged me not to just learn but to become the kind of person that I am capable of some of these are: Dr. Coble-Temple, Dr. Carroll, Dr. VanOot, Dr. Vogel, Dr. Mattar, Areil Giarretto, Steven Hoskison, Kathy Kain and many many others.

My partner Maureen Harrington who has seen me in challenging moments and offered presence, care and direct feedback. My dream team of friends who's heart and love helped me find what I am capable of Juliette Cutts, Rebecca Cohen, Statoko Shiabo, Sara Durbin and Vannetta Sandu (and others... you know who you are).

There are so many friends who have helped me develop this book and bring it to this point. Some of these are Brad Kammer, Ellen Byrne, Andrea Smith-Gage, Marcia Black, Noelle Morris, Brandy Vanderheiden, Katie Uemura, Catherine Hurly, and the list goes on and on.

There are also so many people who I do not even know personally who support the health and the vibranceof those I know and have been held by.

Moment by moment life is always wide open. Because of the love, dedication care, cajoling and clear eyed feedback from so many this book became a possibility. It is my deepest hope that it helps us find a way as a culture, health professionals and as individuals to understand the vital role touch plays in our life and to adapt the insights from research to practical tools for living a vibrant connected life.

About the Author

Dr. Changaris is the founder and director of the International Institute of Touch Training and Research (ITTR). ITTR is an organization that supports the development of touch interventions in evidenced practices for health care settings and professionals as-well-as ongoing research into the role of touch in health and mental health.

Dr. Changaris is the training coordinator for an integrated health psychology training program with the Wright Institute. The Integrated Health Psychology Training program trains psychology students in an interdisciplinary collaborative approach to healthcare. He is a clinical psychologist with a specialty in the biological bases of behavior, stress physiology, psychobiology of neurodegenerative disorders and the neurobiology of PTSD. Dr. Changaris is the current chair of Somatic Experiencing Research Coalition (SERC).

Michael Changaris, Psy.D. completed his post-doctoral fellowship with the child, family and adolescent intensive outpatient program with Kaiser Permanente in Antioch. He obtained a doctorate in psychology from John F. Kennedy University. He works closely with medical providers to support effective diagnosis, tolerance of medication regimes and to address the complex interaction between medical and psychological interventions.

Dr. Changaris can be reached:
www.touch-neuroscience.com/workshops.html

Index

BODY-CENTERED PSYCHOTHERAPY *by Ron Kurtz*
The Hakomi Method
The Integrated Use of Mindfulness, Nonviolence & the Body
ISBN 978-0-94-079523-5

REIKI *by Bodo Baginski & Shalila Sharamon*
Universal Life Energy
ISBN 978-0-94-079502-0

LIVING REIKI: TAKATA'S TEACHINGS *by Fran Brown*
Stories from the Life of Hawayo Takata
ISBN 978-0-94-079510-5

RETURNING TO HEALTH *by Anna Halprin*
with Dance, Movement & Imagery
ISBN 978-0-940795-22-8

THE POWER OF RHYTHM—*TA KE TI NA by Reinhard Flatischler*
Includes the companion CD with musical examples
ISBN 978-0-94-079526-6

EROS, LOVE & SEXUALITY *by John C. Pierrakos M.D.*
The Forces That Unify Man and Woman
ISBN 978-0-94-079505-1

**THE AUTHORITATIVE GUIDE TO GRAPEFRUIT SEED
EXTRACT** *by Allan Sachs D.C.*
A Breakthrough in Alternative Treatment for Colds, Infections, Candida,
Allergies, Herpes, Parasites, and Many Other Ailments
ISBN 978-0-94-079514-4

THE COSMIC OCTAVE— Origin of Harmony *by Hans Cousto*
ISBN 978-0-94-079520-4

CORE ENERGETICS *by John C. Pierrakos M.D.*
Developing the Capacity to Love and Heal
ISBN 978-0-97-743940-2

LifeRhythm and Core Evolution Publications
PO Box 806, Mendocino CA 95460 USA · Telephone 707. 937.2309
www.LifeRhythm.com · Books@LifeRhythm.com